PREACHING ISLAMIC RENEWAL

PREACHING ISLAMIC

RENEWAL

RELIGIOUS AUTHORITY AND MEDIA
IN CONTEMPORARY EGYPT

Jacquelene G. Brinton

 UNIVERSITY OF CALIFORNIA PRESS

University of California Press, one of the most distinguished university presses in the United States, enriches lives around the world by advancing scholarship in the humanities, social sciences, and natural sciences. Its activities are supported by the UC Press Foundation and by philanthropic contributions from individuals and institutions. For more information, visit www.ucpress.edu.

University of California Press
Oakland, California

Library of Congress Cataloging-in-Publication Data

Brinton, Jacquelene Gottlieb, 1965- author.
    Preaching Islamic renewal : religious authority and media in contemporary Egypt / Jacquelene Gottlieb Brinton.
        pages cm
    Includes bibliographical references and index.
    ISBN 978-0-520-28699-3 (cloth : alk. paper) —
    ISBN 978-0-520-28700-6 (pbk. : alk. paper) —
    ISBN 978-0-520-96321-4 (ebook) —
    1. Islamic preaching—Egypt.   2. Television in religion—Egypt.   3. Sha'rawi, Muhammad Mutawalli. I. Title.
    BP184.25.B75 2016
    297.3'70962—dc23

                                        2015024792

24   23   22   21   20   19   18   17   16   15
10   9   8   7   6   5   4   3   2   1

I dedicate this book in loving memory of Selma Leabman and Ralph Marcoccia. My only regret is that neither of them will be able to share this accomplishment with me.

CONTENTS

ACKNOWLEDGMENTS

There are many people to thank.

First of all, I would like to thank the many people in Egypt who helped me understand Shaykh Sha'rawi over the years. From the Egyptian-Dutch woman I met at the Red Sea who gave me her beloved book of transcribed Sha'rawi sermons, to Sha'rawi's disciples and son who shared their memories of him with me. Most especially thanks go to 'Abd al-Rahim al-Sha'rawi, Engineer 'Abd al-Rahman, 'Abd al-Ra'uf al-Hanafi, Nur al-Din Attia, and Rida al-'Arabi.

I would also like to thank Abdulaziz Sachedina, Peter Ochs and Elizabeth Thompson for seeing me through the dissertation stage of this project. Thanks to Rizwan Zamir, Adham Hashish, and Reza Hemari.

This book is a testament to the power of love and to the support my family has given me over the years. Thanks go to my mother, Linda Marcoccia, who is my greatest cheerleader. To my husband, John Brinton, this book would not have been more than an idea if it weren't for your constant love, support and assistance. To my children, Lilias, Maya, and Noah, you truly make my life worthwhile.

NOTE ON TRANSLITERATIONS
AND TRANSLATIONS

In general, the transliterations throughout the book follow the *International Journal of Middle East Studies (IJMES)* system, although there are some exceptions. One exception that appears throughout the manuscript is my spelling of the Arabic word *'alim*. For Arabic names, I have omitted diacritical marks and I have transcribed Arabic names from Standard Arabic instead of following local pronunciations. There are two exceptions to this in the book. First, I transliterate Sha'rawi's name as Muhammad Mitwalli Sha'rawi. Second, I spell the name of the Algerian Sufi Shaykh Muhammad Belkaid according to its local pronunciation. Names that are easily recognized by English speakers, such as Gamal Abdel Nasser, are written as they are known. Transliterations of colloquial Egyptian Arabic are done according to *A Dictionary of Egyptian Arabic: Arabic-English*, by Martin Hinds and El-Said Badawi, Librairie du Liban, Beirut, 1986. All Qur'anic translations are based on those of Muhammad Asad from *The Message of the Qur'an*, Dar al-Andalus Limited, 1980. Muhammad Asad's translations are also readily available online. I have adapted his translations to make some Qur'anic verses more readable and I did the same in cases where I felt the English words he chose needed updating or where they needed to be changed to fit the sense in which Sha'rawi interpreted them.

Muhammad Mitwalli Sha'rawi

Authority and Media in Twentieth-Century Egypt

In 2006, while walking the streets of Cairo, I repeatedly saw the image of one religious scholar (sing. *'alim*, pl. *'ulama'*), Shaykh Muhammad Mitwalli Sha'rawi (1911–1998). During his lifetime Sha'rawi was primarily known as a preacher who interpreted the Qur'an and hadith on his popular weekly show, which aired on state run television every Friday afternoon from 1980 until shortly before he died. But his presence in Cairo nearly a decade after his death was still ubiquitous; in addition to the reruns of his sermons that played on Egyptian television many times during the week, his books were for sale on street corners and in bookshops, and his picture was hung outside shops and in kiosks throughout the city. Although Sha'rawi remains one of the most popular Egyptian preachers, he is not the only 'alim one finds when looking at religious material available in Egyptian bookshops or when watching television. The continued success of the television shows of religious scholars trained at al-Azhar, the oldest and most prestigious Sunni university in Egypt, and the profusion of different media versions of their lessons (*durūs*) and sermons is evidence of their extensive celebrity and marketability among the people.

Despite being called the father of Arab television preaching and despite his immense popularity in Egypt and throughout the world, little serious academic work on the importance and legacy of Sha'rawi has previously been published. Although there is no shortage of studies on Islam in the modern world or even specifically on modern Egypt, most of them ignore or at best briefly mention Sha'rawi. He is often dismissed as someone who merely enjoyed widespread support among the Egyptian public who tuned into his show each week. He is also overlooked because he does not fit neatly into the categories frequently used to analyze contemporary Muslim religious figures. Whether these figures actively engage in antigovernment activities or can be labeled fundamentalists, Wahhabis, modernists, or Islamists, for example, often determines if they are deemed worthy of study. Yet these criteria are so broadly defined that they link disparate agents with different agendas, hiding the nuances that help differentiate them from one another.

Categories that seem to be descriptive are often limited in their usefulness because they are presented as binaries, a favorite being the modernist–fundamentalist binary. The term *modernist* is associated with liberalism, but it also implies "'modern' values ... explicitly associated with the modern world, especially rationality, science, constitutionalism, and certain forms of human equality ... not simply modern (a feature of modernity) but modernist (a proponent of modernity)."[1] Fundamentalism is a term long recognized as controversial when used to refer to Muslims seeking religious authority. Roxanne Euben uses the term in a minimally problematic way to connect various religious movements synchronically. She defines fundamentalism as:

> contemporary religio-political movements that attempt to return to the scriptural foundations of the community, excavating and reinterpreting these foundations for application to the contemporary social and political world.[2]

Therefore, according to Euben, fundamentalism is political, not otherworldly or mystical. It is limited to scriptural traditions, and it rejects commentary in favor of the original texts themselves, which for Muslims are the Qur'an and sunna.[3]

A study of Sha'rawi's thought quickly problematizes the use of terms like *fundamentalist* and *modernist* by exposing their limits. Sha'rawi could easily be considered a modernist who followed in the path of Muhammad 'Abduh (1849–1905), an al-Azhar-trained 'alim who is considered the father of Muslim modernism. Both used new media to disseminate their messages of reform, and both were proponents of treating every human being with dignity, regardless of religious affiliation.[4] However, Sha'rawi vetted all knowledge through his exegesis, a method 'Abduh would not have condoned. 'Abduh instead believed that responding to modern problems by searching the Qur'an would not yield solutions unless human reason was used to supplement the knowledge gained from scripture.

Because Sha'rawi insisted that all aspects of life—past, present, and future—should be understood by reading the Qur'an, he could easily be dismissed as a fundamentalist. According to Euben's definition, however, Sha'rawi does not fit the description of a fundamentalist for two reasons. First, he insisted on the importance of the past interpretative methods and expertise of the Sunni 'ulama'. In fact these claims are foundational to his entire program. Second, Sha'rawi's scriptural interpretations were often premised on his mystical orientation. His esoteric orientation also means that, even though he spent many years teaching in Saudi Arabia, he cannot be considered a Wahhabi.[5]

Sha'rawi is also overlooked for the very reason I will argue that he is essential to understanding Muslim authority in modern Egypt: Not only was he grounded in a traditional Sunni worldview—one he learned at al-Azhar—but he was also admired by millions of ordinary people. The one full chapter previously written on Sha'rawi in English is entitled "Muhammad Mutawalli Al-Sha'rawi: A Portrait of a Contemporary 'Alim in Egypt." In it the author claims that Sha'rawi was indicative of the decline of the religious scholars of al-Azhar in general because of both his beliefs and his audiences: "[T]his decline is illustrated by the rise of men like Muhammad Mitwalli al-Sha'rawi who do not have the thorough grounding in Islamic scholarship . . . [and so] pander to popular feelings and superstitions with literalist interpretations of things such as jinn and miracles appealing to a very low religious common denominator."[6]

In this statement Sha'rawi is characterized as gaining popularity by distracting people with what they desire: literalist interpretations of the Qur'an. It not only demeans Sha'rawi, but also his audiences and the central importance of the Qur'an to many Muslims. The author of this quote equated the problem of "literalist interpretations" with the unseen (ghayb) elements of the Qur'an, such as miracles and jinn, to demonstrate that belief in such things is false, a result of feelings and superstitions. By impugning belief in the Qur'anic exposition of the unseen as low, however, the author dismisses an essential tenet of Muslim belief under the pretext of dismissing Sha'rawi. When Sha'rawi spoke about the existence of jinn and miracles, he did so through his exegesis. The unseen is an essential element of the Qur'an and is a subject that even the most highly trained religious scholars accept and write about. Sha'rawi was therefore representing conventional beliefs, which were grounded in his Qur'anic worldview.

The quote in the previous paragraph is also troubling because the author assumes that being grounded in scholarship—something she expresses as belonging to the past—is distinct from having influence among the people in the present. Except among his harshest critics, Sha'rawi was recognized as a specialist in Qur'anic Arabic, but he also spoke in Egyptian dialect (especially early in his career as a television personality), told stories from his village, and reaffirmed local beliefs and customs. Linguistic exegesis was his scholarly enterprise, an enterprise with a long history among the 'ulama' that entails particular rules for dissecting Qur'anic language. Sha'rawi's scholarly limitations were not caused by a lack of "thorough grounding in Islamic scholarship" nor by his appeal among the people; they were instead related to the breakdown of the legal functions of the 'ulama' in Egypt, which makes the issue of Sha'rawi's influence a much more complicated matter. For the type of authority he had as an 'alim-preacher, he relied on a different sort of expertise than what would have been required in the past.

The 'ulama' in Sunni Islam have a long and varied past. Marshall Hodgson connected the rise of an 'ulama' class in Sunni Islam to the beginnings of the four legal schools, but he claimed that the precursors of the 'ulama' were the "piety-minded." Hodgson used the term *piety-minded* generally to refer to those in late Umayyad times (692–750 C.E.) who "expected Islam to carry with its own law, its own learning, its own etiquette, its own principles of private life and public order . . ." According to Hodgson these piety-minded would later be called 'ulama' when they began to systematize these ideals and focus on shari'a through jurisprudence (*fiqh*) in order to answer legal questions.[7] This common way of viewing the rise of the Sunni 'ulama' connects them specifically to *'ilm* (exoteric knowledge), but it also acknowledges that the meaning of the word, along with the vocations and responsibilities of the 'ulama', developed over time. In terms of their overall authority, it wasn't until later, and after much contestation, that the 'ulama' in Sunni Islam came to be defined according to a well-known hadith, as the "heirs to the Prophet."[8] Understanding how 'ulama' authority arose as part of the general competition for religious authority in early Islam is useful. It demonstrates both precedence for contestation and that authority was partially determined by the concerns of a particular time period and situation. But 'ulama' authority was not limited to the realm of legal expertise.

A common typology used to explain Muslim religious authority more generally divides realms of authority according to knowledge (exoteric); access to the spiritual realms (esoteric); pious, exemplary behavior (piety); and the claim to lineage (traditional).[9] While Muhammad was understood to have possessed all of these qualities, religious agents do not need to have all of them to exert their authority; in fact, academics treat these areas as distinctive. For example, the Sufis are often said to rely on lineage and access to the esoteric realms, and the 'ulama' on exoteric—specifically legal—knowledge.[10] Yet confining 'ulama' authority to 'ilm and separating authority according to vocation and religious commitments is problematic. Defining 'ulama' authority as that which relies on exoteric knowledge has led to the idea that there was constant conflict between most 'ulama', as the exoteric and normative representatives, and the Sufis, as the esoteric and antinomian. In actuality many 'ulama' have claimed to possess both exoteric and esoteric prowess, and many Sufis are also experts in law. Al-Azhar provides intellectual lineage for its graduates, but it is also known to have had 'ulama' who are affiliated with different Sufi orders among its highest ranks.[11] Sha'rawi was someone who grounded his discourse in his 'ulama' training, but his sermons are replete with references to esoteric knowledge. In his attempt to renew religion, the brand of Islam he presented to the people was representative of the Azhari tradition of blending Sunni theological and legal concepts with a mystical orientation, or the "Sunni-Shar'ia-Sufi synthesis."[12]

Religious authority depends not just on how agents express that authority. In general, and chiefly through the influence of the theories of Max Weber, it has been recognized that religious authority is noncoercive.[13] Once the Sunni 'ulama' established themselves as the heirs of the Prophet, being "in authority" meant that they had to "obtain compliance with their commands by displaying the marks or insignia of authority that communicate to others that they are entitled to issue such a directive or command." Once recognized through the display of such marks, their authority rendered personal judgment secondary to their decisions.[14] When compliance was obtained, their authority became effective. The fact that the 'ulama' had to display marks of authority indicates that exhibiting particular characteristics and obtaining the acceptance of the people have both been central to 'ulama' authority for a very long time. Evaluations of authority are not always based solely on the abilities of the one seeking authority; they also rely on the perception of those who formulate those assessments. Or, to understand it slightly differently, those seeking authority rely on and display symbols in order to receive compliance. Through interaction, authority is at once effective, interdependent, and intangible; it is generating and generated.

For the 'ulama', receiving compliance could mean either being accepted by other religious scholars or being accepted by the public. Although a single scholar could receive the respect of both, the approval of peers and the adulation of the public were often associated with different functions. In the first case, and on a practical level, some 'ulama' had the responsibility of regulating others, meaning that there were different classes of 'ulama' with different types of responsibilities. For example, the 'ulama' preachers and their sermons have been critiqued and regulated by more highly ranked 'ulama' since early in Islamic history.[15] Many preachers did not belong to the most educated of the 'ulama' classes; often the content of their sermons did not come from acceptable texts and at times were even antithetical to doctrinal foundations. As a result, a literature of internal critique began as soon as preaching became an institutional responsibility of the 'ulama'.[16] The most highly trained 'ulama' also worked out disagreements in law and theology through a vast and complex literary tradition in which they spoke mostly to one another. In the second case, local imams issued legal opinions (fatāwā), taught school, took care of mosques, and performed many other community functions.[17] Preachers transmitted knowledge to adherents through admonitions or warnings (waʿẓ or tadhkira), stories (qiṣaṣ), or by delivering sermons (khaṭāba) from mosque pulpits after communal prayers on Friday.[18]

Depending on their exhibition of valued attributes, and on the compliance they attained as a result, those seeking authority could achieve ascendancy among the competition by displaying the qualities that the public or other 'ulama' accepted as being preeminent in the religious realm. While this characterization of religious authority is in many ways correct, it ignores the fact that, at times, the elements even of noncoercive authority are coupled with institutions and historical contingencies that have an impact on how claimants convince people of their authority. Those influences work not just on those seeking authoritative guides but also on the guides themselves—on the way they compel and attain compliance. When traditional authority is connected to institutions of power, those institutions can both constrain and aid discourse, but they often go unrecognized by those who view religious authority as noncoercive.

In contemporary Egypt, beginning in the nineteenth century, changes were set in motion to reform religious institutions for the sake of modernizing the country. These changes led to a reshaping of the 'ulama' in both direct and indirect ways—they lessened 'ulama' influence in society by removing knowledge transmission and religiously based social regulation from their control. Also in the nineteenth century, many intellectuals began to call for the removal of interpretive, revelatory authority from the specialized realm of the 'ulama'. They wanted people to interpret the Qur'an and hadith for themselves as a way of combating Muslim intellectual stagnation. Stagnation was posited as the answer to the question of why Europeans were able to succeed in subduing regions of the world that had only recently been ruled by Muslims. Thus, the shift in authority began as an attempt to combat European ascendancy through modernization, that is, as an imitation of European models of government and of knowledge production and distribution. Concerning knowledge, it was posited that the stagnation of Muslim societies could be rectified by giving those who were not religious scholars the opportunity to partake in activities seen to exemplify Muslim intellectual production. As a result, rational capacity—and not specialized learning in centuries-old interpretive techniques—became the criteria for interpretive rights. Although the call for individuals to interpret the revelation for themselves came under attack by Muslim legal scholars, the scholars' attempts to maintain control over the transmission of religious knowledge became more difficult—in fact, almost impossible—as time went on.[19]

The notion that rational capability, exemplified by any type of education, was all that was needed for one to be able to extract correct rulings from the Qur'an and hadith in order to introduce change into society led to the idea that training in the methods and rules used by any authorized legal scholar (*mufti*) for this task was unnecessary. In Egypt and in many other places, these ideas were coupled with the notion that such procedures had been a hindrance to true understanding and that they needed to be changed precisely because they were limited to those who had the specialized knowledge to regulate them and restrain their use. The regulating 'ulama', especially the legal scholars, were therefore read as having succumbed to stagnation by restricting the possibilities for change. Stripping the 'ulama' of their regulating rights over the production and distribution of religious knowledge resulted in the despecialization of knowledge; this change, paired with the "invented tradition of stagnation," gave rise to the widespread acceptance of interpretations made by those who were primarily motivated by political contingencies.[20] Many who came to be accepted as religious authorities did so by finding relevant knowledge in the Qur'an and hadith, which helped make their interpretations applicable. The ability to make the text relevant—something that was once an outcome—became the object and description of learnedness.

Sha'rawi positioned himself somewhere between necessary acceptance of already embedded shifts and attempts to prevent further slippage. His role as renewer was best illustrated by his attempt to reinforce the primacy of the "Sunni-Shari'a-Sufi synthesis," which was associated with the mainstream Sunni *tajdīd* (renewal) movements of the eighteenth and nineteenth centuries. These movements represented the schools of law and "conservative" Sufi orders.[21] At the same time he did not renew through the specialized techniques used in the past. Therefore, I refer to him throughout this book as an 'alim preacher,[22] a term meant to signify his attachment to al-Azhar and the tasks he felt his training made him, and others like him, uniquely qualified to undertake. But, the term *'alim preacher* is also meant to refer to the reorganization of 'ulama' functions. Sha'rawi found himself in the midst of the transformation of the 'ulama', yet this overhaul had mixed repercussions for him. Although the 'ulama' lost their regulating functions, and therefore control, over the transmission of knowledge, Sha'rawi benefitted from and even originated some of those changes. Through the use of new technologies, he tried to reestablish the Sunni Azhari position as the dominant religious position in a time when it was increasingly threatened. In his broadcasts, he challenged threats by using language to direct societal conversation about religion. His rise as an authoritative 'alim, as an 'alim-preacher, and as a preacher of the people (*'alim al-sha'b*) therefore signifies disruption and the opportunity it offered to non-legal scholars trained at al-Azhar as they attempted to keep the boundaries of learnedness from being generalized further than their own claims. Thus, in the Egyptian context, men like Sha'rawi centered their claims to societal interpretive authority in the institution of al-Azhar, adjusting to its gains and losses. Sha'rawi used the language derived from his interpretive strategies and his access to the people to try to ensure that those losses did not become permanent.

It is precisely in times of disruption that "discursive coherence" can be deployed to establish discursive dominance. Discursive coherence refers to the attempt to "represent the present" within a particular, cogent perspective that is based on tradition.[23] But achieving dominance through coherence can also result in subtle changes to tradition. Sha'rawi sought discursive coherence by responding to events and discussions taking place in his society. In an attempt to control the import of those conversations, he tried to subordinate them to his Qur'anic readings in order to preserve the underpinnings of the system that helped perpetuate Azhari religious authority. To maintain the viability of the 'ulama' claim to be the true representatives of Qur'anic understanding, however, Sha'rawi employed tactics, such as embracing language fluctuations and television, that subtly altered what he sought to preserve. His television shows were the texts of suitability; they influenced and were influenced by a combination of religious elements as they were transmitted and received. His preaching represented, and still represents, an expression of tradition in its time primarily because of how people engaged both Sha'rawi and his orations.

Preacher texts serve as a paradigmatic example of why hermeneutics, or an emphasis on interpretation, needs to be combined with a focus on the everyday to provide a more complete picture of how religion actually functions.[24] To depict the state of religious engagement in modern Egypt, I assume the interdependency of textualized meaning and immediate presence, presentations focused on God and television watching, the persuasive quality of authority and how adherents substantiate that authority, constraints of history and how people navigate within those constraints, and even esotericism and tools of communication such as language use and media.[25] A lot has been written about the importance of understanding Islam from below, not defining religion through the study of texts alone, but also by how religion is animated in the lives of practitioners.[26] Scripture is part of the everyday lives of devout Egyptian Muslims, who recite verses from the Qur'an in prayer multiple times each day. But the Qur'an and hadith are also seamlessly woven into the quotidian. Anyone who rides the metro in Cairo will see people reading and quietly reciting verses from pocket editions of these texts. This example is interesting because it demonstrates how scripture has been incorporated into daily activities, taking its place in communal mundane space. But the insertion of religious texts into the everyday is also made possible by the material form of those words as print media. The actual content of the books as well as how people's senses are engaged when reading in this environment, influence the understanding they derive from God's words or the Prophet's example. This derived, and potentially adjustable understanding is as important to the entire scene as the circumstances themselves. The fact that passages of revelatory texts are integrated into ordinary practice with the help of modern technologies illustrates that societal, personal, and even political contexts help animate words.

In examining how religious language is integrated into the lives of adherents, its significance becomes apparent. The increased popularization of religious talk, or the increased ability of adherents to pick texts, passages, and preachers according to their liking, is an important aspect of contemporary religion. It means that the 'ulama', or anyone who wants his or her discourse to reach people, needs to conform to public expectations. Popularization is partially the result of an increasingly literate public, who have access to a proliferation of religious perspectives and voices and who are thus better situated to distinguish between competing claimants. For someone like Sha'rawi, competition increased the need for confirmation among the public and decreased the importance of getting approval from other 'ulama'. He did not introduce innovation to the scholarly debates that the 'ulama' have among themselves. As a preacher, he focused on influencing discussions taking place outside al-Azhar by affirming standard Azhari views. As an element that helped to establish his authority, popular support enabled Sha'rawi—and therefore his commentary—to thrive and assured him influence and longevity. Throughout this book, I will explore how Sha'rawi was unique and was also a paradigm of 'ulama' resiliency. His precedent serves as a means of exploring different manifestations of religious authority in modern Egypt more broadly and among the 'ulama' particularly.

Popularization of religious authority also allowed the public to use different types of criteria to decide who was and who was not an appropriate religious guide, and their opinions were often based on personal inclination. The presence of diversity is reflected in the popularization of claims made through language, mass media, and other modes, but it means that those who wanted to speak about religion authoritatively, and those who wanted to understand that language in terms that related to their own lives helped redirect the very notions of authority. This opening is often referred to as a fragmentation of religious authority. The notion of fragmented authority, or even of a marketplace of religious ideas, posits authority as measurable and limits consideration of the components of religious authority that make it fluid and flexible by nature. Those who use such terms often do so to point out how new religious movements or actors have benefitted in the contemporary Muslim majority world, and how the 'ulama', because of their previous definitive claim to religious authority, have suffered loss.[27] Yet the reconfiguration of religious authority was not merely a consequence of its fragmentation; instead, authoritative claims were now developed through displays of multiple elements combined in different ways, elements that have come to determine whether claims will be recognized or rejected. Many have gained authority by combining factors such as affiliations with popular organizations, particular styles of writing, language cues, interpretive strategies, and modes of transmission and reception with their abilities to quote scripture, reference the past, and react to government policy or societal forces. It is how those seeking authority become recognizable, how they appeal to certain publics, and how they distinguish themselves from others that determine their influence.

Religious authority is not a measurable entity, neither is it always an either-or proposition that is limited to a singular choice. It is instead accepted as an amalgam of characteristics that consists of stable and shifting markers, or formative and re-formed habits. It is interactive and blended. Because it exists in the agreement between those who live it—both those displaying characteristics and those who legitimate particular qualities through their choices and proclivities—it can be said to exist when the two are effectively combined. Those seeking authority may rely on certain elements to assert their claims, but because of the increasing diversity of adherent interests, they have no guarantee of success.

Authority, according to this view, is not finitely distributed but differently applied by individuals and groups within populations. It is the proliferation of defining factors that leads to increased struggle, but also to multiple forms of acceptance. Distinct claimants, for example, often complement one another even while they seek dominance, and sometimes they do so inadvertently. In Egypt, this complementarity is also accompanied by distinction. Sha'rawi was admired by many for his expertise in Arabic, his simple and understandable exegesis, his humility and gentle manner, his pious behavior, and receiving special gifts from God (karāmāt). But he rarely offered readings that countered the Egyptian government, he was not associated with any new religious movement, he had close ties with the leaders of Saudi Arabia, and he rarely engaged European and American ideas concerning governance and society. The prominent Islamist Sayyid Qutb, who was executed by the Egyptian government in 1966, had neither exoteric training in nor esoteric connections to religious knowledge; in fact, he had disdain for both. But he was known for defending his beliefs no matter what the consequences, becoming a martyr as a result, his anti-Western polemics, and the solutions he posed for the ills of his society. Yusuf Qaradawi, a global satellite personality, is known for his al-Azhar training, his expert legal opinions, being exiled from Egypt for his beliefs, and his association with the Muslim Brotherhood.

Why, or how, might some people decide to take advice from one or a mixture of these figures? People often choose guides who fit their expectations, and their choice is aided by the rapid increase of messages available through television, print media, and the Internet. However, this increase also means that adherents can combine guidance culled from different sources, even those that represent incompatible views. For example, although Sha'rawi and Qaradawi may have disagreed on the relationship between religion and politics, people might listen to Sha'rawi for his Qur'anic interpretations and tune into Qaradawi's program for juridical advice. They might also admire both out of a sense of national pride, simply for the fact that they both are Egyptian. Access to an ever-increasing pool of competitors allows for numerous factors, including social pressures and institutional influence, to influence how people engage those making authoritative claims.

Sha'rawi was directly connected to two powerful Egyptian institutions: al-Azhar and the government. His discourse was therefore circumscribed by his centrist perspective and by governmental and societal forces. He was restrained and enabled by the construction of his vocation and its discursive history, by societal expectations of the 'ulama', and by the government that employed him. Yet these elements were coupled with the noncoercive aspects of his authority, which included reliance on his expertise and training in Arabic, his public displays of piety, his visible charisma, and his connection to *karāmāt*. He navigated between the authoritative claims he made, especially those that resonated with the people, and the constraints of his time and place until he was even able to affect the functioning of both.

Although I argue that Sha'rawi used the fact that the 'ulama' continue to be associated with knowledge, piety, and charisma to claim his authority, I am not arguing that he reinstated that typology as a singular indication of authority throughout society. Nor am I arguing that his example can be used to make general assertions about the current state of 'ulama' effectiveness in Egyptian society. Both competition for authority outside the 'ulama' ranks and diversity within those ranks make it hard to point to specific characteristics as being the deciding factors in the formulation of religious authority in Egypt today. In this environment it is more accurate to examine how authority becomes effective in particular instances and what it signifies in those cases in relation to broader trends in society. The fact that Sha'rawi's connection to 'ulama' claims evoked recognition of him as authoritative among the people demonstrates that the traditional typology of religious authority remains an important part of the larger picture of religious authority in Egypt. But the fact that Sha'rawi also had to blend those significations with other, more recently embedded changes to the working of authority in Egypt is also telling.

Therefore, Sha'rawi did not become an authority merely by being connected to the Sunni typology. He also struck the right balance between not being overtly political and having the necessary qualities to gain the respect of the people. Adaptation was the key. During his lifetime, Sha'rawi used his discourse to counter what he thought were the greatest risks to the stability of his society. While he rarely responded directly to political and social controversies—especially not in his sermons—he did embed his opinions about them in his articulations. Among the threats he sought to controvert were Islamism, rationalism, and communism, and throughout this book are numerous references to why he thought these positions were dangerous and how he attempted to counter them. Ultimately, in all three cases, he believed that ideas that originated in the human mind and contradicted God's words posed an imminent threat to belief in the primacy of those words. He wanted to reassert that truth could be found in the Qur'an and that the interpretations of trained experts were needed to demonstrate Qur'anic primacy if and when it was undermined by rationally generated ideas.

But Sha'rawi was not without his critics, and he remains a controversial figure among certain segments of the Egyptian population until today. Some saw him as too closely tied to the Egyptian government, others thought his use of the Qur'an as the premier source for deciding the veracity of all information was simplistic. His defense against what he saw as major political and societal threats, which correlated with his role as a government appointed spokesperson, together with his innovations in language and use of technology were more successful than his attempts to fold scientific knowledge into his theological renderings. To demonstrate Sha'rawi's knowledge of science, his son, 'Abd-al Rahim al-Sha'rawi, told me that Sha'rawi would often go to doctors not because he had medical problems but to learn about biology and genetics. Rather than demonstrating that Sha'rawi gained knowledge of medicine through this method, the story instead demonstrates that Sha'rawi's scientific information was gathered haphazardly, which is evidenced by the fact that his attempts to defend the Qur'an from scientific claims did not engage those claims in any sustained way. Sha'rawi struggled to make a convincing case for the view that science could be judged in light of the Qur'an.

The two modes of inquiry have very different groundings, and he never endeavored to explain the difference between them, which even constrained his Qur'anic perspective. It is necessary to examine what he said about these issues in order to ascertain the content of his program of renewal, which helped define the tradition of relying on revelatory knowledge as a primary source of truth in the contemporary era.

The fact that Sha'rawi and his orations were presented on television ultimately determined his reach throughout society and thus determined his impact. In his television appearances, Sha'rawi molded and transmitted fragments of diverse approaches, Ash'arite theology, Qur'anic exegesis, mystical renderings, common stories and folktales, and reactions to contemporary problems. He was the first to deliver in-depth theological postulations and esoteric interpretations amid nationalist messages and advertisements, an innovation that should not be overlooked. Media, specifically television, influenced his discourse in production and reception, but, just as important, it influenced how he, as a man of authority, entered the lives of his viewers. Television transmission, with all of its political, societal, and material aspects, created the phenomenon of Sha'rawi.

Sha'rawi's disciples referred to his innovations in language and mass media techniques when they told me that he was "the renewer of the scientific and technological age." However, his technological innovations had mixed repercussions when considered in light of his goals. When he stated that he became a media preacher to spread his message to as many people as possible, it does seem like he succeeded in achieving what he set out to do. Yet his media success also came at a cost to that message. In many ways, Sha'rawi's use of television justifies the idea that the medium dominates the message.[28] Religious broadcasting changed the way people experienced speech about the Qur'an: from the way people interacted with one another while listening to sermons to how television recordings enabled Sha'rawi's words to live on, to how government intentions helped defined Sha'rawi's sermons. Sha'rawi's books also helped in this regard, but almost all of the writings attributed to him were taken from his televised sermons and interviews, many of which are now posted on YouTube. In addition, video is a neutral transmitter: It does not favor presenters based on what they say as much as on how they say it. Sha'rawi's religious broadcasting basically sanctified visual media as an appropriate place to talk about God. But by doing so, he introduced an opportunity for an increase in competition with his point of view: other television content and other presenters of religion. While television worked well for him because of his charisma, charisma is not limited to people who are connected to al-Azhar. And while having charisma is not a new necessity for a preacher, it is a deciding factor in television success.

The time when national television broadcasts dominated the airwaves passed at almost exactly the same time as Sha'rawi's death, in the late 1990s. The site of media competition among religious authorities has shifted twice since then, first to satellite programming and then to the Internet. Because of his appeal, Sha'rawi has been successfully repurposed through both. Satellite now dominates the realm of television, and the diversity of presenters and content on satellite television is even greater than on state-run media. The celebrity status that television afforded Sha'rawi, and the influence it gave him throughout society, is now shared by many, both on satellite television and on the Internet, whose opinions he would have seen as dangerous. An argument can be made, however, that the integration of technology and theology ensured that Sha'rawi, his sermons, and his perspective would endure after his death. For Sha'rawi's legacy, and certainly in terms of the long-term implications for the 'ulama' generally, media continues to be a dominating factor in the determination of authority among claimants.

My book is structured to highlight the different elements of Sha'rawi's adaptation, the environment in which he worked, and the repercussions of his innovations. Each chapter analyzes a theme but also explains how Sha'rawi can and should be distinguished from other religious authorities, past and present. In chapter 1, I begin with Sha'rawi's historical and biographical context. I examine how that context shaped his life, his public persona, his message, and his legacy. Chapter 2 discusses his reactions to some of the social and political issues of his day and how he influenced public opinion about them, often to the displeasure of the government. Chapters 3 and 4 cover how Sha'rawi, through his vocation, remained grounded in past 'ulama' concepts and methods, yet his association with them marked a distinctive change in how they were understood and in how they functioned. Chapter 3 deals with preaching—both its history among the 'ulama', and Sha'rawi as a preacher in his time in relation to his government and media connections. In this chapter I also compare Sha'rawi's and Yusuf Qaradawi's use of media to explain how their different messages fit the type of broadcasting each chose. Chapter 4 covers the issue of renewal—this concept was associated with the 'ulama' in the past, but its association with Sha'rawi helps expose its transformed meaning. Many Egyptians told me that Sha'rawi was the renewer of Islam in the twentieth century, which means they associated that task with a popular preacher instead of with a trained jurist. Sha'rawi renewed by repeating past Ash'arite theological understandings and making them accessible to the people; he did not innovate by rethinking them. To better understand how the popularization of once specialized terms came about, I begin chapter 4 with an exploration of the thought of Muhammad 'Abduh, who was the most influential 'ulama' reformer of the late nineteenth century. Chapter 5 is centered on understanding shifts in knowledge and how Sha'rawi sought to reclaim exoteric knowledge as primarily Qur'anic in order to make an argument for the indispensability of those trained at al-Azhar. Because his knowledge claims were partially devised to counteract Islamist thought, in this chapter I compare Sha'rawi's ideas about knowledge to the ideas of different types of Egyptian Islamists. I look at Sha'rawi's connection to esotericism in chapter 6: his affirmation of certain beliefs about esoteric knowledge, his association with miracles, and how the retelling of his life exemplifies typical Sufi hagiographies. This chapter also puts Sha'rawi's connection to esotericism in context through a discussion of the rise of Salafism in Egypt, the influence of the movement on al-Azhar, and its vehement anti-Sufi rhetoric. Chapter 7 focuses on the ideological use of language, especially as it pertains to modern Egypt. This chapter takes the elements discussed in earlier chapters related to Sha'rawi's attempt to exercise discursive dominance and helps explain that attempt by looking at language instead of content or context. A comparison of Sha'rawi's struggle for discursive dominance is compared to Sayyid Qutb's similar attempts in this chapter, which helps to distinguish their ideologies. Chapter 8 focuses on the visual aspects of television and how dependence on visual engagement and media rituals both heightened Sha'rawi's authority as an individual and removed that authority from his 'ulama' connections. I use affect theory to explain that seeing, as a bodily act, changes how viewers perceive someone presented on television. Affect and language ideology are related because the form of the message helps determine the message. Each is a site of likely contention when authoritative structures are engaged, and both can result in multiple reactions. But they are also related to one another because there is a back and forth between language and the senses, which means that the senses play a crucial role in how religion and religious authority is experienced. Yet, there are elements that help situate that experience before it takes place. Multiple uses of linguistic expressions, or heteroglossia, in any given society will help determine the reception of sacred speech. In terms of affect, social conditioning helps determine how one uses visual and auditory stimulus. Both affect and language use offer the opportunity to examine how influences, sensual, linguistic, cultural and historical, work on religious reception. In the Conclusion I briefly discuss where religious media has gone since the time of Sha'rawi's death.

I lived in Cairo during the summers of 2006, 2007, 2008, 2010, with a follow-up trip in 2013. I was able to gather information about Sha'rawi through the formal interviews I conducted, and the informal conversations I had about him. The advantage of doing research over many years, as opposed to doing it all in one year, is that I was able to see how the reception of Sha'rawi changed as the political and social environment in Egypt changed, an issue I deal with in the conclusion of this book.

The interviews I did and the conversations I had about Sha'rawi help structure the book because they determined the areas of inquiry I pursued. I did extensive interviews during my time in Cairo with Sha'rawi's followers—those who continue to look to him as a religious guide—and his disciples—those who have tasked themselves with keeping his legacy alive. The disciples I interviewed included Sha'rawi's son, 'Abd al-Rahim al-Sha'rawi; one of Sha'rawi's main disciples, 'Abd al-Ra'uf Hanafi, and his wife, Mrs. Nour El Din Attia; and the director of the Sha'rawi Center in Daqadous, Engineer 'Abd al-Rahman. I also attended numerous lectures given by 'Abd al-Ra'uf and by 'Abd al-Rahim al-Sha'rawi in different places in Cairo. During my time at these lectures, I met and spoke to many who continue to follow Sha'rawi's teachings, although these gatherings did not usually have more than thirty or forty people in attendance.

One of the bonuses of doing research on Sha'rawi is that I cannot mention his name to Egyptians without getting some kind of reaction, by which I mean I have rarely met an Egyptian who does not have an opinion about Sha'rawi. I learned early in my research to listen carefully when I tell people, and not only Egyptians, that the object of my research is Shaykh Sha'rawi. People of many nationalities have recounted stories of watching Sha'rawi when they were young or even of watching him today, and opinions are always mixed. I was able eventually to loosely categorize the comments and opinions I heard because many of them were repeated again and again. I did so in the following manner. First were the disciples and followers of Sha'rawi, as I mentioned. His disciples tended to exaggerate his importance, seeing him as more central to changing Muslim discourse and more appealing to intellectuals and al-Azhar elites than he was. Something I heard commonly was that Sha'rawi spoke on many different levels and that people learned from him what they were capable of understanding. Sha'rawi's disciples also told me wonderful stories about him, many of which are recounted in this book. Second were his followers, who without fail recounted to me how correct Sha'rawi was, how kind and gentle his manner was, how he explained complicated Qur'anic verses in simple language, and how when he died the Muslim world suffered because there was no one to take his place. His disciples and his followers, along with those who respected Sha'rawi but did not follow his teachings, also recounted stories of Sha'rawi's *karāmāt*, stories that are still well known throughout Egypt. Third, I spoke with a limited number of al-Azhar graduates, one of whom was of Sha'rawi's generation. In general they were grateful to Sha'rawi for teaching people in the manner that he did, but they did not find what he said to be relevant to them because they didn't consider it very sophisticated. Some even critiqued his time as an official at al-Azhar. Fourth, there were the educated elite in Cairo and other parts of Egypt. The opinions of this group were mixed: Some saw Sha'rawi as simple and not very interesting; some even regretted his influence among what they called the common people. Others thought of him as anti-intellectual and perhaps even dangerous because he bragged about only reading the Qur'an in the last years of his life. Some people told me that Sha'rawi should have spoken up against the government; many of them considered him a proxy of the presidents he worked for. One person told me that Sha'rawi's sermons helped him return to Islam, but that he had moved on to other teachers once he became more devout. Many people of all classes were impressed with the depth of Sha'rawi's knowledge of the Arabic language, which was sometimes the only quality people admired about him.

In general, however, I found no evidence that those who respected and even received religious guidance from Sha'rawi came only from the lower classes of Cairo, as is usually asserted. Although much of Sha'rawi's devoted public did come from the lower and lower middle classes, Sha'rawi was able to reach across class lines in Egypt because of his Arabic expertise, common sense interpretations, and the perception of him as a person who practiced what he preached. Seeing that Sha'rawi is so often characterized as a preacher of the common folk, I was surprised to find that many of the people who showed up to hear lectures about him were well off and well educated.

The comments made about Sha'rawi show that, even for those who protest his influence, he was at the very least recognized as one of the prominent Egyptian religious authorities of his era, for better or for worse. Throughout the book, I try to address the wide spectrum of opinions about Sha'rawi by investigating religious authority as fleeting and unstable, relying on vestiges of the past, and referencing contestations and future configurations. In any instance, authority is comprised of interactions and elements of complexity that are embedded in a singular society and the interaction of those elements both create discourse and are created by it.

CHAPTER I

Muhammad Mitwalli Sha'rawi

An Egyptian 'Alim Preacher of His Time

Retelling the life of Muhammad Mitwalli Sha'rawi, Egypt's most popular television preacher, also means retelling important parts of Egyptian religious history from the perspective of one man's experience. While Sha'rawi's life story was particular to him, his fortunes were tied to the state and affected by historical shifts in Egypt, a situation common to the 'ulama' of his time. The political changes that affected the religious scholars in Egypt beginning in the nineteenth century can be examined both from the perspective of history and also in how they manifested in the life of Sha'rawi. The choices he made depended on the policies of those in power, and he positioned himself in relation to those policies. Although reform of religious institutions began in the decades before his birth, Sha'rawi personally experienced the most radical alterations made to al-Azhar and to the 'ulama' more generally. Through the people Sha'rawi met, the movements he became involved with, and the rulers he worked for, he was directly connected to—and sometimes even helped influence—the instruments of change that dominated modern Egyptian society.

From his early education in his village of Daqadous to his time at al-Azhar, Sha'rawi's life story is typical of those told about religious figures throughout Islamic history. Although he began his life in a village, he was able to get an al-Azhar education and eventually become an important religious figure in Egypt because of his early ability to memorize the Qur'an and his other intellectual skills.[1] Historical events, however, made Sha'rawi's experiences as a student unlike what they would have been in the past. While still a student,

Sha'rawi became involved in protests and with the nationalist movement, which were common experiences for those involved with al-Azhar from the late nineteenth century onward. For a time he also joined Hasan al-Banna, the founder of the Muslim Brotherhood, which was then a new religious movement.

Later in his life, as he moved between teaching in Saudi Arabia and government jobs, his career was determined by the rulers of Egypt: first Gamal Abdel Nasser (ruled 1956–1970) and then Anwar Sadat (ruled 1970–1981). Nasser placed Sha'rawi in various government posts, including sending him to teach Arabic in Algeria as a representative of al-Azhar. When Sadat became president, Sha'rawi's fortunes changed. During Sadat's rule, Sha'rawi was appointed to what would be the most important jobs of his career, first as head of the Ministry of Endowments (*wizārat al-awqāf*) and then as a television preacher. His different relationships with these two presidents also express Sha'rawi's changing attitude toward the state. Although he obediently went where Nasser sent him, Sha'rawi sometimes spoke out against Nasser. When Sadat came to power, however, Sha'rawi decided to back him and his policies, often to the detriment of his own reputation—demonstrating how, over time, Sha'rawi became more keenly aware of the effect that his personal relationships with the rulers of Egypt had on his career.

The direction Sha'rawi's life took was also influenced by the relationship between state and religious institutions. For example, because of the repercussions of the state taking control of al-Azhar, Sha'rawi stopped working at the institution. Although state impositions had mixed repercussions for the 'ulama' overall, Sha'rawi often said that he left his post as the minister of endowments because he didn't like the corruption at al-Azhar. Whether or not that was his real motivation for leaving is not what is important. Corruption among the 'ulama' who worked at the Ministry of Endowments was a result of al-Azhar's financial dependence on the state and of the fact that al-Azhar functionaries were appointed by the state, but it also lessened the stature of the 'ulama' among the public. Sha'rawi chose to portray himself as one of the common people by distancing himself from official institutions and their corruption. This distance helped him reinforce his reputation as a man of the people, a reputation he garnered through the popularity of his television show.

Near the end of his time as minister of endowments, Sha'rawi began appearing as a regular guest on a religious television show, but it wasn't until after he resigned from this ministerial post that he got his own show. Even though this was a transition for Sha'rawi, he remained a government employee and a confidant of Sadat. The behind-the-scenes control of television by the state at the time did not hinder the perception among vast numbers of Egyptians that Sha'rawi, as he appeared on their screens, was one of them. His television persona represented the delicate balance between being a celebrity and an employee of the state—he simultaneously maintained his state connections and his reputation as the people's preacher, both of which depended on his marketability.

When the government shifted again during Husni Mubarak's reign (1981–2011), Sha'rawi entered the last stages of his life, and at this point his celebrity became the focus of his relationship with those in power. During Mubarak's rule, Sha'rawi reached the pinnacle of his influence, but Mubarak was not always happy with how Sha'rawi used that influence. Sha'rawi had become a new type of religious authority in twentieth-century Egypt: someone who, through popular appeal, had secured the devotion of many Egyptian Muslims. The more popular he became, the more freedom he had to oppose a government that could not be seen as trying to silence someone millions of Egyptians trusted as a religious guide. Even at this stage, however, Sha'rawi rarely voiced opposition to the government and never did so directly, which is indicative of how he carefully cultivated his public image but also of his outlook. Sha'rawi's position in Egypt at the time was unique; he navigated between his reception among the people, government control and appeasement, technological advances, and the variety of religious opinions increasingly coming to the fore of public debate.

THE MODERNIZATION OF RELIGIOUS INSTITUTIONS IN EGYPT

The project of trying to modernize—or Europeanize—Egypt began with Muhammad 'Ali Pasha, who ruled Egypt from 1805 to 1848, and continued throughout the twentieth century. Changes to educational and political institutions, the centralization of state power and control, and technological advances were all part of this process. But the process of modernization is multicivilizational; its processes and effects are multiple because they depend on context.[2] Modifications have varied depending on when and where this process unfolds, and who is centralizing, employing technologies, imposing structural changes, and attempting to generate new experiences. Because the locations and people involved in the modernizing process have been varied, the reactions to imposed changes have also been diverse.[3] Egypt has followed its own particular trajectory, which can be traced in the details of how Egyptian rulers sought to modernize education, law, and religion; in the particular repercussions of institutional reformulation on society as a whole; and in how the 'ulama' acted in response to both.

The public responsibilities of the 'ulama' were greatly reduced by a series of rulers, from Muhammad 'Ali to Gamal Abdel Nasser. Each ruler successively curbed the societal functions of the 'ulama', namely, their powers to regulate law, education, and religious institutions.[4] These policies simultaneously increased government control in these areas and made the 'ulama' financially dependent on the state. During the reigns of Sadat and Mubarak, the fortunes of the 'ulama' began to change, but they have never recovered their full independence. Both Sadat and Mubarak helped the scholars of al-Azhar maintain enough authority to legitimate their regimes while still keeping those same scholars restricted.[5] That balance was difficult for the state to sustain, especially in the late twentieth century when the government's need for 'ulama' legitimation increased. This need, along with new technology, provided an opening for the 'ulama' to reassert their importance and therefore their authority, sometimes in spite of the desires of the rulers.

Muhammad 'Ali Pasha was the first Egyptian ruler to engage seriously in modernizing reforms. Part of his vision included making changes to the financing of al-Azhar. Al-Azhar had been the premier institution for Sunni 'ulama' education for hundreds of years, but it was also much more than a university: It was, and still is, the institutional powerhouse of Egyptian religion. Muhammad 'Ali curtailed 'ulama' independence by nationalizing many of the *waqf* lands (*waqf* usually refers to religious endowments, but in this case it also refers to other types of funding) that had historically been used by the 'ulama' to finance religious educational and other institutions. It was Muhammad 'Ali who also introduced secular education into Egyptian schools as a parallel learning enterprise to traditional religious schools.[6]

After Muhammad 'Ali's reign ended in 1848 but before the revolution of 1952, the Egyptian government introduced more changes, which affected al-Azhar and how it operated throughout Egyptian society. A series of reorganizations of al-Azhar took place in 1896, 1911, and 1930. The focus of these reforms was to centralize religious authority within the institution, especially within the office of the shaykh, or rector, of al-Azhar, As a result, al-Azhar's authority over religious centers and religious schools (including the Teachers' Training College and the School of Religious Law) increased.[7] Although these reforms seem to indicate that al-Azhar gained more power, in actuality they had the opposite effect. By centralizing 'ulama' authority, the government increased its own ability to manipulate 'ulama' institutions and to control official 'ulama' religious opinions, or *fatāwā*. By the twentieth century, this manipulation led people to distrust many 'ulama' who held official positions, especially those who issued official edicts. In addition, the 'ulama' who served as officials of al-Azhar benefitted financially as a result of their increased institutionalized influence, which is why they often did not oppose governmental reforms, but it also explains how corruption became common.[8]

Gamal Abdel Nasser instituted a startling reshaping of al-Azhar between 1952 and 1961, which represented a culmination of the process begun by Muhammad 'Ali. First, Nasser created a new ministry of the government—the Ministry of Endowments—to deal with the remaining *waqf* lands, thereby placing all 'ulama' funding under the control of a government bureaucracy. In 1955, Nasser also abolished the shari'a law courts. But it was Nasser's establishment of a new law in 1961 that introduced the most radical changes to the structure of al-Azhar to date. The 1961 law placed al-Azhar under the control of the minister of endowments, essentially giving the president and government-appointed ministers control over both the hiring and firing of al-Azhar employees and the finances of the institution.[9] As a result of reforms begun by Muhammad 'Ali and culminating in the law of 1961, education in Egypt also came under the control of the state. As such, education today—when contrasted with the diversity present in medieval madrasas—is more homogenous and more subject to governmental control than it had been previously.

In the past, the 'ulama' had assumed control over knowledge transmission through education even though, in practice, their training, affiliations, and geographical regions were so varied that they never formed a uniform group.[10] Still, within any region it was the 'ulama' who maintained official posts in universities and smaller madrasas, who oversaw the system of education, and who made the decisions about what knowledge should be transmitted and to whom.[11] Although the more expert, regulating 'ulama' sought to regulate education by expressing and enforcing standards, diversity persisted.[12] The training of the 'ulama' corps was not consistent, which meant that they could not be controlled locally by a set of centralized standards. Thus the knowledge that was transmitted was inconsistent. Over time, the boundaries of what was considered a proper religious education changed depending on historical and political circumstances.

The law of 1961 also changed the educational degrees available at al-Azhar by expanding its colleges from the three dealing with religious sciences (Qur'an, law, and Arabic language) to include colleges devoted to the study of subjects such as business, science, engineering, and medicine. Many reformist 'ulama' and Egyptian intellectuals had advocated for adding secular subjects to al-Azhar's curriculum, even before Muhammad 'Abduh, as mufti of Egypt from 1899–1905, tried and failed to push such changes through. Reformers like 'Abduh believed that if the 'ulama' were educated in modern science and technological innovations, they could use that knowledge when making religious decisions about modern life; he and many others thought this education was essential to modernizing the 'ulama' corps. But incorporating scientific learning into the curriculum of al-Azhar had unforeseen negative effects. It weakened religious training by draining resources away from the religious colleges.[13] An al-Azhar education, although still respected, does not carry the weight it once did because the religious education is not as strong as it once was.[14] This mixing of subjects also took place in secular schools where religion is now taught as one of many subjects.

The alteration of Egypt's education system, specifically the mixing of religious and secular learning, was a crucial part of the transformation of 'ulama' authority in the modern era. It meant more than just institutional change; it also transformed assumptions about the purpose of education. This shift led not only to the denigration of specialized religious training but also to the bolstering of science and related specialties. Introducing religion into the public schools as a subject equal to math or science meant that it was taught as a reified system, leading to the objectification of religion.[15] This objectified understanding of religion emphasized the memorization and re-articulation of past decisions and rules. Presenting religion as a subject also engendered a need for religious material, both spoken and written, geared toward extending the limited information students received in their public education. The effect of the mixing of epistemologies, religious and secular, also meant that ideas about knowledge that came to be accepted in modern Egypt stood in contrast to traditional epistemic formulations.

Traditional epistemology presents knowledge according to a bipartite division between human knowledge (both secular and religious) and God's knowledge. Religious knowledge is thought to be gained through the religious sciences (al-'ulūm al-dīniyya) and is distinguished from secular knowledge through a direct link to God. Making religious knowledge practical through the religious sciences meant deciphering God's will and intentions as they were disclosed in the revelatory sources.[16] According to the tenets of this view, the transmission of religious knowledge relied on various modes of acquisition, which were associated with the different ways it can be attained. Humans are thought to acquire knowledge through proper action, but it can only be bestowed when, and on whom, God desires.[17]

In this epistemological formulation, three elements are involved in the procurement of knowledge: pursuing human knowledge associated with the religious and nonreligious sciences, proper behavior, and God's bestowal on the pious. These three modes of acquisition are not just considered interdependent in procurement and use—when they manifest concomitantly, they authenticate one another. Accordingly, this close association assumes the connection and complementarity between behavior and knowledge, both exoteric and esoteric,[18] as is demonstrated by the saying "every scholar is a mystic and every mystic is a scholar."[19] This view assumes that knowledge needs to be discerned, or constantly brought forth, through particular methods and procedures, which, in the case of 'ulama' hermeneutics, are constructed to minimize the appearance of human intellectual interference.

Seeing religious knowledge as something that must be acquired through constant endeavor, and as embedded in the relationship between God and humanity, is very different than presenting Islam as a system of codes standardized according to a particular set of beliefs and practices, and therefore as void of dynamism. Yet reducing religion to a stagnant set of codes means that those codes can easily be regulated through government apparatuses, including education.[20] The reformulation of religious and educational structures thus empowered the government to take both actual control of institutions and intellectual control over presentations of knowledge. In the realm of religious representation, however, many policies of the state—including the attempts to systematize religion and lessen 'ulama' influence in society—had a very different effect than was intended.

THE REPOSITIONING OF 'ULAMA' AUTHORITY IN LATE-TWENTIETH-CENTURY EGYPT

Although the 'ulama' are now said to be weak both intellectually and institutionally, too submissive to the government and unable to deal with social change, they have always been politically and socially relevant.[21] The 'ulama' in Egypt have responded in remarkable ways to state impositions, doing everything from openly opposing to cooperating with the government.[22] They were involved in political opposition when Egypt attempted to resist Napoleon in 1798. They were also associated with the 1805 overthrow of the Mamluks, the Orabi uprising in 1881 1882, and the revolution of 1919.[23] (An argument can be made that this pattern was continued in the 2011 uprisings as well.) As early as 1897, some of the 'ulama' of al-Azhar were active in the early stages of the Egyptian nationalist movement;[24] they became involved in order to defend "both religion and the homeland." Defense of religion was about defending Islam and the perfect revelation, and defense of the homeland meant advocating for an Egyptian identity that included all subjects and was not limited to particular religious groups.[25] Ironically, the 'ulama' were integrally involved in the formulation of a brand of nationalism that was justified on religious grounds. They even saw nationalism as inextricably linked to their concerns for the continued preeminence of Islam.

As a result, the 'ulama' were inevitably drawn into the conversation concerning the relationship between faith and political power, formulating their own reactions to the changed environment in which they found themselves. These responses speak to both 'ulama' activism and to diversity within their ranks.[26] So while there is no doubt that changes in the nineteenth and twentieth centuries weakened the influence of the 'ulama' as disseminators of religious knowledge and also affected their stature among the people, this does not mean that they remained passive. Indeed, in the late twentieth century the 'ulama' reasserted themselves publicly as the disseminators of true religious knowledge in the contemporary world, although this time among new and varied competition, even for the designation of the term 'ulama'.

The 'ulama', religious scholars trained at al-Azhar (here adhering to the historic understanding of the term 'ulama'), were able to gain public influence in the latter part of the twentieth century because of the shifts caused by government control of religious institutions. The rise of Islamist groups, in their mild and extreme forms, was facilitated by the fact that the regulatory and intermediary roles of the 'ulama' in society were reduced. Once the Islamists had gained a substantial following, their influence appeared to contribute further to the loss of 'ulama' stature because they were competing with the 'ulama' for religious authority. But this loss did not materialize to the extent that was first postulated for a couple of reasons. First, the divide between 'ulama' and the Islamists, particularly the Muslim Brotherhood, was not so stark. Some 'ulama' (for example, Muhammad Ghazali and Yusuf Qaradawi) went on to become prominent Islamists, but there were also many who decided to receive training at al-Azhar after joining the Muslim Brotherhood. Although they did not become a dominant force at al-Azhar, al-Azhar's leaders were typically not interested in criticizing the government and were mystically inclined; the Muslim Brotherhood did win many student elections. The involvement of members of the Muslim Brotherhood in al-Azhar is an indication of diversity within the institution, which did not consist of scholars of only one religious orientation or political affiliation. Second, as the Islamists rose to prominence, they began to question the legitimacy of the Egyptian government on religious grounds, with extremists groups even attempting to overthrow the government violently. Once Sadat and Mubarak realized that the increasing popularity of Islamism was a threat, they used the voices of the conciliatory Azharis to publicly counter it. So while changes undertaken by the state resulted in 'ulama' dependency, by integrating them into the Egyptian bureaucracy, the government then easily brought certain scholars forth as the official representatives of Islam in Egypt.

Although the 'ulama' lost their economic and political independence, Nasser's modernization attempts did not deal the final blow to the 'ulama' but actually helped them reemerge as powerful political actors.[27] To prove this point, Malika Zeghal emphasizes the difference between the "periphery" 'ulama'—those trained at al-Azhar who join Islamist groups such as the Muslim Brotherhood—and the "center" 'ulama' those who work as government employees within al-Azhar and therefore stay within acceptable political bounds (for example, Sha'rawi).[28] She goes on to say that, even if the center 'ulama' were not, those in the periphery were able to become politically relevant once they removed themselves from the control of the government.[29] But by making this distinction, Zeghal posits that the 'ulama' could regain influence, or be political, only when they removed themselves from the effects of Nasser's policies. Yet many of the Azhari-trained 'ulama' who asserted themselves in the late twentieth century did so within the boundaries set up by Nasser and the modernizers who came before him. What the periphery and center 'ulama' had in common was the use of their al-Azhar training to assert their rights as guides of the people in religion. Although some periphery 'ulama' became directly involved in formulating new social and political ideals, many did so by claiming to be the rightful interpreters of texts and legal opinions as 'ulama'.[30] They differed from the 'ulama' who chose to remain within government-controlled institutions because they decided to gain prominence or relevance through new religious movements.

For many 'ulama', no matter what their leanings, involvement in the institutional functions of al-Azhar still proved to be the best way to exert their influence. As a result of the government takeover of al-Azhar, those affiliated with it tried to maintain or reinstate its main institutional goals: gaining back autonomy, legitimacy, and status among the public for the credentialed scholars, as the rightful representatives and interpreters of Islam, and preserving and propagating a vision of an Egyptian Sunni Islam. After the rise of radical Islamists in the late twentieth century, those who sought to defend al-Azhar were given the opportunity to further those goals.[31] As violence escalated throughout Egyptian society, the government could not be seen as interfering with the output from al-Azhar or its scholars without undermining al-Azhar's appearance as an institution interested in making decisions for religious and not political reasons.

Thus beginning in the late 1970s, as a direct reaction to the threat of violent groups, the government made subtle accommodations toward al-Azhar, giving the institution enough autonomy for it to appear independent from the state. But the condemnation of extremists by al-Azhar was not merely for political reasons. Along with seeking the overthrow of the government, these groups belittled the scholars affiliated with al-Azhar, directly challenging their authority and their history of mediation. By the late twentieth century, the relationship between al-Azhar and the Egyptian state was no longer about the state's control of al-Azhar. It was now characterized by the symbiotic needs of these two powerful Egyptian institutions; the long-term viability of both was now interdependent. Sha'rawi's situation in many ways set the precedent for this accommodation. The fame Sha'rawi gained among the people meant that the government could not oppose his statements without undermining their own reasons for broadcasting him in the first place: to counter Islamists by bolstering the claims of a politically conciliatory, prominent member of al-Azhar.

By the 1990s, al-Azhar had gained enough autonomy from government control to make decisions clearly against the official policies of the state.[32] The Islamic Research Council, which was reinstituted by Jad al-Haq 'Ali Jad al-Haq, Shaykh of al-Azhar from 1982 to 1996, helped al-Azhar became a more influential and conservative institution. The Islamic Research Council was the more independent body of al-Azhar scholars, in contrast to the Fatwa

Council, which was known for issuing fatwas that justified controversial government policies. Under the guidance of Jad al-Haq, the Islamic Research Council was given the power to ban print material, films, and television content it considered "offensive to Islam."[33] It was also the Islamic Research Council that condemned Farag Foda's writings as blasphemous, which eventually led to his assassination.

In 1993, another group of 'ulama' from al-Azhar, calling themselves the Mediation Committee, published a statement not only condemning the violence of extremist groups but also opposing their severe treatment by the government; they offered themselves as mediators to help resolve the problem. Making the most of the government's need for their legitimation, the Mediation Committee was able to further their own goals by condemning the extremists who opposed them and appearing to be autonomous from the state. Of the forty-one shaykhs who signed the document, some were directly involved with the running of al-Azhar and some were not, but they all came together in defense of al-Azhar. They were clearly designing a new relevance for themselves as independent spokespersons for the Egyptian nation, even though they did not all gain influence among the people in the same way. For example, three of the most famous 'alim-preachers of the day—Sha'rawi, Muhammad Ghazali and 'Abd al-Hamid Kishk—were all were a part of the Mediation Committee.[34] But both Ghazali and Kishk were Islamists; Ghazali was a member of the Muslim Brotherhood; and Kishk was known for his speeches against the Egyptian government, its secular policies, and its usurpation of the powers of al-Azhar. Because of his views he was imprisoned in 1965 and again in 1981. Meanwhile, Sha'rawi was preaching on state television to millions of Egyptians every Friday afternoon.

RELIGIOUS AUTHORITY IN CONTEXT: THE LIFE
OF A TWENTIETH-CENTURY EGYPTIAN 'ALIM

Muhammad Mitwalli Sha'rawi (his nickname was al-Shaykh al-Amin al-Sha'rawi) was born on April 16, 1911 C.E., in the Egyptian village of Daqadous. Daqadous is situated in the province of Mit Ghamr in Daqaliyya along the Nile delta. It is about a two-hour drive north of Cairo. Sha'rawi studied in the primary religious institute and secondary school in Zaqaziq, where he memorized the Qur'an by the age of ten.[35] In recounting his life, Sha'rawi said that he always expected to become a farmer like his father, but his early talents in Qur'an memorization and his aptitude for religious learning meant that he was singled out as a candidate to go onto higher learning at al-Azhar University in Cairo.[36] The director of the Sha'rawi Center in Daqadous, a disciple of Sha'rawi, relayed Sha'rawi's early life in this way:

> From a very young age God prepared Shaykh Sha'rawi for the job of *da'iyya* [someone who summons others to the faith].When he was very young he was already reading and understanding very difficult books about Islam and he would sit with scholars who were very advanced and read these books with them. It was also clear to his mother that he was special. She married him off at a very young age so that he would be taken care of.[37]

At al-Azhar, Sha'rawi enrolled in the college of Arabic Language. He graduated in 1941, and two years later he went on to attain a degree in teaching (*ijaza 'alamiyya*) from al-Azhar.

The retelling of Sha'rawi's early life is very much like the retelling of the lives of many 'ulama' throughout Egyptian history. Even though the years of his youth came after the process of modernization had begun, the system of getting ahead through education had not been disrupted. It was Sha'rawi's early political involvement that signaled a change. Sha'rawi's first political experiences came in the 1930s when he took part in student uprisings. Even before he entered al-Azhar in 1937, he played an important role in supporting nationalism as a student leader in his al-Azhar–affiliated school in Zaqaziq. He recounted this experience:

> When the nationalist movement began the committee of youth from . . . al-Azhar was formed. I was elected head of the committee by Professor Deputy Mahmoud Abdul Min Am Khafaji and Professor Muhammad Fahmi Abdul Latif of the treasury office. . . . The leaders of the movement were thrown in jail. Muhammad Fahmi, Abdul Latif and I were thrown into solitary confinement in the jail in Zaqaziq where I spent 30 days.[38]

Supporting nationalism at the time meant fighting for an independent unified Egypt and against the British military presence there. Sha'rawi's vision of an independent Egypt led him to join the nationalist Wafd party. Sa'd Zaghloul was the founding leader of the Wafd Party, and Mustafa Nahas was the party leader and prime minister of Egypt off and on from 1928 to 1952. From its very start in 1918, the Wafd party envisioned a unified Egypt. The Egyptian revolution of 1919, sparked by the British exile of Sa'd Zaghloul and given further strength by his return in 1919, was a seminal moment of national unity. Revolutionary demonstrations were diverse and included women, Christians, Jews, and a variety of social classes. During one demonstration an "Azhari Sheikh was seen carrying a picture of the Coptic Christian patriarch along with the flag depicting the cross and crescent." Rabbis also protested and made speeches about the nation.[39] Much of the revolution was planned from al-Azhar itself because the British, who feared further protests, didn't dare enter any religious space to arrest people.[40]

In recounting the importance of the Wafd and this type of inclusive nationalistic ideal, Sha'rawi later said in a televised interview:

> I was Wafdi such as it was. And in the year 1938 we attended a celebration of the memory of Sa'd Zaghloul . . . we considered the memory of Sa'd [important] because according to his brand of nationalism we [were able to say] what we wanted to say. At this celebration I recited a poem in praise of Sa'd Zaghloul and his deputy Mustafa Nahas. But what we expected did not happen, instead the opposite of what I expressed with this poem welcoming the revolution happened.[41]

The way Sha'rawi recounted his experiences and his attachment to Sa'd Zaghloul years later demonstrates that he still idealized the early Wafd movement. He endorsed their vision of national unity regardless of religious affiliation. In the quote above, Sha'rawi also made it clear that the nationalism of the Wafd Party was in no way contrary to Islamic values. He stated that, as long as those in power allowed the 'ulama' the freedom to "say what they wanted," they were acceptable leaders. This model of when to accept political authority would crystallize later in his life. When he accepted the job as national television preacher, he did so based on the understanding that he would not make political statements in his sermons and that the government would let him transmit religious knowledge as he saw fit. Even though he recounted this story only later in his life, he claims that, early in his life, he formed his Wafdi ideas about every Egyptian belonging to the nation no matter what their religious affiliation.

Even though the Wafd Party and its government represented the only viable political alternative to the king and the British early on, by 1937, they began to lose support, and in particular the support of the students of al-Azhar. Other groups began catching the attention of the students, especially the Muslim Brotherhood and the Nationalist Party.[42] Because the Wafd, the Brotherhood, and the Nationalist Party all opposed the British presence in Egypt, students who were primarily concerned with seeing an independent Egypt could choose among them. This made for fierce competition among the groups and among their leaders and members. It also helps explain why, in 1938, Sha'rawi was working with Hasan al-Banna, the founder of the Muslim Brotherhood (al Ikhwan al-Muslimun), even while remaining attached to the ideals of the Wafd Party. Among the publications of Hasan al-Banna at the time was a leaflet explaining the basics of the organization, and Sha'rawi originally handwrote the contents of that leaflet.[43] But Sha'rawi did not remain with the Muslim Brotherhood for very long. Later in his life, when he was asked about his relationship to Hasan al-Banna and why he separated from the Muslim Brotherhood, Sha'rawi answered:

> When the story of the poem I recited in praise of Mustafa Nahas reached Hasan al-Banna he was angry and he admonished me about this poem. I said to him: "Ya Shaykh Hasan, if we examine the leaders of the nation today to see who is closest to God's way, so that our souls and spirits can be with him, then we will find only Nahas, as he is a good man. He does not smoke cigarettes nor engage in other negative behavior. If we must pursue one of the politicians, then it has to be Nahas. He is the [only] politician we [can] follow." Shaykh Hasan answered saying: "He is one of our enemies. Because he has the support of the people (sha'b) he alone is able to hinder our [progress]" . . . And from that moment I separated from the Muslim Brotherhood.[44]

During the time that this story took place, al-Banna and his supporters were in a serious, sometimes violent struggle with the supporters of the Wafd, which helps explain his reaction to Sha'rawi's praise of Nahas.[45] Although ties between Hasan al-Banna and the al-Azhar students were strong, his relationship with the officials of al-Azhar was strained. In 1942, a high-ranking official of al-Azhar went as far as to recommend that provincial branches of the Brotherhood be forced to close.[46]

When Sha'rawi recounted this period of his life, he did not speak of these broader political struggles, even though he participated in them. Even so, Sha'rawi did not retell these early experiences merely to recount how he was involved with historical figures and controversies. He used them to elucidate his views about the role of religion and politics in the nation, and he spoke as someone who had spent most of his career in the service of the Egyptian government. From the way Sha'rawi told the story, he portrayed himself as rejecting Hasan al-Banna's political goals even while he was working with him. As was his usual style, he did not explain the point of the story but merely alluded to it. He recalls telling al-Banna that Nahas was *the politician* who was closest to God and was therefore the only person fit to rule, implying that al-Banna and his associates either should not have been politicians, or that they were not as close to God as Nahas and therefore not as fit to rule. Sha'rawi stated that, once he discovered al-Banna's animosity toward Nahas, he left, which was meant to signal his attachment to the Wafd Party. In the above quote, Sha'rawi also advocated for judging politicians based on how they lived their lives according to very minimal standards, a view that was antithetical to the views of Hasan al-Banna. At the same time, referring to Hasan al-Banna during an interview recorded in the early 1980s (now one of the most viewed YouTube clips of Sha'rawi and one that gained in popularity after the 2013 overthrow of the Muslim Brotherhood in Egypt), Sha'rawi said: "May Allah accept the martyr who planted the tree [of the Muslim Brotherhood]."[47] Although he regretted the fact that al-Banna became focused on political rule, Sha'rawi never lost his respect for al-Banna as a religious reformer.

In the same quote, Sha'rawi also identified the national political representatives he could support by distinguishing between the two political forces at the time: the Wafd Party and the Muslim Brotherhood. Although Sha'rawi did not remain a member of the Wafd, his nationalist commitments stayed with him. He also remained committed to the idea that religious and political leaders should function separately in society. Sha'rawi's son, 'Abd al-Rahim al-Sha'rawi, recounted that Sha'rawi left the Muslim Brotherhood because he did not believe in resorting to violence for the sake of changing the government, especially for Islamic purposes.[48]

In 1943 after Sha'rawi received his teaching certificate, he was appointed to teach at the religious institute in Tanta, later at the primary religious institute in Zaqaziq, and then at the religious institute in Alexandria. Sha'rawi recounted how he felt when he graduated from al-Azhar, conveying his ideas about the behavioral responsibility of the 'ulama':

> I was always aware that in every place I was a [member] of al-Azhar and therefore that I was an example. So I behaved [according to this status] in my movements, [in all] circumstances, dress and actions stemming from my surety that the 'ulama' of al-Azhar are examples to the people. I carried on my shoulders, with my 'ulama' colleagues, the responsibility [to engage in] model behavior, which must reflect a scholar of al-Azhar. There was an awareness of the extent of the [importance] of the [al-Azhar] degree, which we carried around our necks, concerning the book of God and the sunna of his Prophet.[49]

In this quote, Sha'rawi indicated that his authority as an 'alim was comprised of a combination of elements: knowledge and behavior, or mastering the religious sciences and acting according to that knowledge. Looking back, his sense of the image he portrayed to the people, and the importance it had to him is clear.

In 1950, after seven years of teaching in Egypt, Sha'rawi went to teach in Saudi Arabia, where he worked as a professor of shari'a and theology at the College of King 'Abd al-'Aziz in Mecca. Sha'rawi taught theology and law in spite of the fact that his original degree was in the Arabic language. He rose through the ranks of the 'ulama' in Saudi Arabia and eventually came to the attention of King Sa'ud ibn 'Abd al-'Aziz.[50] The following is a story that was told to me by 'Abd al-Rahim al-Sha'rawi. In 1955, the Saudis decided to enlarge the holy shrine at the Ka'ba. They wanted to move the stone believed to contain the footprint of Abraham because the area around it often became crowded during Hajj rituals, which caused many problems. The Saudi government, following the advice of the council of religious scholars known as the Council of Enjoining the Good and Forbidding the Evil had decided to move the footprint to a different area where it could be accessed more easily. When Sha'rawi heard about the plans to move the footprint he became "annoyed and surprised." He told King Sa'ud that it was forbidden for him to move Abraham's footprint because:

> God has placed Abraham's footprint where it is now, therefore you cannot change it. Even though it was moved before [it was moved by the second Caliph 'Umar ibn al-Khattab] we cannot reach the degree of 'Umar so we cannot do such things [i.e., move the footprint from where he placed it].[51]

Sha'rawi advised the king to put the footprint inside a large transparent glass box, which would expand the viewing area and allow people to see it and pray at it. The king, much to the annoyance of the Council of Enjoining the Good and Forbidding the Evil, took the advice of Sha'rawi and built a new encasement according to Sha'rawi's specifications.[52] After the solution was reached, the Saudi king offered Sha'rawi a monetary reward, but Sha'rawi refused to take it. Instead he told the king:

> I know that the gift of kings cannot be refused and cannot be given back but I told God [that I would issue] this fatwa for his [sake alone]. So please help me; I desire to be sincere and I do not want to take this money. Sha'rawi began to cry, and the king gave him his coat as a reward instead.[53]

This story is interesting for a couple of reasons. First, because accepting money for a religious decision would have meant that Sha'rawi's intentions were corrupt and that he was beholden to the king, the story positions Sha'rawi as a moral model even though he had close relations to those in power. This positioning was important to Sha'rawi's legacy because Sha'rawi has been critiqued as someone who was unduly influenced by these relations. At the Shaykh Sha'rawi Center in Daqadous, many pictures of Sha'rawi and Muslim heads of state were prominently displayed. His close relations with these leaders were a point of pride for his devoted followers, even though they fueled the allegations of his critics. Second, from a practical perspective, the story demonstrates how Sha'rawi was able to maneuver among the powerful through his clever use of language. He did not refuse the gift; instead he affirmed the ruler's power and invoked his religious sentiment. Again, this portrayal of Sha'rawi was at least partially meant to counter those who have portrayed his association with political power as unscrupulous.

In 1963, Nasser and King Sa'ud had a disagreement, so Nasser prevented Sha'rawi from teaching in Saudi Arabia. Sha'rawi was subsequently appointed as the director of the office of the Shaykh Al-Azhar who was, at the time, Hasan Mamun. According to Sha'rawi, during his time as office director, he clashed with Nasser because he opposed Nasser's close ties with communist Russia. Sha'rawi's relationship with Nasser was contentious. Not only did he criticize Nasser's relationship with Russia, he also said that Egypt was defeated in the 1967 war because it was God's will, owing to the fact that Nasser had ties with a communist country. Besides the influence of Islamism, Sha'rawi perceived communism—because of its rejection of religion—as the biggest threat to Egypt. Nasser for his part was interested in developing Egypt as a modern state and not necessarily in affirming its identity as a Muslim nation. As a result, Nasser removed Sha'rawi from his position at al-Azhar and sent him to Algeria to head an official delegation of al-Azhar graduates who helped the Algerian government reestablish the primacy of the Arabic language after the revolution.[54]

The scholars that were sent to Algeria were very unpopular, which resulted in their mistreatment. Sha'rawi attributed their unpopularity to Egypt's disastrous role in the 1967 war with Israel and to the defeat of the Arab armies. But the Algerians disliked them mainly because the Egyptian teachers who were sent to villages all over Algeria were inadequate. Many of these Egyptians acquired the reputation for being substandard teachers, which added to the Algerian rejection of anything associated with Egypt.[55] Sha'rawi recounted that the Algerians even rejected the sale of Egyptian bread, forgetting Egypt's role in, and support of, the Algerian revolution.[56]

During his time in Algeria, Sha'rawi met the Sufi Shaykh Muhammad Belkaid of the Hibriyya Sufi order in the Tlemcen region, along with many other Algerian Sufi masters. Belkaid was a spiritual guide for Sha'rawi, although Sha'rawi never officially entered the Hibriyya Sufi order by promising allegiance to the Shaykh. As their relationship was explained to me, Sha'rawi had many dreams about Belkaid beginning twenty years before they actually met. In these dreams Belkaid would give Sha'rawi advice on matters that were confusing him. In recounting these stories, however, Sha'rawi's disciples always stressed that, in some ways, Sha'rawi was also a teacher of Belkaid.[57] Sha'rawi was not widely known as a Sufi in Egypt either during his lifetime or after his death. Most of the people I spoke to about him did not associate him with any Sufi order, despite the fact that when one listens to or reads Sha'rawi's sermons it is obvious that he had a mystical orientation. It was important for Sha'rawi, and his disciples, to keep this aspect of his life private for a couple of reasons. First, Sha'rawi spent a lot of time in Saudi Arabia, a country that is founded on a religious ideology that is extremely hostile toward Sufism. Second, and perhaps more important, in late-twentieth-century Egypt, many of the practices associated with Sufism had become controversial, including the idea that a Sufi master can serve as an intercessor between an adept and God (see chapter 6).

While in Algeria, Sha'rawi began his life as a popular preacher: "In Algeria when he spoke the mosques would fill with people and sometimes the crowds would spill onto the streets."[58] When Sha'rawi returned to al-Azhar after his time in Algeria, he was appointed by the minister of endowments as the director of preaching and thought (da'wa) at al-Azhar. A few years later he returned to Saudi Arabia to again teach at the University of Malik 'Abd al-'Aziz in Mecca. He returned home to Egypt in 1976, this time because he was selected by Sadat to become the minister of endowments.

Sadat obviously judged the usefulness of Sha'rawi's opinions differently than Nasser did because, unlike Nasser, he saw the identity of Egypt as closely tied to Islam. As a result he did not agree with many of the changes Nasser had made while he was president. Almost as soon as he became president, Sadat released the Muslim Brothers that Nasser had imprisoned. Although he later reinstated the policy of imprisoning the Muslim Brothers, many of Sadat's policies remained focused on making Islam a societal force in Egypt. At first Sadat saw Sha'rawi as someone who could help him with this project, but later the two developed a strong relationship. (The controversial aspects of Sha'rawi's relationship with Sadat will be discussed in chapter 2). When Sadat appointed Sha'rawi to head the Ministry of Endowments, he wanted someone in the post whom he trusted to help him make religion a more influential part of society.

Sha'rawi accepted the position, but as minister he witnessed extensive corruption, which he blamed on the four previous ministers:

> Neglect and bribery were prevalent in most sections of this Ministry. I released some of the directors who were making large profits from accepting bribes, which was equivalent to selling the Ministry. Previously they [the corrupt members] had the ability to remove any minister from the Ministry if he did not comply with their advice, and if he did not implement their orders. . . . I was shocked in my first days in charge of the ministry due to the bribes and falsity, which had openly eaten away the wealth of the nation. . . . Therefore my time as the Minister of *Awqaf* was difficult. My task proved impossible and I left the Ministry in 1978, after less than two years in office.[59]

After leaving this post Sha'rawi began his television show *Nūr 'alā Nūr* (*Light upon Light*). In the 1970s Sha'rawi appeared as a guest on the show, which was hosted by Mahmud Faraj. He was invited back many times, and his appearances were so popular that in 1980, at the age of sixty-nine, it became his show. He instantly changed the format from a question-and-answer show to a show containing his "thoughts" (*khawāṭir*) about various topics in light of his Qur'anic interpretations; essentially he became television preacher. The show was run on state-sponsored television as part of the Egyptian government's attempt to counter the rise of extremist rhetoric with a more moderate religious message. Several Egyptian preachers were broadcast at this time, but none of them enjoyed the popularity of Sha'rawi. At certain points in his career, his sermons could be seen on television four times a week, which was also the case a decade after his death. He continued his television preaching until he became too ill to broadcast, right before his death in 1998.

SHA'RAWI AS TELEVISION PREACHER

Egyptian president Gamal Abdel Nasser began in the 1960s using state-run television to further his goal of engendering nationalist sentiment.[60] By the time Sha'rawi began his broadcast career in the 1970s, the medium of television had become integrated into Egyptian daily life and was immensely popular among the public.[61] But television was most often used by the government to help Egyptians understand what it meant to be members of the nation.[62] Religious broadcasting in Egypt was from the beginning interwoven with these intentions. In Egypt, school and home have been the primary places of conditioning subjects in the language of the nation. Because television has become an important part of family life, it has aided in that conditioning.[63] Preachers like Sha'rawi, who became part of Sadat's attempt to make religion a guiding force in the nation, helped enforce the association between religious and national goals. The project of creating national religious preachers through television complemented the goals of presenting religion as an easily definable system through education. Thus television preaching was encouraged in Egypt because the government hoped it would help with morally educating the nation and simplifying Islam in order to teach Egyptians "the basics of morality and religious duty."[64]

Sha'rawi never directly spoke about political controversies in his television sermons. In the beginning of his career, that may have been because he did not want to anger his government employers, especially Sadat. But this is not a convincing argument for his later life because once Sha'rawi had become a religious guide to millions of Egyptians, his fame protected him from repercussions. Mubarak even grew to regret that the Sadat administration had helped to create the phenomenon of Sha'rawi.[65] Sometimes, later in his life, Sha'rawi subtly raised questions about government policy, but he did so on religious, not political, grounds and only in interviews and occasional writings.

Sha'rawi's lack of outright political response was due to three factors. First, all during his career as a television preacher, he understood the government expectations of him. When Sha'rawi was hired by Sadat, he and his administration were already familiar with Sha'rawi's political and religious perspectives. Sha'rawi's willingness to help further Sadat's agenda was apparent by the time was given his own television show. Second, Sha'rawi's embrace of nationalism and the way he expressed his rejection of Hasan al-Banna affirmed his belief that religious figures should not be directly involved with politics. It was an accommodationist stance that fit Sha'rawi's role as a government appointed spokesperson for Egyptian Islam, but it was not without historical precedence among the Sunni 'ulama' throughout Islamic history. The idea of separating religious and political thought was very important to Sha'rawi, even though he did not recognize how much his close relationship to the Egyptian government cast doubt on his commitment to this stance. Third, Sha'rawi enjoyed his status inside and outside of Egypt; a status that came through government opportunities. For him the Egyptian government was preferable to the other groups vying for political power. When he did critique different Egyptian groups and their agendas, it was usually those groups who, like the Muslim Brotherhood, were directly competing with him for religious authority.

CONCLUSION

Although Sha'rawi's life story does not tell the story of the 'ulama' overall, it does illustrate how the religious scholars of al-Azhar had to reposition themselves in direct relation to state power. Because of historical changes, the 'ulama' were brought under the control of the government, which stripped them of the very elements that supported their authority in society: their claim to transmit knowledge and their economic and procedural independence. The state usurpation of what had once been the purview of the religious scholars is what Sha'rawi and the other 'ulama' of Egypt had in common. As they had done in the past, however, the 'ulama' responded to these attempts to limit their influence in society in many different ways. Some joined Islamist groups, some remained at al-Azhar and worked for the government issuing *fatāwā* or managing funds, and others worked within the institution itself.

By the time Sha'rawi began his career as a representative of al-Azhar, he was also working as an employee of the state. His career demonstrates the possibilities that were opened to someone who was willing to use his official role to find a prominent place in society with the help of the state. This was not the only choice he could have made, but the elements of the choice and how those elements changed over time represent the position of the 'ulama' in Egypt more generally. His life, as a unique story, also illustrates the personal nature of the history of twentieth-century Egypt.

to reframe his initial support for peace with Israel, a policy that remained unpopular with the Egyptian public. Throughout his memoirs, Sha'rawi repeatedly told the following version of the story concerning his support: When Sadat originally decided to make peace with Israel, Sha'rawi was in favor of his decision and even encouraged Sadat to travel to Israel so that he could negotiate a peace treaty in person. Sha'rawi also supported the 1947 United Nations General Assembly resolution accepting the UN Partition Plan for Palestine. The plan called for the partitioning of Palestine into two independent states, one Jewish and one Arab. But, according to Sha'rawi, he later modified his recommendation by publicly stating that as soon as the Arabs were powerful enough, they could demand that the land be returned and, if necessary, at that point they could even fight Israel for it.

In his memoirs Sha'rawi focused on a particular disagreement in 1980 that arose between him and the first Israeli ambassador to Egypt concerning statements Sha'rawi made on his television show. Sha'rawi interpreted some verses of the Qur'an[3] to mean that the Palestinian-Israeli struggle would continue until the end of time.[4] One of Sha'rawi's disciples, 'Abd al-Ra'uf, told me that it was a coincidence that Sha'rawi gave his interpretation of these verses at the same time that the peace treaty—specifically, the provisions dealing with Israel and Palestine—were still unsettled. According to the story, it angered many Israelis who assumed that Sha'rawi was offering his interpretation as a statement against the viability of peace. While it is doubtful that Sha'rawi's interpretation was aimed at undermining Sadat's efforts at this relatively early stage, it is important that he and his disciples recounted that he angered not only the Israelis and some Americans but also, as a result, the Egyptian government. What made the government angry was not Sha'rawi's interpretation of the Qur'an; they could not directly contradict his authority as an exegete without claiming interpretive rights. Instead the controversy surrounded how his interpretation was understood by the other states involved in the peace process. According to an interview with Sha'rawi:

Interviewer: The ambassador of Israel in Cairo was against your Qur'anic interpretation and indeed an American paper circulated the headline 'shut that man up,' which was how they attacked your virtue.

Sha'rawi: That is correct . . . but did the government silence me? No. They reduced my program . . . a little . . . after that there were [only] two programs every week. But then it increased [again] . . . to four times a week because [the dispute] only pertained to one occurrence; it was not my habit [to dispute with the government].[5]

When concluding the story, Sha'rawi said that Sadat told the Israeli ambassador that because Sha'rawi was speaking from his wealth of religious knowledge, he would not ask Sha'rawi to shut up.[6]

Sha'rawi pointed to his discomfort about disputing with the government even while trying to distance himself from Sadat's controversial policy toward Israel. He said that, because of his standing as a truthful interpreter, Sadat could not shut him up, and even though the government sought to punish him, the punishment was slight and did not last. Sha'rawi's recounting of the incident clearly lays out the agreement the two men had: Sadat did not interfere with Sha'rawi's religious mission, and Sha'rawi was not supposed to interfere with the agenda of the government. The "punishment" was probably meant to be a reminder of that agreement. Yet this moment also marks the point at which Sha'rawi's notoriety began to give him more freedom to disagree. Part of the reason the government failed at its supposed punishment of Sha'rawi was because his programs were immensely popular, which meant that they would be broadcast no matter what. It is interesting to note that in his retelling, Sha'rawi was affirming both that he had the freedom to say what he wanted and that he did not want to dispute with the government. Ultimately, Sha'rawi remained loyal to Sadat. He continued to portray their relationship in a positive way, and he also continued to portray Sadat as Sadat portrayed himself: as a pious leader.

SHA'RAWI AND THE CHALLENGE OF USING
SCRIPTURAL READINGS TO REACT TO SOCIAL ILLS

Sha'rawi had an interesting and at times contentious relationship with the Coptic Christian community of Egypt, which comprises somewhere between 10 and 15 percent of the population overall. Although he accepted Christians as people of the book, he did not try to reach beyond the past limitations of Islamic thought about Christianity, especially in regard to the Trinity and other foundational Christian doctrines. He upheld the view that only Muslims have a perfect religion. So even though he was committed to national inclusivity, his theology contradicted the very premise of that view. Sha'rawi's attempt to fold Christian concerns into a Muslim perspective exposed the limitations of trying to avoid sectarian strife through the discourse of a dominant religion.

Sha'rawi often talked about Egypt as a nation of Muslims and Christians, yet he did not see a contradiction between identifying both communities as Egyptian and justifying that identification through Islamic discourse. The opinions Sha'rawi espoused about Christians—whom he saw as a scriptural people that were mistaken in their fundamental beliefs—were devised long ago by a Muslim religious elite who often spoke as representatives of powerful Muslim empires. These sorts of theological hierarchies used to arrange the status of communities in the past could not be easily reconciled with a twentieth-century nationalist ideology. Perhaps even more problematic is the fact that, even though Sha'rawi recognized that Copts and Muslims were equally Egyptian, he did not engage the problems that the Coptic community faced and therefore he was not able to push beyond past restraints with his idealized views of national unity.

Sha'rawi generally took two distinctive approaches to Christianity. The first was to read the Qur'an as affirming the notion that Muhammad did not bring a new message; he brought the same one that Christians and Jews had received from their messengers. The second was to uphold Muslim ideas that, even though Christians and Jews were given a holy writ, those scriptures had since been corrupted. His relationship with the Copts was strained because he held both positions simultaneously. Sha'rawi is often accused of mocking Christians, of supporting the view that only Muslims are saved, or of being someone who thought unbelievers (meaning non-Muslims) should be killed. Nothing in what he said supports any of these views, even if early in his career Sha'rawi was insensitive to, and perhaps even misunderstood, Coptic beliefs. In particular his portrayal of the Trinity has been cited numerous times by Copts as insulting and incendiary. Later in his life, when he began to develop a pubic relationship with Baba Shenouda (the Coptic pope), he was more careful with his words. Sha'rawi is also criticized for his stance regarding Christianity by those who have not done a thorough reading of his Qur'anic exegesis (tafsīr) and by those who are not familiar with the classical positions concerning Qur'anic superiority. This notion of superiority—while it poses its own problems—is not always used to demonstrate that Christians and Jews are not saved, as Sha'rawi's thought demonstrates.

One such example is Sha'rawi's interpretation of the following verse from the Qur'an: "For, if one goes in search of a religion other than self-surrender unto God (*al-islām*), it will not be accepted from him, and in the life to come he shall be among the lost" (Qur'an 3:85). In his commentary Sha'rawi did say that those who do not follow *al-islām* will be lost, but he was not referring to other religions of the book.[7] If one continues reading in the commentary, it is clear that he means any Muslim who follows a system that seems to be Islam but goes against the precepts of Islam, or corrupts the true meaning of Islam, will not be favored by God. He uses as an example the wrong application of the Qur'anic rule for cutting off the hand of a thief.[8] Ultimately he was concerned with what he perceived as the wrong, harsh representation of Islam in his society, not with condemning Christians. Sha'rawi also used the term *unbeliever* (*kafir*) to refer to atheists, those who denied the existence of God. He did not associate atheists, as unbelievers, with any particular religion, and he did not say they should be executed. In his usual manner he countered what he perceived as a threat with theological discourse, saying that unbelievers are merely hiding God's existence, thus proving that God exists as that which they are attempting to hide.[9]

Sha'rawi's view of different scriptural religions is more clearly laid out in his other interpretations. To explain the idea that God gave the same message to all prophets, he used the Qur'anic verse 5:48:

> We sent you the scripture in truth, confirming the scripture that came before it, and guarding it in safety: so judge between them by what God has revealed, and follow not their vain desires, diverging from the truth you received. To each among you have we prescribed a law (*shir'atan*) and an open way (*minhājan*). If God had so willed, he would have made you a single people, but his plan is to test you in what he has given you: so strive as a race in all virtues.

Sha'rawi interpreted this verse to provide an example of how different religions function:

> *Sharī'a* is the path to water. *Minhaj* (open way) is the path on the earth. The fundamentals of human life [come] from water and from the nourishment of the earth. Because of that God placed value in both of these, the law (the path to water) and the open way (the path on earth). God has prescribed for us a law and an open way, which is why he said in another verse: "In matters of faith, he has ordained for you (*shara'a lakum min al-dīn*) that which he enjoined upon Noah—and what we gave you [O Muhammad] through revelation" (Qur'an 42:13). This means that there is agreement in the fundamentals of the principles of faith (*'aqīda*), which do not ever vary in different time periods. . . . So, when God says: "The same law for you that he enjoined on Noah," this is limited to the principles

of faith. . . . What is important is the unity of the legislative source [God]. . . . If God had made the positive and negative commands the same in every *minhaj* [system of religion], that would not have been suitable to different time periods and individual groups of people. So it is logical that the laws that were given were appropriate to the illness [they came to correct].[10]

It was important to Sha'rawi to make a distinction between the principles of faith, which were always the same (belief in one God being one of those principles), and the variation that occurred in different religious systems. Each religion had a divine legislation and a method, which had been taught to humanity through different prophets. For Sha'rawi, a hypocrite was someone who denied the basics of belief, the common thread that ran through all prophetic religions since the time of Noah, including those who followed Muhammad.

Although Sha'rawi recognized the common thread in all religious systems as it related to God, he did not view all methods of religion equally. He believed that Islam was the only perfect religion:

> Truly submission (*islām*) is the final religion and submission (*islām*) is the first religion. Abraham is the father of the *muslims* (submitters) . . . so be as God has called you—the submitters (*al-muslimun*). The end result of your submission (*islāmukum*) is the perfection of this Islam. The Prophet will be a witness for you on the day of judgment according to what he informed you concerning [your] religion and [according to] what he taught you, so that you will be happy in this life and in the next life. In this way we see that God named us the Muslims (*al-muslimun*) and did not [only] describe us as the submitters, because Islam is for the believers (*mu'min*) a description, a noun and a proper noun. This has a clear meaning; the religion that is with God (*al-dīn 'ind Allah*) is Islam because the name has become a description and a proper name for us. But submission (*islām*) in relation to those who came before us is a description only. Truly all of the religions are described [by the word] submit (*islām*) but we are the followers of the Prophet Muhammad.[11]

Thus for Sha'rawi, Muslims were special because they followed Muhammad, and following Muhammad was the "religion with God." Only the manifestation of God's prescribed method as it was given to Muhammad was perfect, and only the Qur'an was complete and unchanged. Although it is hard to reconcile the idea of superiority with the view that the religions that came before Islam were not invalidated by Muhammad, Sha'rawi stipulated that neither God nor God's universal method belonged to the Muslim community alone. He believed that Christianity was imperfect but that Christians were still meant to follow their own method because it originated with God. At best, this view protects Christians from the title of unbelievers; at worst, it makes their continued commitment to Christianity in the face of a more perfect religion seem unreasonable.

Sha'rawi's scriptural perspective did not take into account that his views were insulting to Copts. Even Sha'rawi's ideas about nationalism were taken from his interpretations of Islamic sacred texts because he believed that only those texts contained untainted truth. Sha'rawi advocated for the participation of all Egyptians in decisions about how the nation should be run, and he did not believe in imposing the *jizya* (the tax levied on non-Muslims living in Muslim empires) on Christians, as has sometimes been said about him. But he also did not advocate for equal consideration of each individual within the nation. When Sha'rawi stated that the Muslim majority, as the majority, had the right to make decisions through means such as voting, he assumed a necessary split between the desires and goals of the two communities. Even though he referred to this control as that of the majority and not in religious terms, his views were based on the notion of religious allegiance because he assumed a unity within groups and disagreement between them.

Sha'rawi's basic premise of understanding Egyptian identity as being related to religious affiliation had become prevalent in Egypt among Muslims and Copts, and has helped shape the concept of what it means to be Egyptian in the contemporary period.[12] The polarization of religious communities in Egypt actually originated in the process of solidifying minority status for the Copts as a group separate from Muslims.[13] As religious difference became intertwined in the language of citizenship, it had the effect of making identity confessional, which translated into increasing sectarian violence.[14] The idea that political status should also be based on "proportionate minority representation" means that not all individual Egyptians are considered equal citizens. Not all people within each group agree on political matters, and identifying populations based on group affiliation within the nation leaves little room to address problems within communities. For a community to form a shared sense of belonging there must be inclusiveness in the political process, including legally ensuring power sharing among majority and minority populations.[15] In a parliamentary system, this means allowing individuals to vote for candidates they believe represent their interests instead of centralizing involvement by having the government appoint and give power to representatives of the minority community.

It is often said that Sha'rawi added to the increasing sectarian violence in Egypt in the late twentieth century because of his discourse of Islamic superiority when in fact it seems to be his mixing of that rhetoric with his notions of nationalism that fed into the increased separation of community identity. When Sha'rawi argued for religion not to influence politics, he did not explore the full implications of the problem. His Qur'anic and nationalistic ideologies translated into the notion that sectarian affiliation and not Egyptian citizenship should be counted as the main marker of identity.

SHA'RAWI'S OPPOSITION TO ORGAN TRANSPLANTATION

Besides the fact that Sha'rawi's discourse influenced and reflected issues pertaining to relations between religious groups in Egypt, reaction to his words also highlighted fissures among Egyptian Muslims. Sha'rawi became popular at a time of transition in Egyptian society, when the very definition of Islam was being contested through conversations about the role that religion should play in society and politics. One of the most well-known and controversial opinions Sha'rawi expressed was his opposition to organ transplantation, and the notoriety of his opinion was a result of the influence he had among his followers. Sha'rawi based his opinion on the idea that the body belongs to God; as God's possession, no part of the body should be given away by any human being, a view that was controversial for a couple of different reasons. First, the government was trying hard to pass a law allowing organ transplantation. Second, the religious underpinning for the law was based on juridical arguments about the public good, arguments Sha'rawi did not engage. And third, Sha'rawi's opinion became influential in society overall, making the law and the very idea of organ transplantation unpopular among many.

For those who accepted Sha'rawi's disapproval of organ transplantation based on the notion that the body belongs to God, his opinion did not seem strange because it fit with the notion of God's absolute dominion over creation. For those who believed human beings must play a more active role for the sake of the public good, his opinion seemed outdated. There was also a related disagreement concerning the rational human sciences. It wasn't necessarily a conflict between those who agreed with the use of science and those who trusted in God; devout Muslims argued for both sides of the issue. It was instead a conflict between Sha'rawi, who maintained that God retains absolute rights over creation, and those who saw independent human knowl-edge as a necessary component of improving life.

Perhaps most telling is that Sha'rawi was able to sway public opinion in spite of not being a legal expert. Besides opposing the government's desire to make organ transplantation legal, Sha'rawi did not argue from Sunni legal rea-soning concerning the sanctity of the body and when that sanctity can or cannot be overridden for the sake of public good (maṣlaḥa).[16] Legal scholars in Egypt and elsewhere had been arguing for a while that the body of the dead had both inviolability (ḥurma) and dignity (karāma), which had to be weighed against the good that might be derived from cutting open the body and vio-lating those principles.[17] The principle of maṣlaḥa is an accepted Sunni juris-tic tool, one that allows new information to be incorporated into the law through new rulings or that allows the suspension of earlier rulings when the good of the community is at stake.[18] In the case of supporting organ trans-plantation, the argument of the legal scholars was based on the idea that the good to be derived overrides the harm of violating the dignity of the body. Sha'rawi, by contrast, made his argument based on what he saw as a fixed theological principle: ownership of the human body. In this case, Sha'rawi endeavored to respond not only to scientific and political views but also to Shari'a-based juridical opinions by trying to subsume all of these into his theological point of view.

Sha'rawi's view of organ transplantation annoyed many Egyptian medical professionals, government officials, and even the mufti of Egypt, Shaykh Muhammad Sayyid Tantawi because, unlike Sha'rawi, they agreed with the standard bioethical view that the body belongs to the individual, which also contrasts with standard juridical opinion.[19] A closer look at Sha'rawi's opin-ion reveals that what he advocated was a normative Sunni ethical ideal:

> It is God who gives the gift of life. Those who have permitted organ donation do not have the justification to say that they are "saving the life" of another. Saving life is an imperative owned by God alone. . . . My plea to those scholars and doc-tors for whom the humanitarian spirit and love has dominated their work, is for them to stay far away from arrogance and rebelliousness toward God's creation . . . don't destroy the religions in order to "save life." . . . Now this does not mean that we do not take precautions or cures, or that we do not take medicine for illness, for it is God who created illness and God who created its medicine.[20]

This quote exemplifies Sha'rawi's method of clinging to a position he came to through his interpretation of the Qur'an and then applying that position to

a contemporary problem. At the same time it gives only a hint of his larger theological positions. For Sha'rawi, maintaining God's control was essential, and it
was the height of human arrogance to claim God's powers as one's own. In his
view the survival of religion depended on the recognition of human deficiency.
However, Sha'rawi did not make clear the difference between saving a life with
surgery and saving a life by taking medicine. It seems from the quote that it was
the rhetoric of "saving a life" that bothered him: It was language that threatened faith in God. If humans claimed power over life, it meant that they were
claiming that rational human capacities were equal to, or perhaps could
even override or exceed, God's capacities. Because Sha'rawi believed that God
controlled life and death no matter what humans did, he did not think that
surgeons could take that control from God, so they should not say that they
could. Sha'rawi saw claims of scientific knowledge as a major threat if they had
the potential to undermine theological principles.

In another quote, Sha'rawi talked about the impossibility of anyone killing another human being:

> Death is different than murder because in the case of death, it comes first and only
> after that the structure of the body (binā' al-jusud) breaks down. But in the case
> of murder the body must collapse or break down first and the consequence of that
> is death. [This is the case] when someone hits his head or is shot in the heart or
> head or some other place [on the body]. So in the case of murder, the body must
> collapse [in some way] first. Then the soul leaves and [that is when] death occurs.
> Death takes life first and then the body breaks down. But this cannot happen
> unless it [comes] from God (the exalted and most high); no human being can
> control it. Murder demolishes the body first and then it takes away life. This is
> how it was with the Prophet Abraham when God gave the king [dominion]. He
> [Abraham] said to him [the king] when they were discussing the issue of life and
> death: "My Lord is he who gives life and causes death" (Qur'an 2:258).[21]

This Qur'anic passage is one of many that Sha'rawi interpreted as saying that
only God gives life and only God can actually remove life from the body, caus-
ing death. In bioethics it is believed that medical processes should be used
to defeat death,[22] making those processes of primary concern. It is a position
that regards human action as capable of staving off death. In contrast, Sha'rawi's
views on specific biomedical issues were secondary to his views of life and
death, and he insisted that both were absolutely determined by God.

The focus on reinforcing his views about God's control over human life
led Sha'rawi to devise arguments in a logical progression, but often they also

contained ambiguity and sometimes even internal contradictions. In the quote above, ambiguity is derived from the fact that Sha'rawi used a physical process to make a nonphysical argument. He wanted to say that God was in control by making the argument that, even in the case of murder, human beings cannot actually take life. For him, the difference between death and murder was God's action—death occurs only when God removes life from the body, which, of course, is not a visible difference. But it is difficult to sustain the view that death by murder and death by other causes are always distinct: It is not impossible for people to die after the body begins to deteriorate even if they are not murdered. Sha'rawi was asking his audience to believe in what was unseen and to understand physical processes based on the premise that God's actions can and do take precedence over what appears to be otherwise. His statement was meant to undermine the primarily physical nature of the process in order to make his theology work.

In another instance Sha'rawi again used the issues of life and death to make similar theological points. In interpreting the Qur'anic verse 2:28 ("How can you refuse to acknowledge God, seeing that you were lifeless and he gave you life, and that he will cause you to die and then will bring you again to life, whereupon unto him you will be brought back?"), Sha'rawi said:

> God used the word "how" in this verse not as a question word but to help explain a very difficult matter. . . . What is the evidence of those who disbelieve? They have no evidence and they cannot argue with logic. . . . No one can argue with "you were lifeless and he gave you life" as God has created us from nothing. No human being can claim that he created himself or others. . . . And when God says "he will cause you to die," no one can doubt that he will die. . . . We can use the matter of death when we confront nonbelievers . . . when they deny the existence of the unseen world. . . . Life constitutes [only] one period of time between two ranges: the first is when God creates us and the next is when life ceases and we die. . . . When they talk about "test tube babies" as the best solution for parents who cannot conceive they describe it in an ignorant way. They merely collect the egg from the womb that prohibits fertilization, fertilize it with the sperm of the husband, and then implant it [back] in the womb. But what they took, the egg of the mother and the sperm of the father, were the creations of God. All that takes place [in this process] is fertilization . . . they created nothing.[23]

Sha'rawi's perspective can be summed up in his statement that "no one can argue with 'You were lifeless and he gave you life.'" The Qur'an, in the way he interpreted it, was for him absolute truth. In this quote, Sha'rawi also affirmed God's existence in another seemingly logical argument, but it exemplifies exactly what Sha'rawi's detractors saw as his weakness. He took a Qur'anic verse and interpreted it to apply to a medical procedure despite having only limited medical knowledge. He only used the information that supported his interpretive position, which is rhetorically but not substantively effective.

Although his opposition to organ transplantation was based on the idea that all of creation ultimately belongs to God, his pronouncements had actual repercussions in Egyptian society. Sha'rawi's opinion resulted in many doctors and clinics refusing to perform the surgery and in the parliament at least temporarily refusing to pass a law allowing the procedure. This backlash against the Mubarak government's attempt to make organ transplantation legal in Egypt was even more striking considering that Tantawi, the highest ranking religious scholar in Egypt at the time, had already issued a fatwa claiming that the procedure was permissible under Islamic law. Not all government officials disagreed with Sha'rawi, and not all state-appointed 'ulama' agreed with him, demonstrating differences within sectors of society and similarities among those often considered at odds with one another.

SHA'RAWI AND WOMEN

I recently met a young Egyptian woman who came to the United States as part of a young women's leadership program. She was educated, articulate, and a devoted follower of Sha'rawi, even fifteen years after his death. When she spoke about Sha'rawi she displayed an excitement I had seen many times, a dedication to both the man and his message. She told me that there is no one today who can take Sha'rawi's place. Not only was he knowledgeable, he was also gentle and understanding.

Among Sha'rawi's many books and pamphlets, by far the best-selling ones are those that deal with issues relating to women. While it would seem to be an objectification of women to have male preachers telling them how they should behave, many young Egyptian women continue to take advice from the "old bearded shaykhs" who were born in villages and trained at al-Azhar, men like Sha'rawi, Yusuf Qaradawi, and Muhammad Ghazali.[24] Yusuf Qaradawi uses the Islamic legal tradition to put forth a modern view of a gender-equal Muslim society; for example, he argues that women have the right to full political participation under Islamic law.[25] Sha'rawi's appeal to young women, in contrast, was due to his definition and explanation of piety and to his persona, not to the political or legal implications of his message.

In the edited version of Sha'rawi's opinions about various matters, one of the topics covered is titled "Circumcision and Female Circumcision" (*al-khitān wa al-khafāḍ*). Included in the explanation of the fatwa is a brief appraisal of the opinions of the four Sunni schools of law on the procedure. Basically, in the legal literature (if not in common Egyptian parlance), *al-khitān* refers to male circumcision and *al-khafāḍ* to female genital cutting. As an ancient Egyptian practice, *al-khafāḍ* entailed removing the entire clitoris and the entire labia. As a Muslim practice, its justification is based on the hadith (considered sound by most jurists) in which the Prophet is said to have declared: "Circumcision (*khitān*) is *sunna* for the male, and an honor (*mukrama*) for the female."[26] Even so, scholars in the four Sunni schools of law (Hanafi, Shaf'i, Maliki, and Hanbali) disagreed on whether it should be performed on females. Hanbalis think circumcision should be performed on males only, and Shafi'is believe that it is necessary to perform both *al-khitān* and *al-khafāḍ*. Malikis and Hanafis stayed closer to the apparent meaning of the hadith and said that it was obligatory for the male and recommended for the female.[27] As the fatwa book explains, Sha'rawi took the latter position and saw *al-khafāḍ* as both a custom for reducing female sexual appetite and as recommended for females according to Islamic law. He believed that *al-khafāḍ* should be performed on the female according to the principle: "Reduce or minimize the two parts (clitoris and labia), but do not go too far."[28]

Sha'rawi disagreed with Shaykh Mahmud Shaltut (Shaykh al-Azhar from 1958 to 1963), who according to some "denied the Shafi'i position that the procedure should be performed on both sexes" and instead ruled that it should be illegal in Egypt.[29] In 1996, the government of Egypt made the procedure illegal,[30] but they have not been successful at curbing the practice, partially because shaykhs like Sha'rawi continue to recommend it. It is estimated that more than 80 percent (and perhaps as high as 95 percent) of Egyptian women have had their genitalia cut as children or adolescents,[31] even though some of the highest ranking muftis in Egypt have ruled that the practice be prohibited.

As with the issue of organ transplantation, Sha'rawi proved to be a hindrance to the Mubarak government's attempt to change practices that they believed slowed Egypt's progress toward becoming a modern nation-state. Sha'rawi thought that *khafāḍ* should continue as something both authentically Muslim and authentically Egyptian in order to stave off the West's sexualizing influence. Although he was not alone in his decision about the practice among the old bearded shaykhs of al-Azhar, Sha'rawi did not make this decision as someone who had training in issuing *fatwāwā* (legal opinions). Most of Sha'rawi's opinions about legal matters in his fatwa book were examples of how he took the opinions of his peers or past legal decisions and made them relevant to the public.

The issue of shaykhs defending the practice of female genital cutting is an example of how male jurists and religious experts have continued to make judgments about the female body without recourse or reference to women's perspectives on their own lives.[32] Although it can be said that generally Islamic jurisprudence is less concerned with the conditions of life and more with the linguistic and textual exactitude of rulings, the point is that it is another example of how male religious authorities like Sha'rawi use their knowledge and training to exert influence over women. In his presentation of women's piety, Sha'rawi had other opinions that might also be characterized as undermining gender equity. For example, he taught that husbands are responsible for the behavior of their wives:

> God teaches that every person has power and responsibility over others. The husband is responsible for his wife and children. . . . Because of this God requests that the eyes of the one in charge be fully aware of what those they have responsibility over [are doing]. He must try to see the beginning of any type of deviation, face it with decisiveness, and remove it from the life of the individual. . . . The husband must ask his wife if she is possessed of anything he did not buy and the mother must ask her daughters about what they possess. . . . The principle of "from where did this come to you" (Qur'an 3:37) is Qur'anic legislation. Every individual [must] implement it within his circle of responsibility. God wants us to seek the answer so we can know. Carelessness with this principle is the reason for the corruption that harms the universe. . . . It must be asked in order to straighten the movement of life in the universe and to establish the good for all. . . . Carelessness begins with keeping quiet; if the matter is ignored deviation will spread.[33]

For Sha'rawi a woman was not only subordinate to her husband, her life had to be under constant scrutiny as part of her husband's responsibility over her. A husband's scrutiny over even seemingly small daily matters, such as making purchases, was not just related to the health of the couple's relationship, it had other repercussions. Sha'rawi's blatant support for gender differentiation makes it difficult for academics to understand how women could feel devotion toward him, especially in a climate in which there is an increasing availability of diverse religious material.

Yet in speaking of issues like gender equality and the question of women's dress in the context of a Muslim society, one must be aware of the historical connections this discourse has to colonialism and missionary activity. What is needed is an alternative discourse based on an understanding of how women differ throughout the world.[34] Muslim women's involvement in contemporary Islamic movements directly contradicts feminist theories of equality and liberation. Women in present-day Islamic movements have concepts of "self, moral agency and discipline" that are able to function amid what might be called patriarchal religious systems. Therefore it is not correct to view women involved in these movements as seeking "freedom from relations of domination." It is more accurate to say that moral agency is enabled by women's engagement in these relations.[35]

The focus on becoming more virtuous by performing and embodying righteous acts is, according to Saba Mahmood, "not . . . an Idea, or . . . a set of regulatory norms, but . . . a set of practical activities that are germane to a certain way of life."[36] Practices and the dispositions formed by those practices help an individual become happier or more pious, not as an individual per se, but according to societal expectations. In Mahmood's study, however, she claims that the *telos* of those she studied was to behave according to

> the exemplary conduct of the Prophet and his Companions . . . aimed not so much at . . . establishing a personal relationship with God, but on honing one's rational and emotional capacities . . . to approximate the exemplary model of the pious self.[37]

Mahmood does not consider the theological imperatives of the revelation, or what sort of role seeking the pleasure of the divine in action might play in how and why one might strive to become virtuous. In the quote above, Mahmood repeats the understanding of the rational self as necessarily excluding any theological motivation for action. She juxtaposes the idea of "establishing a personal relationship with God" with the idea of becoming more rational and more emotional—something usually associated with the pneumatic but here re-appropriated as a cultivated capacity. Sha'rawi's model, in contrast, helps explain how the focus on self-cultivation can rely on understandings of divine expectations, and how a personal relationship with the divine—as a normative idea and a discourse of dominance, if not an activity—can contribute to and become a practical means of cultivating an embodied pious self.

Sha'rawi saw his purpose as helping women fulfill their duties as proper Muslims according to the highest status they could attain: that which God laid out for them. He had recourse to invoke the most effective and powerful discourse; he talked about how a woman ensured a happy life in this world and in the hereafter when she fulfilled her God-given duties.[38] For Sha'rawi, these duties, such as modest dress for women, were proper because they were suitable. God ordained what was best, and human beings should simply try to understand and live by those commands. Even though his expressions of God's commands were based on his interpretations of the Qur'an, he presented them quite effectively as God's own will, which made them seem imperative.

Sha'rawi also related God's will to the good of society. He said that carelessness with God's principles caused "corruption that harms the universe." God's principles must be followed to "straighten the movement of life in the universe and to establish the good for all" because if they are ignored, "deviation will spread."[39] For Sha'rawi, becoming pious through practice was directly connected to the notion of God's orders, which in turn had repercussions throughout society and the universe. When one practiced according to God's system, one implemented and realized that system; the responsibility, according to Sha'rawi, was primarily to God. Thus a husband's scrutiny of his wife was presented as necessary to ensure that God's system was in control, and the wife's acceptance of this surveillance was presented as being ordained by God in the same manner.

It is important to recognize that Sha'rawi made two simultaneous assumptions as a shaykh who defined women's (and men's) responsibilities. What Sha'rawi said was proper for women—that they submit to their husbands, for example—was presented as God's actual intention, as a God-given ideal norm that therefore had to be enacted, not as law, but also not as opinion, even though he formulated that norm according to his personal understanding based on past interpretations. Women chose whether to enact his guidance, which was geared toward helping them become righteous. It was a discourse of authority legitimated by those who believed in Sha'rawi as a loving, caring, knowledgeable person.

Even though many women chose to follow Sha'rawi's description and definition of Islam, some in Egyptian society worried about the influence he had among women. Many people were not happy with Sadat's attempt in the 1970s to re-Islamize Egyptian society, an effort that helped to reestablish gender roles as they had existed before Nasser pushed for more gender equality in society and government. Sha'rawi played a large part not only in Sadat's program but also in the overall trend in Egyptian society toward increased public expressions of piety and attachment to Islam. He had a strong impact on women choosing to become *muḥajjibāt* (women wearing the hijab). In Sha'rawi's early guest appearances on television, his audiences consisted of men and of women without headscarves sitting together in the studio. Once he starting broadcasting his own show, however, he preached exclusively to male audiences from inside a mosque. Sha'rawi led a larger trend in Egyptian society: In the 1970s less than half the women in Cairo wore the headscarf, but by the time Sha'rawi died, the headscarf had become the standard dress for most women. The increase of Egyptian *muḥajjibāt* is often mistakenly attributed exclusively to Wahhabi (Saudi) influence spreading throughout Egyptian society.[40] While this may be the case for the face veil (the *niqāb*), it is not the case with the increasing number of women wearing the hijab in Egypt in the late twentieth century.

Sha'rawi was not an advocate of the Wahhabi ideology, but he did think that Muslim women should wear the hijab. According to his son, Sha'rawi introduced the beautiful, colorful headscarves many Egyptian women wear today. He did so by asking a friend of his, a shoemaker in Alexandria named Muhammad, to "produce beautiful Islamic clothing for women in bright beautiful colors so that they will love hijab." His friend protested, telling Sha'rawi that he was merely a shoe specialist, but Sha'rawi insisted and eventually his friend complied. This shoemaker went on to become one of the largest Egyptian manufacturers of hijab and other religiously sanctioned clothing for women, specializing in suits and the production of scarves with beautiful colors.[41]

Although Sha'rawi's advice to women about proper behavior was a powerful discursive presentation of religious norms, ultimately that discourse became effective only when women made it their standard dress. To take a more specific example, Sha'rawi, among other influential Muslim preachers, is often criticized as someone who is responsible for wealthy Egyptian women— including movie stars and entertainers—becoming *muḥajjibāt*. Critics repeat the idea that women were unduly influenced by male preachers like Sha'rawi, explaining the phenomenon as if women were merely vehicles for the establishment of a radical agenda and relying on the familiar category of radicalism to make the claim that shaykhs control female subjects.[42]

In expressing this phenomenon for herself, however, the former Egyptian movie star Hana Tharwat framed her decision to leave her profession and begin to wear the hijab very differently. She described a meeting she had with Sha'rawi in an Arab newspaper:

"Al-Sha'rawi was a wise scholar and very patient as he first listened to all my excuses about how I ensure that my job does not contradict Islamic principles." Al-Sha'rawi gave her an example that shattered her concept of herself as a devout Muslim. Al-Sha'rawi told her that a person could not ask a tomato vendor to choose the best from among his wares. Similarly, she was choosing to abide by certain principles and ignoring others. "At this point, I felt God's truth and realized how ignorant I was. So my husband and I decided to stop acting . . . life is an earthly test to determine whether one prefers to be obedient and choose the everlasting life or to enjoy this life and be a loser in the metaphysical one. A true Muslim is one who sees God in his heart. Everything in metaphysics is right and everything in real life is false because it fades and vanishes. It is God who led me on to the correct path," she added.[43]

Tharwat told her story according to how the goals of her life shifted from a concern for this world to a concern for the afterlife, something she may have heard Sha'rawi refer to in one of his television shows but not something she recounted him telling her in this meeting. She said that what she originally desired was to be a devout Muslim but that she came to understand through a "realization" that, in order to achieve that desire, she had to be obedient in her dress and actions. Sha'rawi used an allegory to help her understand her position; his words, as she said, led her to "feel God's truth." How Sha'rawi's simple example accomplished this remains unclear. What is clear is that even before meeting him, Tharwat had an attachment to Sha'rawi, and he acted as she expected a wise scholar to act (listening patiently). According to Tharwat, Sha'rawi also served as an intermediary, leading her to God's wisdom, with what must have been more than the story of a tomato seller. She wanted to become a more pious person, and as she tells it that desire came directly from some feeling established between herself and God through Sha'rawi. God led her on the straight path, which in turn led her to strive to be obedient in her dress to please God.

CONCLUSION

The controversy surrounding Sha'rawi has not been limited to the issues I discussed in this chapter. His support of Islamic banking, his connection to Saudi Arabia, his belief in devils and *jinn*, and his pride in the fact that he read only the Qur'an in the last years of his life have also been debated. The way I have presented the issues in this chapter are meant to offer a framework for understanding how and why debate over Sha'rawi's intentions, opinions, and actions continues. Sha'rawi's Qur'an-based nationalist opinions as well as his opinions about organ transplantation are clear examples of how he chose to respond to relevant social issues from the assumption that his knowledge was superior. This assumed superiority is what kept him from fully considering the challenges posed by intercommunal tensions or from considering the potential good that could be gained from certain medical procedures. Still, Sha'rawi was popular enough to sway public opinion by bringing forth past ideas and fitting them to larger social issues. That others in Egyptian society disagreed with him shows the diversity of public opinion. His relationships with Sadat and Mubarak, sometimes as supporter and sometimes as adversary, and the debate Egyptians had over the meaning of these relationships also expose deep disagreements over the relationship between politics and religion, which were ubiquitous in Egypt at the time. Sha'rawi's thought about how he should interact with the government developed over time, making it difficult to label him as either a lackey of the state or as someone who offered an Islamist challenge to it.[44] The influence his fame brought him made it impossible for him not to have political leverage, no matter how much he insisted that, as a religious leader, he should not seek to influence politics.

Sha'rawi's ability to influence many in Egypt, despite his detractors, is a prime example of how, even in one society, people differ dramatically in their definitions of Islam, which are partially derived from opinions concerning the relationship between religious tradition and society. Sha'rawi made scriptural, creedal, and theological ideas the primary measurement of truth, in contrast to science and human reason. Neither position ignores the other; they merely differ in their assessment of what is most beneficial.

But it is important to see Sha'rawi as someone involved in more than controversy. Although all the issues explored in this chapter are indicative of his particular worldview, he did not respond to them as individual issues. Assuming that his importance was limited to his involvement in controversy assumes that he had nothing interesting to say otherwise. Even worse, this view removes any possibility of seeing his followers as thinking individuals because it sets up a false divide between those who can critically assess his ideas and therefore can easily see their flaws, and those who follow along because they are uneducated or do not know better.

To understand Sha'rawi's importance, one must look further into his thoughts, linguistic abilities, place in the history of Islamic tradition, and charisma. His fame meant that he could and did voice his own ideas about what it meant to be a good Muslim in modern Egypt, and he combined and reacted to common problems through his sermons and Qur'anic worldview. Sha'rawi's ability to gain a cadre of devoted followers came down to his personalization of the notion of virtue, centering on how each individual relates to the divine in every moment of life. He based this idea on his interpretations of the Qur'an, and he presented those interpretations as representations of God's thought. He therefore positioned himself as a uniquely talented intermediary.

CHAPTER 3

Preaching as a Nexus of 'Ulama' Influence

INTRODUCTION

Sha'rawi's television preaching earned him his celebrity, which enabled his opinions about societal issues to have deep and lasting influence. Preaching events, regardless of venue, are often sites of apposite response, which include practitioners, orations, definitional rules, suitable praxis, and intended audiences. They exemplify how authority depends on popular support. In the past, Muslim preachers, most especially those who delivered the Friday mosque sermon (khuṭba), but also the less formalized admonishers and storytellers (wa'aẓ or tadhkira and quṣṣāṣ), were judged according to a set of standards concerning proper style, content, and delivery.[1] But successful preachers do not have to possess in-depth learning or adhere to particular regulations; at times even resistance to power can garner admiration. A preacher instead needs to demonstrate characteristics that are less systematically acquired, such as the ability to make complex ideas understandable or to be an engaging performer. Because preachers rely on autonomous, impartial, and often personally regulated traits, their ranks—both inside and outside the cadre of 'ulama'—tend to be varied and disagreement among them tends to be common.

While the preaching event presents the preacher as expert, preaching is, in actuality, a community practice: All of the participants aid in determining its nature—and as such it provides an example of how the power of an authoritative agent is at once effective and constrained.[2] In the past, 'ulama' institutions were sites of social control, and decisions about the workings of those institutions were removed from the common people. Yet preachers have always depended on the proclivities of the populace, which means that the details of orations delivered outside the mosque and other official settings were usually left to their discretion. Spectators and their concerns exerted influence on the specifications of orations: when, how, and why they were delivered, and often their content. This in turn made it difficult for the regu-lating 'ulama' to enforce their standards on those who preached, even though they consistently attempted to do so. Sermons and orations displayed the in-teraction between official and unofficial practices because they were com-prised of both elements.

Since the beginning of the twentieth century, contestation and diversity among preachers has been enhanced as questions concerning religious au-thority became further entrenched in public choice. The breakdown of 'ulama' institutions such as al-Azhar in twentieth-century Egypt and the rise of new government institutions in their stead removed the social regulatory power of the 'ulama', which had once been taken for granted and incorporated into religious oratory. Religious messages are now delivered through media that record and spread opinions to vast audiences, which further encourages dif-ference. The ease of reaching the public, and the concomitant reconfiguration of religious authority, has meant that many contemporary preachers must be understood beyond the broad and hard-to-centralize categories of the past. Discord is no longer about normative standards and the struggle to maintain control by enforcing conformity. Now the focus is on establishing a hegemonic definition of Islam and therefore on discrediting competitors by bolstering one's own claims and visions. The more media outlets that transmit religious content, the more crowded the field gets and the more complicated alliances and oppositions become.

PREACHING IN ISLAM

The responsibility of Muslim preachers has always been to "provide Muslim believers with the minimal means to observe the precepts of their religion and to run their lives in accordance with Muslim religious law."[3] But they also had other tasks, including admonishing believers about the consequences of not following the shari'a, transmitting knowledge about behavior and belief, encouraging modest living, reciting the Qur'an, and telling stories about the lives of the prophets.[4] Many preachers also reminded believers of the idea that this world is fleeting and that reward comes in the afterlife. Thus they encouraged people to prepare for the Day of Judgment.[5] Ibn al-Jawzi (1201 C.E.)[6] discussed this aspect of the preacher's vocation in his book, *Kitab al-Quṣṣāṣ wa al-Mudhakkirīn* (*The Book of Islamic Preachers*), where he stated that preachers were meant to remind the people of the importance of the afterlife. To illustrate this point, he quotes Ahmad ibn al-Hanbal (d. 855 C.E.), whose name is used for one of the four Sunni schools of law and who said of Islamic preachers:

> The true preachers [here *quṣṣāṣ*, storytellers] are those who speak about paradise and hell, who arouse people to fear, and who are upright in intention and honest in matters of hadith . . . untutored persons who have no knowledge should listen to these people; perhaps they might take a word to heart and repent.[7]

For Ibn al-Jawzi, the connecting thread between believers and the fear preachers were supposed to inspire in them was the revelation. He therefore stated that quotes from the revelation should begin and end every utterance.[8] But this did not mean that preachers were supposed to teach rejection of the world for the sake of the afterlife; instead, preachers were supposed to couple their reminders with a call for the modification of behaviors, making worldly life a tool for securing positive results in the next life.

Ibn al-Jawzi and his student, Ibn Taymiyya (d. 1258 C.E.), worried about the influence of preachers among the people and wrote about the need to regulate preachers according to the expectations of intellectuals and traditionalists. Ibn al-Jawzi also discussed the linguistic nature of the preacher's tools—preachers were meant to inspire change in their listeners through the power and correctness of their words—and he warned against the common practice of telling false hadith. He also believed that the spotless behavior of preachers was essential to their success: Preachers had to be living examples because the purpose of popular preaching was to establish acceptable practices among the uneducated.[9]

The vocation of preaching and the content of sermons have been subjects of controversy throughout much of Islamic history.[10] Preachers were hard to control: As orators they often decided what they would say without regard for the concerns of men like Ibn al-Jawzi.[11] As a result, a literature of critique began almost as soon as the institution of preaching began. While the literature of "denunciation"—especially of storytellers—started early, it became especially prevalent in the fourth Islamic century.[12] The controversy among the 'ulama' resulted from the fact that even official preachers could practice their craft as long as they could get people to listen—spreading knowledge through sermons depended on oral and not written forms of edification. 'Ulama' preachers were known to use unconventional language, tell folkloric stories about the prophets, and to deliver messages in unique ways.[13] Besides preaching manuals written by the regulating 'ulama', juridical literature and discourses about rhetoric stipulated that it was the sunna—the example of the Prophet Muhammad, the original preacher—that must be the model for official preachers.[14]

Although norms were espoused in official settings, the regulating 'ulama' had a hard time controlling preachers who stood far outside acceptable practice: those who admonished or warned and especially those who told stories (qaṣṣa).[15] Part of this difficulty was because the literature that sought to establish an ideal for preacher behavior and oratory often focused on impractical minute details. In one case, someone who delivered a sermon (khaṭāba) from the pulpit of a mosque after communal prayers was said to innovate (bid'a) because he could not claim the title khaṭīb or imam (leader), even though he preached according to the rules laid down in preaching manuals.[16]

Those 'ulama' who sought to regulate rhetoric, content, and form also recognized that in order to be influential, preachers had to "effectively communicate,"[17] a skill that could not easily be regulated. So while they sought to maintain control over the vocation of preaching, they also had to allow for some creative strategies, which, when they got out of hand, created the need for further attempts at control. The indeterminacy of preaching made the preacher effective and also made social control impossible. Preachers engaged in a structured practice, a play of power relations that required assent but also allowed them to master their experiences and not merely be molded by them.[18]

The ability to resist control through performance is further exemplified by the fact that besides 'ulama' preachers—both those who sought to regulate preaching according to normative standards and those who broke free of those standards—there were preachers who did not claim any 'ulama' credentials. These preachers appear to have had little or no official training in the religious sciences, yet they enjoyed popularity among the people.[19] Regulated preachers, therefore, had to compete with renegade preachers for audiences, which meant further adaptation outside institutional control. One example of the renegade preacher was the storyteller.[20] Storytellers often told stories that came not from acceptable texts but instead from texts that could even be antithetical to Islamic doctrinal foundations. There were also Sufi preachers who claimed direct knowledge of God in order to justify contravening standard doctrine and belief.[21]

Tension between constrained and renegade preachers gave rise to various configurations of preacher types. This tension exemplifies how language meant to reinforce a certain vision of religion incorporates the ideals and linguistic practices of agents and practitioners who may agree only on the necessity of such talk but not on the content. Variation and diversity among Muslim preachers has persisted into the modern age, as has the concern that sermons be appropriate and competitive. Richard Antoun, studying a modern preacher in Jordan, has said that the social organization of tradition is a "two-way flow of ideas" between the learned men and women of society and the folk or peasants, and that preachers are therefore "culture brokers."[22] In a similar way Patrick Gaffney, in his book on modern preaching in Egypt, emphasizes the distinction between religious institutions and popular forms and expressions of religion. Yet Gaffney tries to avoid clearly separating the different strata of Islamic discourse into categories like high and low, or official and popular, and instead shows horizontal or vertical connections between the various traditions in order to recognize a complex and interwoven reality. These interweavings are enmeshed into layers and therefore cannot be separated easily.[23] Thus Islam for Gaffney becomes both multiple and singular, and belief systems "shape" and are "shaped" by circumstances. The preacher is the one who, in the local context, combines the recent and present developments of his society with a type of social authority.[24]

But sermons are not subject only to historical, social, and political circumstances; they are primarily part of religious discourse and in contemporary times the means by which preachers attempt to assert their discursive dominance over others in a very crowded field. Many authoritative elements are at work through discourse, and by invoking some and not others, those striving for dominance seek recognition. The 'ulama' engage past understandings of theological, doctrinal, epistemological, and esoteric renderings not just as authoritative past but also as the relevant present. Sha'rawi utilized social and political elements to reestablish the primacy of revelation and, by extension, to strengthen and modify 'ulama' interpretations. To this end, he had to stay focused on the purpose of that modification: to increase adherent apprehension and enactment of God's will in a new era. In other words, for Sha'rawi, the purpose of preaching was renewal and concomitantly to be recognized as the one qualified to renew.

In content, Sha'rawi's messages comprised standard elements of Sunni as well as Sufi thought and method, an older form of compromise and adaptation. Yet the popularity of Sha'rawi's orations depended on his use of mass media. Somehow the combination of these two elements the traditional content of his words and his willingness to market or re-form those words through new techniques of communication—increased his influence in Egypt even while competition steadily grew throughout his lifetime. He responded to the problem of increased contestation by inaugurating a particular practice: television as a communal mode of reception and local dialect as a means of transmitting and receiving theological knowledge.[25] He tried to make up for the loss of the societal integration of Sunni epistemological understandings, which he equated with Qur'anic truth, by increasing his influence in other realms of cultural production and everyday life. Sha'rawi established a new practice in order to achieve a particular goal and to solve the problem of 'ulama' loss. But he "misrecognized" how he was reordering the "problematic" by reproducing the very problem he sought to combat because media helped increase the competition for religious authority.[26] He was instrumental in reclassifying the criteria of authority by centering it in media success, choosing a new site for the continued efficacy of the once prominent Azhari worldview. While mass media made Sha'rawi's perspective available to all, it further neutralized religious authority.

PREACHING MODERATION ON TELEVISION: COMPARING SHA'RAWI AND YUSUF QARADAWI

While Sha'rawi taught individuals how to read Qur'anic knowledge and apply it to their everyday lives, Yusuf Qaradawi, another Azhari-trained media sensation, advises his viewers on the application of legal prescriptions. Qaradawi was born in Egypt twenty-five years after Sha'rawi and is commonly referred to as a global mufti because he has achieved global fame through his satellite broadcasts. As a legal expert he uses the interactive aspects of television to solve the everyday problems of viewers. Television has carried the messages of both Sha'rawi and Qaradawi to the public in a way that has strengthened the particular goals of each. Both have used television to argue for the indispensability of the 'ulama'. Qaradawi defends the legal prowess of the trained scholars, and Sha'rawi defended their interpretive rights. Qaradawi also believes that the 'ulama' are the only class of Muslims capable of formulating an Islamic awakening (al-ṣaḥwa al-islāmiyya). He reaffirms the centrality of the 'ulama' as possessors of a specific type of knowledge (the true "foundations of Islam") that can be used for societal goals, and focuses on applying that knowledge to social and political "movements."[27] By transmitting his views on satellite television, he hopes to present a palatable version of Islam to the worldwide community.[28] But neither Qaradawi nor Sha'rawi understood that television would help contribute to the partial undoing of what they sought to bolster.

Qaradawi's life went in a very different direction than Sha'rawi's did. He was forced out of Egypt in the 1970s because of his association with the Muslim Brotherhood, and he currently lives in Qatar, where he records his television program, Al-Shari'a wa al-Hayat, on al-Jazeera. While his preaching style is not typical, the advice he gives, and the fact that he gives it directly to an audience, means that he engages in practices that helped define preachers in the past. In many ways he has been the prototype of Muslim religious authority on satellite television, blending interactive legal advice with popular public presentation.

Sha'rawi, on the other hand, was an Egyptian, rather than global, preacher. Although his shows eventually became global, and his exegesis was appreciated by audiences all over the world, he originally spoke to Egyptian audiences and often in Egyptian dialect. This local orientation suited Sha'rawi's notion that 'ulama' expertise was centered in an al-Azhar education, one he took great pride in as an Egyptian. Sha'rawi's local emphasis also served his view that performing religious obligations was not primarily for the sake of changing the Muslim community. Instead he believed that, because knowledge was eternally revealed through the texts, one of the main tasks of the 'ulama' was to bridge the gap between the constant disclosure of God's knowledge and what those disclosures meant for individuals.

One way to understand the different orientations of Sha'rawi and Qaradawi is through the concept of wasaṭiyya, or moderation. Both men have been characterized as being moderate, or between extremes (wasaṭ). Sha'rawi was given the title of moderate by his admirers, and Qaradawi began to characterize his program as moderate in 1990s, although he insists that he has defined his ideas this way since the beginning of his public career.[29] There are some similarities between Sha'rawi's and Qaradawi's concept of a middle way, including the push for moderation in political and social outlook as well as in religion. Both have based their ideas on the principle that religion is easy by referring to the Qur'anic verse 2:143 and to the hadith in which it is narrated that Muhammad said:

> Religion is very easy and whoever overburdens himself in his religion will not be able to continue in that way. So you should not be extremists, but try to be near to perfection and receive the good tidings that you will be rewarded; and gain strength by worshipping in the mornings and at night.[30]

But when viewed more closely, Sha'rawi's program of renewal differs significantly from that of Qaradawi and other Islamists. As a global preacher, Qaradawi presents Islam as a particular type of religion among other religions. He has been primarily concerned with the negative portrayal of Islam in the European and American media and with the extremism of radical Muslim groups. Thus he has used the term *wasaṭiyya* to put forth a "positively viewed Muslim identity in the trans-global framework" on satellite television.[31] Sha'rawi's association with the term *wasaṭiyya* can similarly be attributed to his use of mass media but for the sake of presenting a mild and easy version of Islam to encourage the piety of individual Egyptians.

Sha'rawi's statement, "I do not want to govern by Islam but to be governed by it," highlights the main difference between his *wasaṭiyya* and that of someone like Qaradawi: Sha'rawi was not concerned about rules; he was focused instead on the middle way between extremism and neglect. He believed that moderate behavior helped Muslims keep on the straight path as ordered by God.[32] He also believed that simplicity and mercy, and not difficulty and harshness, were the keys to helping people implement God's method in their lives. Sha'rawi's moderate method also included his gentle way of admonishing. As his son said, he would speak of heaven before he would speak of hell:

> He was not on the right or left but in the middle (*wasaṭ*). He solved many problems by choosing the simplest solution, as did the Prophet; he always chose the most moderate way because he wanted to be welcoming and to make people love religion, [he did not want them] to fear. He always mentioned paradise before hell and he would always say how good deeds lead people to heaven before he would say how bad deeds lead to hell. Many preachers are using this method now in *da'wa* [summoning through preaching].[33]

It is interesting to note that 'Abd al-Rahim al-Sha'rawi understood there was competition to establish who was the originator of the contemporary use

of the term *wasaṭ*. This competition to claim *wasaṭ* signals the popular acceptance of the middle way as the right way—the "true Islam"—and the resulting
widespread use of the term in public discourse. He also presented Sha'rawi's
ideas about what constitutes the middle way as primarily theological, not just
in the idea of God as lawgiver but also in the idea of God as concerned with
the well being of humanity, a personal God. He emphasized, as Sha'rawi
himself did, that the way to God is not only through a concern for the specificity of the laws but to live them out of love for, and devotion to, God.

Sha'rawi and Qaradawi, two shaykhs of al-Azhar born nearly a century ago,
were both well suited to media performance. Even though their programs
differed, both approaches proved to be effective and, to some viewers, even
complementary. Together, these two men originated a new public role for
the 'ulama' through television in a time directly following the severe curbing
of 'ulama' influence through the usurpation of their institutional power.

SHARED LINGUISTIC TECHNIQUES: METAPHOR

Sha'rawi used linguistic techniques particular to preachers to help his audience assimilate complicated theological ideas. Among those techniques are
metaphor, repetition, and storytelling. Sha'rawi's explication and presentation
of practicable knowledge extracted from the Qur'an and the hadith was aided
by metaphors, which facilitate the assimilation of ideas by changing attitudes
about what is already known. With a metaphor, an existing reality is presented
in terms of another reality and thus alters the original concept. Alteration occurs because metaphors restructure the linguistic formulation of one term in
the sense of a different term—what I will call the first and second factors of
the metaphor, respectively. But in doing so, metaphors affect how people talk
about, understand, and enact the original concept because alteration through
language can change actions that are associated with the original reality.[34]
Thus a metaphor, which begins with the stated or unstated goal of the person who devises it, actually has three components, that goal and the two terms
of the metaphor itself.

If the goal of the metaphor's composer is to defend a theological proposition, a previously accepted religious idea can be presented as the first factor
of a metaphor, which can be altered in meaning and applicability by the
second factor of the metaphor. Such a method is especially effective if the
second factor is related to the everyday lives of those receiving the metaphor.

The movement from language to action takes place when novel metaphors are created. These are metaphors that have not been widely used before, and they derive their force from being insightful and appropriate to the "given . . . experiences of members of any particular generation and/or culture."[35]

Novel metaphors have the power to define reality through a "coherent network of entailments that highlight some features of reality and hide others."[36] The acceptance of the metaphor translates into an acceptance of the reality it creates by what it focuses on and what it ignores, which can help listeners accept its propositions as true. But this truth, like the reality the metaphor creates, is relative to the metaphor.[37] Metaphors also depend on culture to animate them, and thus they rely on concepts embedded in cultural systems. By their nature, metaphors hide and highlight the elements that fit the goals of the one devising and using them. They present a certain version of truth because they present a particular reality powerfully grounded in the lives of the cultural group to which they are directed.

By using metaphors as part of his exegetical method, Sha'rawi infused the common understanding of science and politics with the theological. In one sermon, Sha'rawi used two metaphors to point his listeners to the conclusion that the theory of evolution was false. Sha'rawi's first novel metaphor was creation as bread making, and in it Sha'rawi brought together two distinctive elements: The first factor of the metaphor was focused on knowledge about creation, and the second factor was focused on action and experience through bread making. Ultimately, he created a reality to fit his objective: reinforcing the Qur'anic view of creation by hiding and highlighting only certain aspects associated with each component of the metaphor. Sha'rawi began by saying that, because no human being witnessed creation, people must rely on what God has said about it. He continued:

> When God speaks about the creation of humanity [in the Qur'an] he says one time, "I created everything from water." The second time God says, "I created humanity from earth." The third time he says, "I created humanity from clay." The fourth time he says, "I created humanity from fetid clay (ḥama' masnūn)."[38] The fifth time he says, "I created humanity from dry fired clay like pottery (ṣilṣāl)."[39] This is the essence of humanity. After that God breathed his breath into humanity. One might suppose that there is a contradiction in saying one time that human beings are created of water, another time of earth, a third time of clay, a fourth time of fetid clay, and a fifth time of dried clay. However we have emphatically maintained that if one studies these stages together he will find no contradiction in them. It is the same as if I took a loaf of flat bread and said, "This is [made]

from wheat." I would be telling the truth because [wheat] is [present in] the first stage of bread making. When I say that, "This flat bread is made from flour," I am also telling the truth because flour is involved in another one of the stages of making flat bread. If I say yet another time, "This flat bread is made from dough," I am again being truthful, because this is another one of the stages of making flat bread. So we see that even though I said one time that flatbread [comes] from wheat, another time that flatbread [comes] from flour, a third time that it [comes] from dough and a fourth time that it [comes] from leavening, each statement is true. This is because each one is giving name to a stage within the process of bread making. There is no contradiction in the succession of these stages. So when your Lord says, "I created you from water," this statement is true, just as when your Lord says, "I created you from earth," it is also a true statement. Because when water is mixed with the earth it becomes mud. When God leaves mud until it changes [then it is] like what happens with raw dough in which we put leavening, until it reacts and ferments and becomes fetid black clay. When we leave clay it then becomes something like hard clay from which the sculptor can sculpt what he wants . . . when the sculpting of the human being is complete then comes the stage of blowing in the spirit, which is when life enters into the human body.[40]

In addition to using metaphors, Sha'rawi also frequently repeated himself in order to help facilitate the acquisition of difficult knowledge among the people and to prove his point. His use of repetition gave his audience time to assimilate new information, specifically the connection between the two terms of the metaphor. He also used repetition for the sake of clarity and to help with recollection. He repeated words and combinations of words from the first factor of the metaphor in the second factor, which strengthened the connection between the two and directed attention toward these similarities repeatedly. This tactic highlights specific aspects and directs the listener toward the truth Sha'rawi hoped to underscore and away from associations he wanted to avoid. As the sermon progressed, Sha'rawi repeated short excerpts from the Qur'an, which begin with "I created," many times. By repeating the elements he wished to emphasize—what God says about creation—he accentuated God's words.

The use of repetition is common in public preaching and coincides with what one sees when watching Sha'rawi preach. During his sermons, he would often recite a verse from the Qur'an and then he would pause to allow the audience to repeat it with him. The second time Sha'rawi recited the verse, he would stop after the first word; say, "Eh?;" and wait for the audience to repeat the rest of the verse. He also used a similar method of repetition with the main

points of his lessons, even if they were not stated as Qur'anic verses. This interactive participation facilitated memory of the sermon, or the verse.

Sha'rawi's use of repetition also helped him build his metaphor in
stages. At first it seems that his main goal was to defend the Qur'an against
its detractors, who say that it contains contradictions. But as the sermon pro-
gresses, it is clear that his main goal is to explicate creation as a process, the
stages of which are built one upon the other, in order to defend the Qur'an
against doubt and even scientific knowledge. He began by setting out the
Qur'anic passages on which he built his interpretation of the stages of creation.
First he introduced the original concept: the elements from which humans
are made. Then, with the metaphor, Sha'rawi reiterated that, not only are
Qur'anic statements not contradictory, they stand for a process, which can be
understood in terms of another everyday process.

Although Sha'rawi never gave full voice to his opponent, the presence of
the opposite view is still in his sermon. Even though he omitted any support
for the stance that the Qur'an is contradictory, that fact that this sermon was
a defense implies that he assumed that his audience was familiar with what
he was defending against. In building up the argument for the truth of the
Qur'anic account before even mentioning the ideas of the doubters, he solidified his view first. Only after solidifying his view did he mention the potential threat—giving the listener just enough information to identify it.

Sha'rawi was not manipulating his audiences or hiding his real agenda; his
intent was clearly to prove his own truth claim, to convince through language.
He defended the perfection of God's words by referring to a physical reality
and a cultural symbol that all Egyptians are familiar with: bread making.
Bread is called 'aysh in the Egyptian dialect; 'aysh can also mean life (connected
through the meaning of sustenance). By using this process as the second factor of his metaphor, Sha'rawi illustrated how one word can become the building block of a novel metaphor by making it appropriate to the audience. In
the Egyptian language, bread is already connected to life, so it took only one
more step to equate it with God's act of creation; according to Sha'rawi, bread
and creation are formed through a similar process.

Using material arguments to fortify belief and to highlight the limitations
of human knowledge, Sha'rawi stated that, although we can witness the destruction of the human body, we cannot witness the creation of the human
body in its original form. In exploring what death is, Sha'rawi hoped to prove
Qur'anic ideas about the creation of life in reverse because "the destruction

of everything comes in the opposite way of which it was built."[41] To explain this idea further, he used the following metaphor: The stages of the creation of life can be proven through the stages of bodily destruction just like a ride on a train that passes the stations on the return trip in the exact opposite order of how they were passed on the original trip.

> When you travel to Alexandria from Cairo you must pass through Cairo first, then Tanta, then Damanhour, then Alexandria. The last thing you pass going into Alexandria is the first thing you pass when returning from Alexandria. So when God destroys something he does it by the opposite means of its construction. . . . Truly God has said to us that he created humanity from water and earth, then fetid clay and then fired clay into which he blew his spirit. So when death comes the first thing the human being loses is the last thing God put into him when he was created. So we see, first the spirit leaves the body. Second the body is filled with air, which is then released . . . this means it has returned to the stage of being fired clay. After that comes decay and the body rots, which means it becomes hard clay with an odor. After that the liquid and earth come out of it and the residual components disintegrate into the earth. By this I mean (the body) becomes dust (turāb).[42]

In this second metaphor, Sha'rawi supported Qur'anic truth by attaching it to a common experience. He presented the notion that the process of destruction is the reverse of the process of creation by comparing it to a train ride. Thus his lesson was a cultural presentation and was not based on scientific logic; in fact, Sha'rawi's scientific knowledge is completely lacking in this example. As with the example of him using the process of death to prove God's control over life and death (see chapter 2), he was materializing or actualizing through language the unprovable or immaterial in order to substantiate his belief. Sha'rawi used this rhetorical device often, and it made his arguments both understandable and untenable. Here I explore how this device worked, but in later chapters I will focus more on how it undermined some of his propositions.

In this example, Sha'rawi used a metaphor as a self-fulfilling prophecy and attempted to create a new reality as he spoke it according to his own theological goals. He sought to show that the logical progression of the theory of evolution, which states that human beings evolved from fish and monkeys, was false by offering another competing progression: the bodily process itself.[43] His explanation of how the body disintegrates is easily refuted; even simple knowledge of what happens to the body after death disproves his account. Yet he used a linguistic tool—the two terms of the metaphor—to embody the process of creation: a concept even he admitted was a mystery and could not be known by human beings.

STORIES AS NARRATIVE INSTRUCTION

Sha'rawi used stories to engage his audiences because stories are entertaining, are accessible, and can signify broader perspectives than argument or logic. Both stories and metaphors allow preachers to do more than just remind adherents of rules concerning behavior and belief. They expand and specify rules and therefore help adherents build relationships in the world. Principles are not necessarily the "moral essences of stories" because stories can signify a "deeper moral significance."[44] This significance goes beyond directly stating what is right and wrong; it brings the listener into a relationship with the characters of a story, who become moral models.

As signification, stories do not in themselves put forth conclusions but instead present listeners with the opportunity to extract and apply meaning derived from them. According to Sha'rawi, this was the purpose of Qur'anic stories, especially the stories of the prophets (qiṣaṣ al-anbiyā'), a popular genre for preachers. He thought that the qiṣaṣ had a divine connection that gave them special significance and made them universally applicable and capable of teaching listeners about their place in the world through historical example:

> "Out of all the accounts relating to the [earlier] prophets, we convey to you [only] that which makes your heart firm: for through these [accounts] truth comes to you, as well as an admonition and a reminder unto all believers" (Qur'an 11:120).

> The stories of the Qur'an are told to affirm to the messenger and the believers, when their positions are shaken by events. The stories of the Qur'an are not for killing time (qutal al-waqt). Rather the goal of listening to stories is for affirmation in all aspects of life. If we look closely at the stories of the Qur'an we will find that they talk about things that happened long ago as historical incidences. History connects the present to the past. . . . If you read the history of any event you will find that it reflects the point of view of the writer of the story. . . . These stories tell us what happened in history, but they are [also] repeated over time (marr al-zaman). Pharaoh, for example, is every leader who wants to be worshipped on earth. The people of the cave, for example, is the story of every group of believers that escape from tyranny of unbelief (al-kufr), and who are cut off from worshiping God. . . . And that is why the identity of the personalities in these stories are anonymous [in the Qur'an] with the exception of only one story—the story of Jesus the son of Mary, the daughter of Imran, [because] the birth of Jesus is a miracle that will never be repeated.[45]

According to Sha'rawi, Qur'anic stories teach lessons that are always repeated and thus always applicable in different contexts because they are from
God. Therefore Qur'anic stories help humanity apply lessons to every action
in life. They connect listeners not just to their own world but also to human
history and, more important, to the prophets in history. Sha'rawi believed that
stories were a teaching method of God for the purpose of providing eternal
inspiration or renewal because, as God's stories, they were timeless. Learning from the past, seeing the mistakes of the grand figures of prophetic
history—pharaohs and those singled out by God, is a common theme throughout scripture. Thus, according to Sha'rawi, God revealed that their purpose
was to teach humanity.

While Sha'rawi usually retold stories from the Qur'an and hadith, he also
retold stories that were common in Egypt, or ones that contained important
cultural and/or religious symbols. Even with these stories, Sha'rawi led his
audience to a particular meaning, but he let audience members interpret that
meaning themselves. He usually began his storytelling with a proposition
that was not easily understood and then illustrated that proposition through
narrative in order to ease assimilation. In one example, Sha'rawi began by
telling his listeners:

> There is dignity in full obedience to God's law. When the decision comes from
> God then there is no bitterness, no problem and no pain. With this faith it is pos-
> sible for individual disputes to vanish.[46]

Sha'rawi said that, in disputes, God prepares a third side that becomes a screen
(*sitr*) for two disputing parties or individuals in order to protect their dignity, which is necessary for reconciliation to succeed. Sha'rawi went on to
tell the story of a husband and wife who loved each other very much but
had become estranged from one another through their disagreements. The
woman wanted to know what her husband was doing, so she snuck up to his
door to listen.

> The husband was calling to God saying, "Oh Lord, make my wife come to recon-
> cile with me." Then he began appealing to God's saints saying, "Sayyida Zaynab,[47]
> for you I vow such and such if my wife reconciles with me." The wife then returned
> to her room and put on her finest clothes and headed back towards her husband's
> room as if someone was pushing her, while saying: "Why are you forcing me into
> reconciliation with him, Sayyida Zaynab?" In this way we see that the excuse as-
> sociated with (*al-taḥajjuj bi*) Sayyida Zaynab is a screen (*sitr*) for love. The tale,
> even though it is a funny anecdote, illustrates how each side in a dispute loves it

when a third side enters [to reconcile them]. So we see that God wants to preserve for humanity their superiority and their dignity, so he included in the heavenly laws that which assures this dignity.[48]

Although this seems to be a simple story about marital reconciliation that is resolved without either side needing to apologize or admit fault, it is actually more complex. Sha'rawi presented the idea, repeated at the end of the story for emphasis, that when God's law is adhered to, believers do not suffer. But the story takes the listener beyond what is associated with law by bringing forth cultural and religious symbols, leaving open the possibility of multiple interpretations and applications of the original lesson and the story.

The story includes human relationships; the divine–human relationship; and, perhaps most important, an explanation of the intervention of God, reached through the heavenly law. Divine law is often seen as something God decreed and then left to humanity, implying that God's activity in relation to the law ended once it was revealed. But here Sha'rawi was saying that God can actively intervene through the heavenly law, which in this case was the third side. Sha'rawi was not just telling the members of his audience that God was concerned with their lives but that heavenly law protected and ensured their dignity. God's living provisions were part of the heavenly laws, realized in human action.

But Sha'rawi's use of the narrative form meant he did not have to specify the third side. In the story, it is not clear how the law was being followed. The only thing that is clear is that the husband was asking for God's help and that his wife used the opportunity to end the dispute. So while the man did plead with Sayyida Zaynab, asking her to intervene, the saint did not actually intervene as far as we are led to believe because the wife walked "as if" Zaynab was there. But the story can be interpreted to support the belief in saintly intervention because Sha'rawi did not condemn the practice of asking saints for help. Actually he seemed to be saying that, as long as one asked for God's help before supplications were made to the saints, this type of pleading was according to heavenly law.

Sha'rawi spoke of God intervening with a third side, which here was connected to the supplication of the husband and not to an actual intervention by the saint. Sha'rawi was therefore not clear about exactly how God intervened in this case. In the story, the saint served as the screen for God's action (Sha'rawi even used the word *love* to describe the third side that God provided). But what exactly was the third side in the story? Was it the love God placed in the hearts of the husband and wife before they began to reconcile? Was it the idea of the saint? Or was it the husband's pleading with the saint? If it was the last choice, it could mean that the saint's intervention was useful to God's purposes, even though only God could grant the petitions of a believer. Sha'rawi was clear in the story that God granted the petition of the husband, but his opinion about the intervention of the saints is less easy to state.

The narrative form allowed Sha'rawi to use one of the most popular saints in Egypt (Zaynab) and a common practice among Egyptians (calling on the saints for help) to put forth his lesson about how God acts in the lives of believers. The narrative form also meant that Sha'rawi was able to end the story in a way that captivated and satisfied the audience: The husband and wife reconcile, even though Sha'rawi left it up to the listeners to clarify any uncertainties in the story for themselves.

SHA'RAWI'S EXEGETICAL METHOD

Sha'rawi used common techniques to support his perspective or increase viewer involvement in the creation of meaning, and his preaching was comprised mostly of Qur'anic exegesis. Through his linguistic methods of interpretation, he preserved the categories, methods, and results of his hermeneutic predecessors. For example, he used intratextual interpretations to explain the meanings of Qur'anic words and historical occurrences (asbāb al-nuzūl, reasons for revelation). But he did so for reasons particular to his situation: to explain away any suggestion that the Qur'an is somehow imperfect. He used linguistic devices to defend the Qur'an against modern detractors and scientific knowledge.

Linguistic interpretation is one of the major genres of tafsīr literature, and Sha'rawi's method was not novel: He broke down chapters by verse, verses by word, and words by sound.

> In the Qur'an, words sometimes need restructuring in order for accuracy to be preserved . . . [f]or example, when verbs are changed from transitive to intransitive or the other way around. The verb saqā (to water or to quench thirst) is used four [different] ways [in the Qur'an]. One of the forms of this verb is seen in the following verse: "And their sustainer will quench their thirst (saqāhum) with a pure drink" (Qur'an 76:21). Yet in a different verse the word saqā has a different meaning: "If they (the idolaters) tread the right path, we shall give them to drink (asqaynāhum) of water in abundance" (Qur'an 72:16). Although the two words

share a common root, the omission of a letter gives them two different meanings and [therefore] avoids repetition . . . the word in the second example—"we shall give them to drink"—means that God has given humanity many sources of water, but we must find those sources, whether in a well or from a spring. But the words "their sustainer will quench their thirst" imply that humanity will not need to exert effort, for in paradise water comes [automatically] to those who are thirsty. All desires will be fulfilled immediately in paradise.[49]

In this passage, Sha'rawi compared verses with similar words in order to clarify the meaning of a word in one verse in relation to a similar word in another verse, but in this case to prove that the Qur'an in its perfection never repeats even a single sound. Sha'rawi used this intratextual method often, mostly for the sake of clarifying God's intentions. One such example is when he interpreted the following verse: "And fight in the way of God (*qātilū fī sabīl Allah*) against those who wage war against you, but do not commit aggression—for, verily, God does not love aggressors" (Qur'an 2:190). He began his explanation with another common exegetical approach: considering the historical context as a reason for the revelation:

> The reason this verse was revealed (*sabab nuzūl*) to God's messenger was that he and his companions longed to visit the holy place in Mecca (*al-bayt al-ḥarām*). In the month of Dhū al-Qa'da in the sixth year of the Hijra they left [for Mecca]. But they were stopped by Quraysh before they reached a place called Hudaybiyyah. [The people of Quraysh] said: "Muhammad, you and your companions cannot enter Mecca." So the two sides negotiated an agreement. The Prophet agreed to return [to Medina] that year, but only if he could come back [to Mecca] the next year.[50]

Sha'rawi then explained how Muhammad's companions were disappointed by the treaty; they were very close to Mecca and did not want to turn back. This dissatisfaction worried Muhammad, but upon returning to Medina he took the good advice of one of his wives, Umm Salamah, and decided not to speak to anyone about the incident, and his companions quickly followed suit.[51] At this point in the story, Sha'rawi has not explained the verse about fighting in the way of God, although it would seem to apply to the situation because it could have been revealed to keep the companions from entering Mecca lest a fight ensued. But this wandering on and off topic was typical for Sha'rawi; his sermons often took unexpected turns only to make their way back eventually to his original point. Sha'rawi continued by explaining how the verse he began with was revealed the next year, when Muhammad and his community returned to Mecca.

In the following year God spoke to them saying: "Fight during the sacred months if you are attacked: for a violation of sanctity is [subject to the law of] just retribution." Thus God assured them. . . . The Muslims were afraid to go the next year lest the Meccans should break the pact (ʿahd) and fight them [during the month of Dhū al Qaʿda, which was designated as a sacred month in which no fighting should take place]. So God revealed, "And fight in the way of God (qātilū fī sabīl Allah) against those who wage war against you, but do not commit aggression—for, verily, God does not love aggressors" (Qurʾan 2:190).[52]

Here Shaʿrawi finished his explanation of the occasion of the revelation, stretching it out and providing a more complete context for the verse. But the story only partially explains the first part of the verse and does not touch on the second part. He continued by comparing verses:

Let's consider God's utterance: "and fight in the way of God," in which we find that God places emphasis on the words "in the way of God" (fī sabīl Allah) to put an end to human tyranny. The motivation for fighting must be in the way of God, it cannot be for vengeance, or tyranny or oppression. And killing cannot be for one's own gain, or money or revenge, or for economic assurance (ḍamāna al-sūqi al-iqtiṣad). "And fight in the way of God (qātilū fī sabīl Allah) against those who wage war against you, but do not commit aggression—for, verily, God does not love aggressors." . . . Believers should only fight when they are responding to aggression, [they should] not instigate aggression. . . . In another sura, God tells the believers: "Hence, if you have to respond to an attack (ʿāqabtum), respond only to the extent of the attack leveled against you; but to bear yourselves with patience is indeed far better for you, since God is with those who are patient in adversity" (Qurʾan 16:126). And in another verse God says: "The recompense of an evil may be an equal evil (sayyiʾatun mithluhā): hence, whoever pardons [his foe] and makes peace, his reward rests with God—for, verily, He does not love evildoers" (Qurʾan 42:40).[53]

So Shaʿrawi finally answered the question of what it means to fight in the way of God, or in what context the Qurʾan sanctifies war and violence, a question that was at the forefront of public discussions in Egypt. Although there were a variety of opinions among both Islamists and ʿulama, depending on the circumstances of the fighting,[54] many Egyptian extremists in Shaʿrawi's time asserted that the Qurʾan sanctioned violence if that violence was committed for the sake of defeating an unjust ruler in order to establish a Muslim society. Some went as far as to say that such action was the duty of every true Muslim. In contrast, many ʿulama supported the idea of fighting war only for defensive purposes.

In his exegesis, Sha'rawi supported a moderate view and dismissed the radical view without ever referencing the debate. He did so by choosing which verses to highlight and which verses to compare them to. In the first instance, he used the word *qātilū* (fight), a word that has no connotation of holiness on its own. But he also compared *qātilū* to an even weaker word, *'āqaba* (attack), to make the point that violence is only justifiable in self-defense. His interpretation of "in the way of God," which comes after the word *qātilū* in the verse, signified the connection of the fight to God. Sha'rawi narrowed the application of that connection by specifying that fighting for vengeance, tyranny, or oppression, rather than defending oneself against direct attack, was not fighting in God's way.

Besides defining specific Qur'anic words and verses to argue against groups he disagreed with inside Egypt, Sha'rawi also used his interpretations to defend the Qur'an against outsiders who asserted that the Qur'an is contradictory—those he called orientalists. For Sha'rawi critics were only critics because they did not interpret the verses of the Qur'an correctly and therefore could not understand the underlying meaning and purpose of the words:

> What do the orientalists (*mustashriqūn*) say? They say that in many chapters of the Qur'an, the earth and heavens are said to be created in six days, but in chapter (*sura*) *Fussilat* it says that the days of creation are eight. They say that this mistake is caused by human forgetfulness ... What does the Qur'an say in sura *al-A'raf*? "Your lord is God, who created the heavens and the earth in six days" (Qur'an 7:54). And it says in sura *Yunus*, "Truly your lord is God, who created the earth and the heavens in six days" (Qur'an 10:3) ... but when we move to sura *Fussilat* ... and we count the number of days [referenced] in the sura we will find that God says that he created the earth in two days and that it took four days to set the mountains and give it [the earth] sustenance (*aqwātahā*) and two days to set up the heavens ... Thus in sura *Fussilat* God speaks about the creation of the earth, which came about in two stages. In the first stage he created the earth in two days. In the second stage he created the mountains and provided sustenance in two days. The explanation is that the two days and the four days overlap; four days is the total time it took to create the earth with the mountains.[55]

Sha'rawi's orientalists were foreigners, mostly Europeans and Americans, who had for decades studied the Qur'an in order to criticize the Muslim belief in its divine origins. Although identifying foreigners as threatening is a common trope, Sha'rawi's concerns were not unsupported. He understood well that the ideas associated with the methods of the orientalists (such as literary and historical criticism of the Qur'an) had already filtered into his own society.

Sha'rawi responded to and identified threats that were relevant in his time, but he always referenced them as secondary to the main issue: the truth of the Qur'an. He presented other views only as he believed and wanted others to believe them to be. His strength was in defining truth as Qur'anic to demonstrate the lasting relevance of God's message to humanity. For those who accepted his premises, this self-enclosed system was very powerful.

For Sha'rawi, the purpose of the Qur'an was revealed in the first verses of sura *al-Baqara*:

> This is the Book; in which there is no doubt, for those who fear God" (Qur'an 2:2). Although the Qur'an is [primarily] a book of guidance, God has placed in it [every] answer to [every] doubter until the Day of Judgment (*yawm al-qiyāma*). We know only some of the information that is contained in the Qur'an . . . But we can find out which scientific evidence is true through the Qur'an. The Qur'an contains all correct knowledge and [therefore can be used to judge] incorrect scientific knowledge. Science which contradicts the Qur'an is not true . . . but it is wiser not to compare the Qur'an to unproven scientific theories until they are proven without a doubt . . . It is wrong to say something is from God only to find out later that it is proven false.[56]

Sha'rawi also said that scientific revelations that are not yet clear are meant to "discredit those heretics who hail the doctrine of science and decry the doctrine of faith."[57] He explained that, even though God reveals the knowledge of science, this knowledge should not be used to validate the Qur'an for the simple reason that it reverses the order by which truth claims should be evaluated. Using the Qur'an to validate science would make science the primary source of truth. But as with his discussion of evolution, using the Qur'an to "find out what scientific evidence is true" could also prove dangerous to Qur'anic knowledge when scientific evidence became irrefutable.

CONCLUSION

Sha'rawi's concern with explaining the correct way to validate truth claims was central to his defense of the Qur'an but also to justifying his theologically centered approach to all of life. His 'ulama' methods of defense and affirmation set him apart from others. His talent with the Arabic language meant he could present his interpretations as being of the text itself. Many

Muslim television preachers do not have Sha'rawi's talent with language, a sign of his al-Azhar training, and thus cannot signal to their audiences their level of learning. Qaradawi was able to distinguish himself similarly through his legal expertise.

When I was told, as I often was, that Sha'rawi's popularity was derived from his ability to make complex ideas understandable, what people were partly referring to was his ability to devise metaphors and stories and to employ repetition to help people absorb the complexity of the ideas he was trying to convey. While both metaphors and stories help listeners understand a difficult concept in terms of something simpler, they also serve different functions. Novel metaphors can create a particular view of reality, while stories engage through open signification. Stories also allow for interpretation because their references can be broad and various.

Metaphors and stories were not the tools that set Sha'rawi apart, however, from other preachers. The fact that he used typical exegetical methods of Qur'anic interpretation to convey complex theological ideas marked him as a trained 'alim and helped distinguish him from his competition. Contestation was not a new issue for 'alim preachers: Competition has been a feature of Muslim preaching almost from its beginnings as a vocation. The current widespread availability and diversity of preachers and orators further blurs the categories of popular and official. What has fallen away are attempts to regulate preachers according to particular rules and standards (with the exception of official mosque preaching, which is heavily regulated by the Egyptian government) and what is highlighted is the invocation of past primary sources, the Qur'an, the prophet, certain stories, the effectiveness of the preacher, and the incorporation of innovation for the sake of audiences. Language use has helped determine this movement. Sha'rawi is most commonly referred to as a preacher through the term 'alim al-sha'b, translated as "preacher of the people." At the same time, he referred to his orations not as admonitions (wa'az or tadhkira), sermons (khatāba), or storytelling (qaṣṣa) but as his thoughts (khawātir) and as lessons (durūs). The language of thoughts and lessons in reference to an official preacher's orations demonstrates a new understanding of what it means to be learned or a new understanding of religious authority. But it also signifies the shift to individualization through an emphasis on rational capacities.

CHAPTER 4

Renewal as a Nexus of 'Ulama' Discursive Authority

Every hundred years there is an imam who renews, and all of the imams and shaykhs agree that Sha'rawi was [the renewer] of the 20th century. He had a soft way and a sense of humor in his style when he delivered the message. He showed generosity and solved people's problems. He performed good deeds for the last day and followed what he told people to do. He also guided people of other religions [to Islam] by convincing them and not by force, and some of them converted.[1]

INTRODUCTION

The quote that opens this chapter is from a woman I met in Cairo who, like many people I spoke to, felt a deep affection for Sha'rawi. She showed significant knowledge of the tradition of *tajdīd* (renewal of religion when the community has strayed from God's path) and the emblematic elements of authority that solidify the stature of a renewer (sing. *mujaddid*, pl. *mujaddidūn*). She referenced the hadith that specifies that a renewer will come in every century, the necessity for a *mujaddid* to be recognized as such by his peers, and the importance for a *mujaddid* to behave according to the expectations of the community. Yet the elements of authority that she highlighted were very different from the expectations of the past. She did not say that Sha'rawi innovated through legal or theological reasoning; rather, she mentioned his behavior and his ability to convince. Her statement exemplifies how the tradition of *tajdīd* in Egypt has become popularized among people who have had increased access to religious actors and to a myriad of displays and combinations of authoritative assertions. In the quote, no mention is made of how Sha'rawi actually renewed religion, only that he made the concerns of his audiences a primary consideration, a talent that is generally associated with preachers more than with those who innovate to revive the religion. Such innovators were centered in the world of the texts, even though they used real-life situations to provide a purpose for, and to direct the result of, any textual search.[2] But their ability to communicate with and care for adherents did not determine the impact of their works. It is also not the case that all of the religious leaders of Sha'rawi's time agreed that he was the renewer of the twentieth century, not even in Egypt. The focus on Sha'rawi's reception among and relation to his audiences as opposed to his peers signifies a deep shift in the workings of religious authority gained through discursive production.

The chapter-opening quote encapsulates how a term like *tajdīd*, which is related to knowledge and learning, was redefined in contemporary Egypt. Other terms, such as *'alim* and *ijtihād* (independent judgment derived through legal reasoning), also shifted as they came to designate religious responsibilities that could be fulfilled by anyone with any sort of expertise.[3] *Ijtihād* was once limited to the most expert legal scholars, and even though it was sometimes minimally utilized, it was a technique that allowed jurists to incorporate new ideas into the law.[4] The standards necessary to perform *ijtihād* were well developed, and specific rules had to be followed for an 'alim to claim the title of *mujtahīd* (one who performs *ijtihād*).[5] There was also an inherent hierarchy among legal practitioners based on levels of training. The mufti (any jurist) who could perform the highest levels of *ijtihād* was more highly skilled than one who could not, but all muftis were expected to be more highly trained than judges (sing. *qaḍi*, pl. *quḍā*) Muftis were also expected to possess in-depth knowledge of Islamic law and its procedures, sources, and previous rulings.[6] A mufti, whether a *mujtahīd* or not, was also supposed to live an upright life and have an impeccable character.[7]

Both renewers and those capable of performing *ijtihād* appeared throughout Islamic history and, "moved either by ambition or by objection to recognized doctrines," returned to the meaning of *ijtihād* as "asserting the right to form one's own opinion, usually in relation to the law, from first principles."[8] Thus *ijtihād* and *tajdīd* were considered interdependent because renewers needed to issue new opinions to put forth new programs in every century. Like preaching and unlike *ijtihād*, however, the tradition of renewal was animated by inconsistencies, which led to controversies. Arguments arose not only over what constituted true Islamic faith and practice and which practices and beliefs needed to be purged but also over who had the right to renew. Although anyone who performed *ijtihād* or who was considered a *mujaddid* was assumed to represent the highest caliber of leaning, those who performed *ijtihād* were recognized by their peers as being specially qualified, and those who were labeled renewers usually received that title from their disciples after their deaths. Disputes, especially after the first few centuries of Islam, arose over who was the renewer of each century and prevented the establishment of an official apparatus for defining and identifying renewers.[9] The practice of naming renewers exemplifies why standardization was impossible even though a certain level of influence was assumed.

Both independent judgment and renewal, based on the notion that only a few scholars could undertake them, were a means of limiting stature, a limitation that was gradually overridden in the modern era.[10] Today, both are claimed by a variety of 'ulama' and non-'ulama' authorities, a phenomenon that began in the nineteenth century with the call to remove interpretive, revelatory authority from the specialized realm of the 'ulama'. Terms like *ijtihād* and *tajdīd* were re-appropriated and now signify activities that are diversified, have minimum standards, and are even undertaken by those who are not specialists in the religious sciences.[11]

THE TRADITION OF TAJDĪD

In the most cited reference to renewal in the hadith, it is reported that Muhammad said: "At the beginning of every century God will send to this community (*umma*) someone who will renew religion (*yujaddid dīniha*)."[12] This hadith became central to the tradition of renewal and was interpreted to mean that the Muslim community would need to be purified every century because of the human propensity to stray from the basic teachings of Muhammad and the Qur'an over time.[13] At the same time, whatever distanced Muslims from remembering and practicing those foundations had to be expunged. The renewer of any era was supposed to help the Muslim community focus on following the straight path, God's will for humanity, by redirecting the community away from human failings and again toward the revelation. As the definition of renewal developed over time, it also came to signify the purification of the community through the eradication of whatever beliefs and practices could not be confirmed by the authentic sources. The responsibilities of the renewer included reinterpreting scripture, defending tradition, transmitting interpretive knowledge to the public, and especially making independent judgments about legal or theological issues for the sake of deriving new rulings.[14] Before the modern era, all these tasks belonged within the purview of the 'ulama', and many well-known 'ulama', including the influential Sunni thinker Abu Hamid al-Ghazali (d. 1111 C.E.), were considered the renewers of their centuries.

The trend toward looking to the texts to discover the ideal usually kept renewal focused on scripturalism[15] or, perhaps more accurately, kept it discursive. The language of renewal helped a *mujaddid* navigate from past to present, moving from scripture to judgments concerning the specifics of lived reality. Yet renewal was not inherently conservative or inconstant; a renewer sought to limit as much as possible human influence on textual meaning through procedure. Throughout Islamic religious history, *tajdīd* constituted "an authentic part of the working out of the Islamic revelation in history," a definition which recognizes the peculiarities of discrete moments in history, as well as the influence of past movements on the present.[16] Renewal as a pattern has also been used as a way to protest against an existing order, again signifying the importance of historical specifics.[17] *Tajdīd* has been especially prevalent in times of crisis, in which existing institutions are threatened, and it is often focused not only on defense but also ultimately on reconstruction. Today, the idea of using scripture to process historical change is associated not only with the word *tajdīd* but also with the more general terms *nahḍa* (revival) and *iṣlāḥ* (reform).[18] Shifts in meaning demonstrate that crisis not only called forth the need for *tajdīd*; it also transformed the institution of renewal itself.

HISTORICAL CHANGES AND RENEWAL: MUHAMMAD 'ABDUH AND BEYOND

The nineteenth-century call to remove interpretive, revelatory authority from the specialized realm of the 'ulama' began in earnest with Muhammad 'Abduh (1849–1905 C.E.) and his teacher, Jamal al-Din al-Afghani (1838–1897 C.E.). 'Abduh is commonly referred to as the first or most influential Egyptian modernist; even though he was an important Egyptian 'alim, his calls for reform helped lead to the loss of 'ulama' authority in Egypt overall. 'Abduh emphasized the importance of emulating Muhammad and his companions and successors (the pious ancestors or *al-salaf al-ṣāliḥ*) and rejecting that which separated the individual and the community from the first sources, including the determinative authority of the 'ulama' and their methods. In the spirit of returning to the pristine ways of the early community, 'Abduh also said that Muslims should not be affiliated with particular legal or doctrinal schools; instead, they should be unified as one community.[19]

'Abduh emphasized the power of human reason to discover the truth of revelation. His answer to the question of how to reconcile modern innovation and Islam was to discover the correspondence between revelation and rational thought.[20] He and his followers sought to revive the community by downplaying the importance of 'ulama' responsibility and emphasizing the individual's—any individual's—judgment as *ijtihād*,[21] here signifying a re-appropriation of the term. This emphasis prompted many to claim their interpretations of the "first sources" as *ijtihād*, even if they were focused on interpreting the Qur'an and sunna to address present circumstances rather than to incorporate new ideas into the law through specific procedures.[22] It was an epistemological change—'Abduh thought that, through mass education, Muslims could be trained to understand the truth of the Qur'an in accordance "with the principles of science and natural law."[23]

'Abduh's legacy spurred two distinctive movements in the twentieth century: defending the unencumbered use of reason despite revelation and advocating for increased scrutiny of behavior based on judgments derived from individual interpretations of the Qur'an and sunna.[24] Yet these two groups also had much in common. Both questioned the past authority of the 'ulama' and instead advocated for returning to the earliest models and to scripture, and both focused on human capacity, and away from methodology, as the correct means for extracting meaning from the sources.[25] Their extractions were not based on processes, instead their interpretations of scripture were often presented as completed solutions meant to be applied to present societal issues.

Partially as a result of 'Abduh's influence, the transformation of the concept of *tajdīd* as an element of discourse that signifies a function has been acute. Those not associated with the 'ulama' have sought to usurp the right to direct the community back to the truth of revelation. Revisionist, revivalist, or reformist groups often postulate that the revelation needs to be searched for solutions to problems that are the direct result of the mistakes that the 'ulama' have made over the past centuries. These types of reformers see the present era as one in which they have a chance to start over, erasing mistaken 'ulama' methods and reformulating not only according to an idealized past but also according to an original model. For them, this model is distinct from what was authoritative during the time between the era of the pious ancestors and the present moment.

A third, much overlooked group—those trained at al-Azhar—also carried on 'Abduh's legacy. As mufti of Egypt, 'Abduh insisted that the al-Azhar curriculum should be changed to include secular subjects like science, engineering, and medicine. Although secular subjects were not introduced until after 'Abduh's death, the change came about in no small part because the rectors of al-Azhar that advocated for them, like Muhammad al-Maraghi (rector from 1927–1929), were 'Abduh's disciples.[26] 'Abduh's vision for al-Azhar became the legacy of that institution; secular subjects are now taught and religious education has been curtailed. 'Abduh hoped that such changes would help religious scholars learn more about the scientific world and incorporate that knowledge into their rulings and opinions. Instead, al-Azhar students now graduate with both an inferior scientific education and a diminished religious education.

RENEWAL: A COMPARISON OF 'ABDUH AND SHA'RAWI

'Abduh's ideas of reform also influenced individual scholars like Sha'rawi. While Sha'rawi's disciples often told me that Sha'rawi was the renewer of the twentieth century, they also insisted that 'Abduh was the renewer of the nineteenth century, in order to position Sha'rawi as his successor. As a renewer, Sha'rawi repeated and even benefitted from some of 'Abduh's ideas, but there were others he opposed. In many ways, 'Abduh and Sha'rawi addressed the same issues in their works. They both believed that the Qur'an was always relevant and could at any time reveal new information if one read it carefully; therefore, the Qur'an had to be searched anew to find answers to pressing problems. For Sha'rawi, however, the eternality of revelation meant that it was unlimited in application and that human understanding in any one era was limited by circumstances, making renewal necessary. 'Abduh, on the other hand, believed that the Qur'an was timeless but that it could not be read as true merely because it was timeless. The human mind could verify Qur'anic claims at any moment by examining them through reason. He did not deny the truth of the Qur'an, but he asserted that human beings must start by honing their rational skills, which is what the Qur'an demanded:

In the Qur'an God gave us everything we needed to know, everything he permit-
ted us to know, about his attributes. But we are not required to accept what it says
simply because it says it. On the contrary, it offers us arguments and evidence [for
what it says]. . . . It speaks to the rational mind and it requires a vigilant intelligence. It describes how the universe is ordered according to principles and certi-
tude, [but also] requires active scrutiny [by the human mind] in order to validate
its message and its claims.[27]

'Abduh insisted that the use of human reason helped define Islam. In
the quote above, 'Abduh argued that the universe runs according to the
unchanging laws of nature. Sha'rawi, in contrast, held to the notion that
God creates the universe anew in each moment.[28] Sha'rawi's position is
reminiscent of Ash'arism, the dominant Sunni theological school, particularly the ideas of occasionalism and atomism as they are presented in the
works of al-Ghazali. Al-Ghazali thought that no material or created matter
could be the cause of any occurrence in the world. Instead, because only
atoms exist in the world, God must intervene in each moment to bring about
actions.[29]

The difference between Sha'rawi and 'Abduh is also apparent in their
different approaches to scientific knowledge. 'Abduh believed that the laws
of nature, when proven through scientific (rational) inquiry, would verify
Qur'anic claims. He was not an apologist; he did not think the Qur'an needed
proving. Instead he stated that the human mind needed to find its own rational ways of verifying those words, just as rationality was needed to prove the
existence or power of God. For 'Abduh, human reason—as given by God and
verified in the Qur'an—was crucial to humanity and therefore should not be
limited to religious application:

Muslims who are beginning to explore science, see their religion as an old piece
of clothing, and are embarrassed to appear in it in front of other people [scien-
tists]. While others who are deceived and assert that they are the most orthodox
believers, see reason as the devil and science as supposition. In light of this we must
call God, and his angels and all of humanity to witness that science and reason
are a part of this religion.[30]

As an 'alim, Sha'rawi was still grappling with the divide that 'Abduh described
in this quote, but he took a different approach to reconciling the difference. He
did not believe that science was supposition, but he did believe that the Qur'an
could disprove scientific claims. For Sha'rawi, the Qur'an was the religion of
Islam, and science was an outside and potentially threatening force. Renewal

was for judging new scientific discoveries in light of the Qur'an, not for including rationality and science into religion.

For Sha'rawi, renewal also depended on the Qur'an, and the human mind was a vessel through which new information was revealed. He affirmed the need for interpreters who could compare new information to the Qur'an in order to test the veracity of that information. He emphasized God's control over humanity, reaffirming tradition against the idea that human reason is unrestricted. Sha'rawi thus would have disagreed with the idea that rational capacity made one capable of religious reform; for him, individual reasoning could help discover and implement the law, but it was not a first source. Sha'rawi's defense can be seen as a refutation of 'Abduh's idea that tradition and imitation were the enemies of human reason and therefore that they prevented the discovery of truth.[31]

But Sha'rawi also benefitted from 'Abduh's influence. The lack of scrutiny of would-be renewers meant that the word *mujaddid* no longer connoted the intellectual rigor it once did, even when applied to Sha'rawi. Although Sha'rawi was an 'alim, he was not trained to perform the procedural tasks assumed to be the duty of the renewer in the past. Sha'rawi also adopted and benefitted from 'Abduh's focus on individuals rather than schools of law. But in contrast to 'Abduh, he took standard Sunni and Sufi theological ideas and demonstrated how individuals could apply them to their lives, thus focusing on individual problems rather than societal solutions.

SHA'RAWI'S METHOD OF RENEWAL

Sha'rawi saw newer forms of schooling, the elevation of the rational capabilities of individuals, presentations of societal norms as stagnant, and the attack on the 'ulama' and their history as potential threats to the well-being of his society. His response was to speak to individuals about the importance of having a direct personal relationship to God by reasserting the notion that the Qur'an is eternally applicable. Sha'rawi defended what he saw as the crucial elements of Islam, and he sought to bring individuals back to God through an understanding of how human action—every movement in life—was first and foremost related to God and God's justice in the universe. These concerns may seem archaic to those who place social or political concerns above the theological, and Sha'rawi did not counter threats by engaging such people intellectually. Instead he sought to inculcate a new understanding of practices, and thereby cultivate trust in the religious advice of those trained at al-Azhar, by discussing theological complexity with a mass audience. Through a mutually reinforcing process, he made himself the authoritative example in order to reinstate the very authority he exemplified. Yet he also expected his example to influence people in a way that augmented his authority. But there were weak points in this edifice. For example, the loosening of knowledge standards even among the 'ulama' classes increased reliance on public engagement for the establishment of authority, which further weakened those trained in the religious sciences.

Sha'rawi sought to increase public engagement through form and content. His Qur'anic readings were televised community events through which he included his audiences in the practice of understanding the meaning of the Qur'an, an understanding that he implied belonged to every Muslim. He focused his Qur'anic teachings on the human condition because, for him, renewal meant bringing every Muslim back to the truth of revelation through a participatory understanding and application of knowledge. He also taught that the Qur'an was capable of providing whatever knowledge human beings might need at any moment: past, present, or future.

When interpreting a Qur'anic verse, Sha'rawi would often begin by stating something like:

> Let's look deeply at the story of the Queen of Sheba with the spirit of renewed understanding (bi ruḥ al-fahm al-mutajaddid) and firm conviction as God has given us some story or part of a narration with the goal that either will provide us with a ripe lesson.[32]

Sha'rawi spoke of his interpretation as a group endeavor, one he guided with his expertise so that a "ripe lesson" could be derived. Thus he implied that the purpose of renewed exegesis was to find something edifying in the Qur'an for his audience. His concept of the eternally applicable lessons of the Qur'an implied that even if the Qur'an had clarified an issue in the past, it needed to be reinterpreted constantly for every community of believers over time or in different regions. Renewed understandings brought forth by exegetes were always needed because of changes in the human condition and not because of any lack in the Qur'an itself. Thus as an expert exegete he defined his own role as a mujaddid, which he read into the Qur'an:

> Evidence about the truth concerning the universe has been hidden [in the Qur'an] for fourteen centuries, and has only recently begun to yield its wealth of scientific

data. The meaning was not uncovered for the human intellect (al-'aql al-bashariyy) until the present. As I have said, the Qur'an bestows renewed (mutajadid) information in the [following] verses: "In time we will show them (sanurihim) our messages in the utmost horizons [of the universe] and within themselves, so that it will become clear unto them that this [revelation] is indeed the truth. [Still,] is it not enough [for them to know] that their sustainer is witness unto everything?" (Qur'an 41:53). We must pay attention here to the letter s in the word "we will show them" (sanurihim) because it indicates the future tense. But [reference to] the future here has no ending; instead it indicates future generations and generations that will come after, until the end of time. But this meaning does not indicate more than what it currently signifies.[33]

According to Sha'rawi Qur'anic verse 41:53 referred specifically to scientific knowledge in his time, but was not limited to referencing scientific knowledge in the future. For him scientific knowledge had to be understood in light of the Qur'an, which is how the Qur'an's unlimited knowledge would be revealed in the contemporary world. The Qur'an never stops revealing new information, and deriving this information is how those who know how to interpret the Qur'an's constant disclosures renew religion. Thus Sha'rawi positioned himself and his interpretations between the prophetic and the public. He carefully navigated between overtly referring to the commonness of his insights (he referred to his exegesis as his thoughts, khawāṭir) and embedding his special claims to knowledge in his discourse. Sha'rawi said that even Muhammad understood that dissimilar situations required diverse prescriptions. During his lifetime, Muhammad gave different answers to the same questions depending on the situation of the questioner and not simply based on the similarity of the question.[34] Sha'rawi affirmed the necessity of diverse interpretations so that he could maintain that the 'ulama', as those who represent Muhammad, have a right to devise new interpretations as situations warrant.

EXAMPLE OF RENEWAL: THEOLOGY

Sha'rawi sought to reassert points of faith that had been neglected and to clarify them in order to counter oppositional ideas, real or imagined. Both discursive motivations fall under the category of renewal through reaffirmation. Although Sha'rawi defined renewal as bringing forth new information from the Qur'an, he did not say that such information could revise settled matters of belief, although in matters that were not settled he always took a particular side. He never questioned the basic method of deriving truth; he always began his logical arguments with the revelation as the basis of proof. He explained the well-known idea that in revelation God gave humanity everything they needed to know, making the Qur'an the basis of all certain knowledge:

> The method of God (*minhaj Allah*) requires praise from us. God revealed his method to show us the path of the good (*ṭarīq al-ḥayr*) and to distinguish it from the path of evil (*ṭarīq al-sharr*). God revealed his method to his prophets so that we might know that God [is the one] who created this universe for us and then created us (*wa khalaqanā*) in it. The precision and greatness of the creation demonstrates for us that there is an almighty creator. But [the creator] is not able to tell us who he is (*man huwa*) or what he wants from us, so [he sent] his messengers to bring us his message. That is why they have told us that the one who created this universe for us and then created us was God, and that God requires praise. The method of God shows us what God (*al-ḥaqq*) wants from us, and how to worship him, and thus that he requires praise. The method of God is a glory among glories in which he gave us the path and legislation (*al-ṭarīq wa al-shar'*), giving us a way of life as true legislation. God does not distinguish between any one of us, and does not favor anyone above another except according to [a judgment of] piety. All of us are created equal in the eyes of God. Right legislation, right speech, and right judgments are all from God.[35]

Sha'rawi's simplicity in explanation is demonstrated in the positive way he referred to the relationship between God and human beings: God has given humanity a right legislation, everyone is equal before God, and each person should praise God in return. He mentioned the difference between good and evil but focused on the good. Although Sha'rawi did occasionally talk about the negative consequences of not following God's method, he rarely admonished his audiences. Instead, he characterized the God–human relationship as a type of reciprocal affection, one he said benefitted humanity.

In the quote above, Sha'rawi also established that all certain knowledge comes to humanity through the messengers who bring a method, that is, the same method for distinguishing between good and evil. From there he moved to a notion of human responsibility toward God as action-based by making obedience a basic tenet. He set up the idea that, although God created the universe and left the revelation, God expects human beings to use their rational capabilities to follow what has been revealed.

But Sha'rawi's logic was based on the belief that God created the universe and placed human beings in it. Without this idea, he could not prove the existence of the creator and thus could not refer to necessary human behavior.

Why is the idea that God created the universe and placed human beings accepted without question by Sha'rawi? It is accepted because it is revealed; as such, his argument is a tautology. Belief in the existence of a creator is Sha'rawi's version of a premise, or assumption, and the revelation as coming from the creator is offered as proof, leading to the conclusion that humanity must follow the rules God set down in the revelation, a logic with no room for doubt. He also embedded in this quote an argument for the existence of God that originated in early Muslim theology: the idea that the material universe is proof of a creator. He used what could be seen or felt as proof, or signs, of the existence of an unseen creator of the universe.

Once Sha'rawi established the existence of God and the primacy of revelation, then the question became: What sort of responsibility is the praise of God and how is it related to God's method? Because human volition lies at the heart of Sha'rawi's theology of responsibility, he spoke often about freedom of choice:

> We are held accountable for the responsibility (al-taklīf), or the trust (al-amāna), human beings carry. According to God's will, he created us with the freedom to choose (ḥuriyya al-ikhtiyāriyya) . . . There are things that God wanted us to enjoy in the world from the gifts bestowed upon us. We can choose from the wonderful food and drink and clothes and other things [God provided]. But other than in these matters we do not have a choice. We are free to apply God's method (minhaj Allah), the commanded and the forbidden (if'al wa lā taf'al) [literally, "the do and don't do"]. This is the method upon which our accounting in this life will be based because this is the meaning of human responsibility (al-taklīf).[36]

Through a circular strategy, Sha'rawi presented every action in life as an opportunity to create a state of God consciousness in the participant.[37] He did not do this by setting out particular actions as special compared to others but by making the distinction between the dispositions of those who act with theological awareness and those who do not. He was keen to emphasize that following God's orders still allowed one to partake in sensory pleasures—here eating, drinking, and wearing nice clothes—and to associate those pleasures with the exercise of free will.

According to Sha'rawi, God gave humanity a method (minhaj) and freedom of choice in enacting that method.[38] This was Sha'rawi's idea of freedom within limits, or his system of human action, in which God conceives of and creates all things including acts, and after which, or within which, human beings can exercise independent volition. In this instance he was countering the rationalist position, the position of those who, according to Sha'rawi, believed that "the intelligent human being is capable of deciding (*yaṣna'u*) his own destiny and is even capable of deciding his own place in life."[39] Sha'rawi's explanation of human responsibility was also a practical account of virtue directed toward individuals. He did not just present actions as norms, or impositions of control; he presented them as human conditioning resulting from God's bounty. In order to emphasize that human responsibility in the face of expectations and possible rewards was a matter of making the right choice and of developing an awareness of God in each moment, he was purposefully vague and nonspecific.

The mundane choices that Sha'rawi highlighted also represented three pressing issues in late-twentieth-century Egypt, where alcohol and non-halal food were readily available and where women were returning to wearing the headscarf. Even though Sha'rawi presented clothing, food, and drink as choices, he always maintained that no human being has absolute freedom by demonstrating that human beings cannot control what happens; individual choice cannot override God's power:

> Whatever happens in the universe happens according to the power of God, which is the effective intention (*al-murād al-fa'āl*) of God in his universe. No one can prevent or stop or do anything about God's effective intentions in his universe and no one has any choice in it. The events that come about though God's power are beyond the realm of [human] choice just as what happens to you from people other than yourself is beyond your choosing. You have no choice in it, as when you are walking in the street and someone comes up to you and hits you, or flings a stone at you, or fires a bullet at you . . . or assaults you . . . or beats or kills you. All of that is outside your realm of choice.[40]

In this passage, Sha'rawi applied negative, tactile experiences—all of which result in pain—to the theological realm, providing emotional evidence for what cannot be proven physically. This use of affect helped Sha'rawi evoke immediate reaction in his audiences in order to aid their assimilation of theological concepts. It was not meant to be a rationally convincing argument because it is impossible to prove that what holds true in the material world also applies to the theological realm.

The above quote also seems to contradict the one in which Sha'rawi maintains that human beings have the freedom to choose, even beyond the limitations placed by God. He continued his sermon by trying to explain this problem:

Before we continue with this subject [human choice] we must define "the doing" (al-fi'l). There is "saying" (al-qawl), and there is "[human] action" (al-'amal), and there is "what is done" (al-fi'l), and each of them has a different meaning. What is said (al-qawl) is the work of the tongue, whose purpose is speaking, and all utterances (kalām) come from the tongue . . . Doing unifies what is said with [human] action. That is why God says: "You who have attained to faith! Why do you say (taqūlūn) one thing and do (taf'alūn) another? Most loathsome is it in the sight of God is that you say what you do not do" (Qur'an 61: 2–3) . . . But the human being has control over what is said and does not have control over what is done. Why? Because "doing" has conditions that are not subject to human choosing. The first of these conditions is time and [the second] is place. Everything that is done is in need of a time and is in need of a place . . . Time is controlled by God, the creator, thus we do not control time. This means that we cannot remain as children nor can we [control] our growth . . . nor does the human being have the power to restore the past . . . So whether what is done [actually] happens or comes to fruition is controlled by God. None of us has power . . . unless God wills or unless God gives us the life and the power to get it done.[41]

God provides particular conditions, and then humans can choose to unify sayings and actions, but only if the situation is conducive. While this explanation seems simple on the surface, in it Sha'rawi set up something quite complex in order to reconcile free choice with God's control. For him, there were different levels of freedom within control, a metalevel and a subordinated level. Doing is the metalevel of human movement, but God allows it and maintains it until completion. God controls the conditions, but if those conditions are set and the time, place, and environment are conducive and allow freedom of movement, the good must be followed:

> So which movements (al-ḥarakāt) do we call involuntary movements (al-ḥarakāt al-irādiyya) or mechanical movements (al-ḥarakāt al-mīkānīkiyya)? . . . The power of the energy [that makes an occurrence possible] is granted by God. No one can summon it by his own power. God placed this energy inside of you—the energy to move—then he gave you the freedom to direct it. You can direct that energy created by God towards good or evil. You can walk to the mosque, or you can walk to the bar (God forbid). That move you made is not of your own power, but the power of moving is from God and you directed that power to good or to evil . . . That is the scope of choice that God gave you. It is limited to directing the energy towards good or evil.[42]

Sha'rawi was speaking about conditions of time and place, and also saying that God animates human beings by bestowing the power to act. By providing energy, God preordains actions, creates the conditions that makes them possible, and controls them until the end. The reference here is to Ash'ari ideas of occasionalism and atomism. But these positions are never fully explained in Sha'rawi's articulations; instead, he says just enough to reaffirm them. He also does not address the contradiction inherent in the idea that God creates all actions, but human beings still acquire their acts and therefore are responsible for them, an issue that Muslim theologians—before and after Ghazali's time—have grappled with.

Sha'rawi did not engage in an in-depth discussion of theological arguments because he spoke these words to his live television audiences. Instead, he said that once God provides the energy or conditions necessary for human beings to complete any action, people then have the freedom to choose to direct that energy. This was how Sha'rawi explained to his listeners that they were responsible for their actions. But the question of how human beings can be responsible for acts that God controls goes unanswered in Sha'rawi's exposition. It is a question that speaks directly to the issue of God's justice, and Sha'rawi addressed concerns about justice when he stated that, if human beings are forced to do something, that is, if God does not create the right conditions, then human beings are not held responsible for their actions or omissions:

> But a power, which you are unable to resist, might interfere with your choice. I might be under a compulsion (*ukriha*), which prevents me from choosing God's method. We say that in this situation responsibility (*taklif*) is removed from you and you will not be held accountable [on the Day of Judgment]. This is God's justice (*'adl*). God does not hold you accountable for a thing that completely prevents (*habas*) your freedom to direct your energy towards doing good or evil. Suppose a man comes and ties me up with chains so that I cannot pray; am I or am I not accountable for not praying? Suppose a man comes and forces me to prostrate to that which is not God; am I accountable? The answer is naturally no because God has said: "As for anyone who denies God after having once attained to faith—and this, to be sure, does not apply to one who is under compulsion (*ukriha*), while his heart remains true to his faith" (Qur'an 106:16).[43]

Sha'rawi goes on to say that those who are forced to perform their responsibilities are not rewarded. Those who perform their duties for fame or wealth or acknowledgment will also not be rewarded for their actions. To receive reward, one has to perform duties out of love for, and sincere devotion to, God.[44]

This conclusion about the importance of human intentions in acting, and the clarification that the most important intentions are love and devotion distinguished Sha'rawi's perspective from other views of human responsibility. His words, although seemingly theological and a rehashing of notions of God's control, spoke to the political and social situation of his time. To those, like some groups of Islamists, who sought to enforce God's commandments and prohibitions on the population of Egypt through governance, Sha'rawi stated that acts of worship become void if they are regulated by an outside force. To those who thought that human beings have unrestricted freedom and therefore did not see the necessity of adhering to the commands and prohibitions of God, he firmly restated that God is in control. Sha'rawi sought a middle ground between the two positions:

> We must be aware of an important point. God wants to draw (our attention) to the fact that we are granted the freedom to choose in the world, but only by the power of God and his will. If he wanted he could take away what he had granted us by his will. That is why God said about Abu Lahab, the uncle of God's messenger . . . "Doomed are the hands of him of the glowing countenance: and doomed is he! What will his wealth avail him, and all that he has gained? Together with his wife, that carrier of evil tales, [who bears] around her neck a rope of twisted strands . . ." (Qur'an III: 1–5). God announced in the Qur'an—which never changes, cannot be replaced, and was revealed to his messenger for the purposes of worshiping God until the last days—that Abu Lahab will die as an infidel and that he will go to hell.[45]

Sha'rawi is here reaffirming the Ash'arite position that human beings are not given choice because God is compelled to give it, and God does not conform to human ideals of justice.[46] By decreeing in revelation (which Sha'rawi emphasized is valid throughout time) that Abu Lahab will die without becoming a believer, God sealed his fate, taking away his freedom to choose. While this may seem unfair and to go against the entire idea of freedom of choice, God's reasoning is inscrutable because human understanding is limited.

There is no explanation for this in Sha'rawi's words except that it is part of God's capability, implying that otherwise God would not be omnipotent. He also does not recognize the contradiction between asserting both that God's actions are not subject to human scrutiny and that God would not hold someone responsible for actions that they cannot control, which appears to be a human judgment about God's justice. Instead of explaining these contradictions, Sha'rawi made a point using this example of Abu Lahab, a well-known historical figure who is now uniformly recognized as a cursed and hated man and one of Muhammad's staunchest enemies. It seems natural that God should condemn such a despicable man, but questions about God's justice still remain. Sha'rawi's did not dwell on God's power to remove choice because that would have conflicted with his ultimate goal: to demonstrate how human action related to success in the afterlife and to benefits in this life:

> Indeed God gave us ordinances (*ḥudūd*) in order to grant the human being the chance of improvement. In the matters that God left to the independent reasoning (*ijtihād*) of the human being, that person is able to implement those ordinances in order to attain a life of safety and security. In the matters in which human beings have no freedom to choose their movements (*ḥurriyya al-ḥarakat al-ikhtiyāriyya*), in them you will find the universe at the peak of beauty (*al-jamāl*). In most cases corruption grows when humans choose their movements. So when God says, as part of his method, "do" and "don't do," this was necessary to systematize human independent volition (*ḥarakāt al-ḥayāt*) . . . only then are the results of [human] action (*al-'amal*) good, only then do they regularly enjoy safety and security.[47]

Ijtihād of the individual is here defined as making judgments about how to apply God's ordinance, not as making judgments about the ordinances themselves. At the heart of Sha'rawi's system of renewal was his concept of independent volition (*ḥarakāt al-ḥayāt*).[48] Human beings are at fault for ugliness in the world because, when given freedom, they make the wrong choices. Only following God's orders can restore the cosmic beauty originally intended in creation. The limitations God places on humanity are there to benefit human society. Here, Sha'rawi was responding to the critique that religious laws restrict human freedom. He flipped this critique by saying that the freedom to ignore God's ordinances is what harms individuals, society, and ultimately the universe; for him it was a false concept of freedom:

> Justice is the scale of the merciful—why? Because truly the orders and restrictions (*ḥudūd*) of God are a scale of beauty (*mizān al-jamāl*) in the universe. If the human being is able to restrict his [own] goals by perfecting life in [human] action (*al-'amal*) and behavior, then beauty spreads in the earth because the scale of justice (*mizān al-'adl*) is indeed set up. If the human being does not realize the goal of existence, ruination and great loss is the result. . . . Free human volition is a movement governed by the righteous method [of God], which results in the righteousness of the human being himself. If one of the rules of the method is deficient or unsettled, then harm will reach the whole society. The aesthetics (*jamāliyyāt*) of life is a type of harmonizing of the free will of the human being with the original cosmic beauty (*al-jamāl al-kawniyy al-aṣīl*) as it is related to the creator of the universe.[49]

Sha'rawi extended the repercussions of God's method into both the seen and unseen realms of God as creator: The original cosmic beauty exists unseen by humans and yet is directly related to the consequences of human action.

Sha'rawi's theology in relation to human action is now brought full circle. It began with the creation of the human being by God, continued to God's control of the universe, continued to the benefit of God's system for the human being in this life and the afterlife, and ended with how human action reveals the absolute cosmic beauty of God. Worldly and otherworldly benefits result from right behavior in life, which is premised on the idea that human action should be a type of worship through love. God's desire for justice is present in the beginning and the end of human endeavor. Sha'rawi maintained that embodying religion through proper action meant freedom within restrictions or because of restrictions. He redefined the term *freedom* by describing it according to complex propositions embedded in the discourse of Muslim theologians.

Sha'rawi's choice to focus on or gloss over particular theological attributes says a lot about his method of renewal. He explained the good and loving aspects of God, God's gifts to humanity, and God's power to take away human freedom at will. At the same time, he repeated many instances of human injustice, which exemplified for him what happens when humans make wrong choices. In an age of mass schooling and secular competition, Sha'rawi had to do more than tell people to come back to the faith. He had to popularize complicated foundational concepts, making them as simple and applicable as he possibly could. His action-based theology, defining human action and the motivation for action as a response toward (or rejection of) a loving creator, was the center of his program of renewal.

EXAMPLES OF RENEWAL

Sha'rawi used religious reasoning to renew theological ideas but also to rethink obligatory forms of worship. In one case, Sha'rawi extended the wellknown position that Muslims can be offered dispensation from any of the five pillars of worship if they are unable to perform them at the specified time or place. Taking this a step further, Sha'rawi said that it is only the pillar of prayer, which was given directly to Muhammad from Gabriel, that must be performed because, during prayer, all of the other pillars are represented. The performance of the *shahāda* is frequently repeated during prayer. Muslims also face

Mecca while praying, signifying a replacement of *hajj*. One abstains from plea-sure during prayer, as during the month of Ramadan, and sacrificing one's work time while praying is a type of zakat (alms).[50]

To Sha'rawi, this formulation did not break with the rules of religion set down by Muhammad. Muslims have always known that those who cannot afford to go on hajj or pay zakat do not partake in these obligations. Sha'rawi did not focus, however, on the circumstances that mitigate ritual obligation; instead, he focused on the fact that prayer is complete worship. Because his audience consisted of many poor Egyptians, he made what hindered them from full participation in the pillars of Islam the center of his concern. He used well-established rules to present something positive, the possibility of completing ritual duties despite circumstantial barriers.

As an example of deeper change—beyond merely changing focus—Sha'rawi formulated an opinion concerning whether Muslims should repeat hajj. He said that Muslims who want to perform hajj a second (or third or fourth) time should not do so if there are starving people in their communi-ties. Instead, they must give the money they would spend on hajj in charity to the poor. Even if they have already given zakat and fulfilled their duties according to the law, feeding the hungry is a priority over repeating hajj. Sha'rawi justified his opinion by saying that, in the past, repeating hajj was necessary because of the hadith that states that God loves to "see a crowd as it makes him proud before his angels."[51] But today, because so many Muslims repeat hajj every year—Sha'rawi offered evidence that 70 percent of people who go on hajj have done so before—there is no need to fear that there will not be enough people performing the ritual.[52]

In this example, Sha'rawi brought circumstances together with his refor-mulation of duty to warrant change. At the center of his justification was the hadith that, in the past, had encouraged repeated performances of hajj but was no longer applicable. Air travel has made the performance of hajj rela-tively easy; during Sha'rawi's lifetime, more than a million people went on hajj each year. Sha'rawi was also reacting to economic disparity in Egypt, encour-aging those who could afford it to help those in need. He used community concern to justify change based on the situation, not to contradict past uses of the hadith.

With some of his scriptural interpretations, Sha'rawi's adjustments were even more pronounced, although he always maintained that renewal was built on tradition. Like the examples given above concerning ritual and theological renewal, Sha'rawi's discoveries came about when he applied his interpretive skills to both texts and contingencies. This combination led him to discover previously overlooked connections and interpretations in the Qur'an and hadith. In one example, he used his rereading of the hadith to encourage good relations between Muslims and non-Muslims in Egypt. Sha'rawi used the concept of neighborly love to push past previously accepted limitations and to modify past understandings:

> Truly God (al-ḥaqq), praised and exalted be he, wants to give the people a scale[53] and that scale is summarized in:
>
> - "All Muslim against Muslim [violence] is forbidden";
> - "The Muslim is the brother of the Muslim";
> - "Not one of you [will] believe completely until he loves for his brother what he loves for himself."
>
> The Prophet, peace and blessings upon him, wants to disseminate (yanshara) equality (al-musāwā) when he affirms this instruction concerning free passage [between human beings] (al-'istiṭrāq al-waṣā'i) through his hadith. Surely the Prophet is about to connect all of the inhabitants of the world in one hadith when he says, "Gabriel continued recommending that I be with my neighbor until I thought my neighbor would become an inheritor" (Noble hadith). When we contemplate this hadith, we see the whole world almost (kāda) becoming a united human family. When one neighbor cares for the other, and when a neighbor is concerned with trying not to infringe on the rights of another neighbor, we find that the human circle is welded together. We find the whole universe connected in love and order and responsibility and equality, connecting every single believer with the other,[54] connecting whoever loves for his neighbor what he loves for himself. In this free passage between human beings (al-'istiṭrāq) is the benefit of achieving happiness throughout the universe. The happiness of the universe continues when you work for the happiness of others and others work for your happiness.[55]

In this sermon, Sha'rawi stretched the meaning of the first three texts with his interpretation of the fourth. In this last hadith, Sha'rawi insinuated that love of one's neighbor was a religious necessity, although he stopped short of connecting it directly to religious duty. Yet he moved seamlessly from the equality of all believers (brothers) to the equality of all humanity with the concept of the free passage between human beings, connecting the hadith about love of other Muslims to the hadith about love of neighbors. The religious significance of the shift came with his replacement of the word brother in the first hadith he quotes with the word neighbor in the last part of the passage

and then in how he equated the neighbor with the whole human family.[56]
Sha'rawi told believing Muslims that they have the responsibility to weld the
human circle together by extending their love beyond their faith community.
His statement:

> When one neighbor cares for the other . . . we find the whole universe connected
> in love and order and responsibility and equality . . . In this free passage [between
> human beings] (al-'istiṭrāq) is the benefit of achieving happiness throughout the
> universe.

can be read in light of the quote (see above):

> In the matters in which human beings have no freedom to choose their move-
> ments . . . you will find the universe at the peak of beauty (al-jamāl) . . . when
> God says, as part of his method, "do" and "don't do," this was necessary to sys-
> tematize human independent volition . . . only then are the results of [human]
> action good, only then do they regularly enjoy safety and security.[57]

Although Sha'rawi did not directly claim in the first quote that love of neighbor is part of God's commandments and prohibitions, or part of Muslim
shari'a, he would never have claimed that the entire universe would benefit
from neighbor love unless God's method was in control. Thus by discussing
the positive repercussions for society and the universe, he affirmed that love
of neighbor is part of God's method.

As with the hajj recommendation, he took a tenet of faith and used it to
place religious borders around a situation that had already broken free of religious structures. In this case, he focused on improving relations between
individual Egyptians regardless of religious affiliation, but stopped short of
using his new reading of the hadith to make neighbor love a religious obligation and therefore to make it applicable to the Muslim community at large.
Sha'rawi also used the qualifier kāda (almost) when extending the love of
neighbor to include (almost) the whole world. He was not limiting the caring
incumbent on individuals in his audience, but like his notion of cosmic beauty,
he spoke of love in the universe as an ideal, not a reality. Because even for Muhammad humanity was *almost* united together, for Sha'rawi kāda referred to
a postponed possibility, one first conceived of by Muhammad but still not
available. This interpretation of Sha'rawi's version of neighbor love as postponed points to his unwillingness to state that something new was legally
obligated in the present. Instead, he circumvented the issue and reframed
neighbor love as an ethical responsibility toward God.

CONCLUSION

In many of the passages cited in this chapter, Sha'rawi focused on obligation as a relationship, not as rules. He was not a legal scholar, so he did not present notions of obligation according to the typical legal/moral categories. Instead, he implied that it was a moral, individual obligation to become someone who acts to please God. This was apparent in his insistence that following God's commands and prohibitions went beyond personal reward—it applied to the entire universe. According to Sha'rawi, every act affected the entire universe. But Sha'rawi was also responding to the situation in Egypt, making judgments about common practices, or—in the case of treating neighbors well—responding to increasing sectarian tensions. His readings of the Qur'an in light of both tradition and context reflected the limitations of his legal knowledge. But his limitations were also an asset. Sha'rawi took advantage of the fact that notions of religious authority had shifted in his society. Legal scholars and their specialized knowledge had already been undermined throughout Egyptian society. His adaptability also aided his ability to reach people with his message of renewal and added to and reinforced his authority— but in ways he did not always expect.

For Sha'rawi, renewal meant reinterpreting the scripture to reveal the truth about present contingencies. But it also meant presenting past theological debates to his audiences and restating those debates in a way that made them relevant to the public. Two methods that helped him make Ash'ari theology seem applicable to the people he preached to were his use of circular arguments, and his use of emotion, sensation and everyday experience to demonstrate what could not be proven. As a preacher seeking to instruct individuals, Sha'rawi can be compared to Muhammad 'Abduh. 'Abduh called for all individuals to use their rational capacities to find answers in the Qur'an, an idea that opened the field of religious authority to any educated person. Sha'rawi reacted against this effect by making himself a significant example of 'ulama' interpretive authority, and he reinforced it by making public approval the crux of his authority. He also incorporated a focus on individuals that fit with his Sufi orientation, teaching about the love of God as a primary element of worship. He did not want Egyptians to be more rational or more dependent on legal prescriptions, but—through being conscious of God in every action—to align every choice to God's purpose. This was ultimately a circular proposition, presenting consciousness of God as both the intention and the outcome. While circularity reinforces the dominance of the position being supported, it limits the influence of that position among those who doubt its veracity.

But Muhammad ʿAbduh's notion of rationality wasn't the only view of religious regeneration that differed from Shaʿrawi's. When he talked about the boundaries God placed on human freedom, Shaʿrawi was responding to the fact that renewal, like *ijtihād,* was no longer limited to the purview of the religious scholars. With his television presentations of Ashʿari theological positions, he hoped to counter both the rationalist position and the Islamist position without naming either. Both positions used human concerns and thoughts as the starting point for programs of revival, and thus they gave precedence to temporal concerns before eternal ones. Both positions also threatened to undermine what Shaʿrawi saw as the unique quality and theological veracity of ʿulamaʾ knowledge. But Shaʿrawi's program of renewal was no less ideological; he merely reversed the order of concern and rejected the primacy of human knowledge in light of his notions concerning theological intention sometimes even positing his ideas as theological intention.

CHAPTER 5

Sha'rawi's Knowledge Hierarchy

INTRODUCTION

Although the environment in late-twentieth-century Egypt was one of increased authoritative contestations, Shaykh Muhammad Mitwalli Sha'rawi
was distinctive. Besides introducing media sermons to the 'ulama' repertoire
through state-run television, he used his linguistic expertise to assert his
interpretive dominance. As part of this assertion, Sha'rawi often spoke in
epistemological terms; for him, knowledge was a unifying concept, one that
connected God to humanity through understanding. Understanding, he
insisted, must be derived from the Qur'an and hadith, which were the only
credible sources of knowledge. Speaking to his audiences about the true
sources of knowledge was central to Sha'rawi's presentation of himself as
uniquely capable of deriving correct understanding. He not only stated that
true knowledge was deposited in the Qur'an, he also presented his hermeneutic
orientation as the only means of gaining true understanding, or of bridging
the gap between God and humanity. Sha'rawi insisted that God had absolute
control over the universe. He presented God's control as a living system
known only through proper exegesis by explaining it in knowledge terms and
by maintaining that the properly trained intermediary was absolutely necessary to understanding.

Sha'rawi used concepts of knowledge very practically. By molding his
discourse to the capabilities of his audience, his sermons navigated between divinely revealed texts and his assumptions about adherents and

their expectations. For example, Sha'rawi used the metaphor of a washing machine to describe his idea that, in the revelation, God generously gave humanity guidance for life:

> If we truly want to solve the problems of the world with a solution that does not need to be changed or altered we will find such a solution in the method of God (*minhaj Allah*), praised and most high. He is the one who created the disease and its cure (*khalq al-da'wā wa khalq al-dawa'*). He is [also] the one who created humanity, so he knows [best] what benefits them and what harms them. He is the most majestic. He created all of existence, so he knows [best] what benefits it and what harms it. In our worldly responsibilities we seek the manufacturer of a machine to fix it when there is something wrong with it, because he is the one that made it; he knows the secrets of its manufacture. If the one who manufactured it was unable to tend to the machine himself . . . , then he would have technicians trained in how to fix it, and he would produce millions of catalogues to guide people as to how to fix it. But if someone comes to us who has not been trained to fix the machine according to the directions of the manufacturer, has not even read the instructions for repair, he will damage and not repair [the machine]. You would not call a carpenter to fix your television; he would only cause further damage and you would be blamed for not seeking the help of the manufacturer nor of the [specially] trained technician.[1]

In this metaphor God is the manufacturer or creator, the washing machine is creation, the trained technicians are those who have direct access to God or who have specialized training in the religious sciences, and the catalogue is the Qur'an. By comparing a common product and its manufacture to the entire universe and its creator, Sha'rawi suggested that God sent the Qur'an to humanity as a guide to fixing any and all worldly problems that may arise. But trained technicians were needed to derive the knowledge of how to fix the machine from the manual provided. It was Sha'rawi's way of saying that only those whose training was derived from the Qur'an and hadith, a claim made by the religious scholars about their methods, actually follow God's instructions and understand God's cure. Note also in the metaphor that Sha'rawi insists that individuals can attempt to access God directly and that specialists can be trained through direct access to God, implying that esoteric knowledge or direct inspiration from God can be as effective as Qur'anic knowledge. It is also important that Sha'rawi mentioned the manufacturer, the specialist, and the production and distribution of the catalogue in that particular order, giving the specialist an intermediary position.

But the metaphor also makes clear that the owners of the machine (the "we" mentioned) have the responsibility to find and choose proper technicians.

Sha'rawi was telling his audiences that it was part of their duty to recognize and authorize those capable of applying God's cure to solve the problems of humanity. It was an interesting strategy. Sha'rawi presented the recognition of the technician as essential to the correct application of knowledge, thus giving his audiences the sense that they were able to bestow authority. Yet he was simultaneously telling them which specialists to choose and of the consequences of making the wrong decision. This was Sha'rawi's particular talent; he blended the old and the new to present his reaffirmations of theological postulations as personal choice. He did not make compliance merely a physical task. Instead he made duty first and foremost about recognizing God's system of knowledge; second, about distinguishing between correctly and incorrectly derived knowledge; and last, about employing that knowledge in action. Sha'rawi's insistence on the second aspect was partly due to the times in which he lived. He sought to train the public to recognize that the knowledge derived by the Sunni scholars of his orientation was the true representation of God's message. For this task he redirected his focus on the reciprocal responsibility between creator and creation to a reciprocal relationship between mediator and the people, between those who spread correctly derived knowledge and those who accept it. But as with the metaphor of the washing machine, he did so indirectly, by using his rhetorical skills.

Reorienting the public toward accepting the supremacy of the scholars was needed because the lines between religious and secular specialties had become blurred in Egypt. Throughout the twentieth century, the government had been molding schools with an eye to teaching a particular brand of Islam in secular schools[2] and to teaching secular subjects in religious institutions. Thus religious knowledge was released from its previously embedded forms of authenticity, and secular learning was raised to a level once reserved only for religious specialists. It was the transfer of knowledge rights out of the hands of the 'ulama' that bothered Sha'rawi, but he also recognized that the popularization of religious authority could be used to his advantage. He therefore sought to win back his epistemological predominance by taking his arguments directly to the people.

But Sha'rawi did not struggle for control by getting into direct disagreements with other specialists. He understood that people had choice, not just between competitors but also between different orientations toward knowledge. In an attempt to limit who had the right to claim intermediary stature between the Qur'an and the people, he distinguished between those who genuinely represented the Qur'an and those who only spoke as if they did. The first group used particular methods to gain understanding or, as Sha'rawi said, subjected their own thoughts to God's thoughts; the second group merely invoked passages from the Qur'an and hadith to back up their claims. To make this distinction even clearer, Sha'rawi set up a hierarchy based on traditional epistemology. He said that God's knowledge was the source of all other forms of knowledge and that the religious sciences were needed to decipher that knowledge. The secular sciences were at the bottom of Sha'rawi's hierarchy. Because they were derived from human thought, they had to be checked against Qur'anic interpretation to be proven true or false. In his sermons and interviews, Sha'rawi sought to demonstrate that information derived from human thought was still completely dependent on the theological and yet was devoid of the resources needed to understand that dependence. It was God, not human beings, that ordered knowledge, and Sha'rawi's knowledge hierarchy reflected this view. But it also meant that he understood his task to include realigning society with God's order, or exhibiting how exegetes trained at al-Azhar were the gatekeepers of truth and thus the only ones who could claim to represent God's authority in society. Sha'rawi's recalling of the past was a powerful symbol, one he used as a response to the recent redistribution of religious authority in his society. It was a symbol that relied on the once assumed primacy of the 'ulama' and at the same time sought to reinforce it.

In the metaphor about the washing machine, Sha'rawi also represented the people who were trying to fix the machine even though they were not trained to do so as a danger to the divine system. In his usual manner he did not directly identify them; it was important to his overall project that he act as a representative of the divine word and not appear to be struggling for worldly power. Through his exegetical, linguistic and personal ingenuity, he instead combated systems of thought he believed were a threat to his position. He sought primarily to counter the claims of the Islamists, in their mild and extreme forms, who used religious ideas to offer political solutions. But he also sought to counter those who accepted scientific findings to explain the universe. Sha'rawi saw these two groups as similar because they both offered solutions derived from the human mind, not from the revelation, even if they used the Qur'an to justify their opinions. He gained prominence by countering these groups through language. He defended a particular Azhari perspective among the people. This defense, along with his vocation as a government media preacher and his charismatic orations, were what propelled him to the forefront of Egyptian society. He cultivated a perception of himself as someone who behaved in a godly manner, and as a technician who was trained to interpret God's manual correctly for the purpose of solving the problems of the people.

SHA'RAWI'S VIEW OF THE LIMITATIONS OF ISLAMISM

In his sermons, Sha'rawi used his epistemological hierarchy repeatedly to counter the truth claims of Islamist groups, from milder groups like the Muslim Brotherhood to the more extreme groups like Egyptian Islamic Jihad (known in Arabic as *al-Jihād*). Through this hierarchy he argued that truth originates with God, is interpreted by professionals, and can then be applied to worldly matters. Because it was a hierarchy, Sha'rawi was adamant that the order should never be reversed: Worldly concerns derived from the human mind should never be used as a device for interpreting the Qur'an to derive God's truth. Practically speaking, Sha'rawi's idea that religious thought and political or human thought should be kept separate helped him defend his vocation and training; remain loyal to his early commitment to a particular brand of nationalism; and combat what he perceived as dangerous, politically motivated portrayals of Islam.

Sha'rawi's defense of the 'ulama' task of spreading knowledge (*'ilm*) was also a response to prevalent attacks made by Islamists and others against the religious scholars concerning the way they had guarded and presented sacred knowledge over the centuries. Many Islamist reformers claimed that the 'ulama' had lost sight of God's method as it was lived by Muhammad and his followers and instead had favored their own opinions and non-Islamic (foreign) innovations. Some saw the 'ulama' in their current state as no longer able to guide the community either because they had led the community astray over the centuries or because they had been weakened by current regimes. Sha'rawi defended the scholars by saying that anyone who had expertise in any realm associated with the nontheological, what he called *basharīyy* (that associated with the secular aspects of human knowledge), including political training, should not disclose information about God's system. And by the same logic he argued that those who had religious expertise should not get involved in politics. He believed that the two realms should be kept separate, seeing different roles for experts in different fields. As he said in one of his answers to the questions of Mahmoud Fawzi:

Q: Do you approve of the work of the 'ulama' in politics as it is occurring now?

A: I do not approve of this. Because politics is not of religion (*dīn*) . . . I [also] do not accept that the words of political parties can be religious. Politics is the struggle of human thought against other human thought. But religion subjects human thought to heavenly thought. The difference by the very nature of the case is large. Explanation and clarification are therefore not needed . . . I do not say I rule (*ḥākim*) by Islam, but I say I want to be ruled by Islam.[3]

What Sha'rawi wanted was not for the religious scholars to have direct political control but for them to be considered as the purveyors of God's truth, and as such to advise heads of state, as he himself did. To this end he distinguished types of knowledge by their sources. If the source was heavenly, by which he meant revelatory or disclosed, then the knowledge derived from it was religious. Political actors, on the other hand, derived their ideas through flawed human methods. Sha'rawi was also concerned with distinguishing types of knowledge applications. For example, if someone's thoughts and words were primarily political, then that person should not subjugate religion (rule by Islam) to these purposes; for Sha'rawi doing so was the definition of corruption. Nothing better illustrated Sha'rawi's discomfort with mixing the religious and the political than his critique of the Muslim Brothers:

> The thought of the Muslim Brothers (*al-Ikhwan al-Muslimun*) failed . . . when what entered their minds were stories of governance. [That is when] they began to collapse . . . The people [of Egypt] will tell you: It is better to be without the *ḥudūd* laws then to have the Muslim Brothers ruling us [with them] . . . If you ask me what is my opinion of the Muslim Brothers I will say: The Ikhwan was once a tree, noble in struggle and glorious in shade. May God bless the martyr who planted it, and may God forgive whoever hurried its fruits.[4]

For Sha'rawi, the problem with the Muslim Brothers came when they began to use scripturally derived religious ordinances in the service of political goals, something he saw as worse than having no religious ordinances at work in society. As he said, they lost credibility when they began to use their noble and glorious, that is, religious, beginnings for the purposes of governance. He further stated that the Muslim Brothers were not fit to enforce the *ḥudūd* laws (laws concerning capital punishment in the Qur'an) because those laws were Qur'anic and therefore heavenly. As with the idea that one should not hire a carpenter to fix a washing machine, Sha'rawi reiterated that relying on a group like the Muslim Brotherhood to institute an Islamic society was dangerous and could lead to injustice. He feared they would use any political power they gained to force compliance with the shari'a. For Sha'rawi the Muslim Brothers did not understand how to properly apply God's rulings, which would have meant subjecting their thoughts to a divine source. Heavenly thought, according to Sha'rawi and represented by his interpretations, should be transmitted to people as the utmost level of knowledge, and those seeking political power or solutions could never yield this type of knowledge.

For this reason, Sha'rawi did not call for the shari'a, especially not the stricter *ḥudūd* laws, to be instituted in Egypt. He insisted that punishments such as cutting off the hand of a thief could be applied only in a society where all people have enough to feed themselves, that is, where God's justice has been established. In his opinion on the matter, he referred back to a saying of Imam 'Ali abu Talib (the cousin and son-in-law of Muhammad) that stealing means taking something that is not yours only if you have enough to provide for yourself and your family.[5] Sha'rawi said that the law about cutting off a hand as a punishment for theft was meant as a deterrence and should not be applied by those who do not understand its divine purpose, which was to restrict its enforcement.[6] In a society where the sources of charity have been co-opted by the government and citizens walk about hungry, *ḥudūd* laws should not be applied.[7] Sha'rawi used this reasoning to assert that those who rule the nation-state must not enforce the shari'a; it was up to individuals to apply the shari'a in their own lives.

Sha'rawi also thought that groups like the Muslim Brotherhood did not understand the basic principles of when and how the shari'a should be applied. Instead they focused on whatever outcome they could implement according to their desires, which for him was a sign of immaturity. Sha'rawi identified what he thought was the primary threat to the state of religious authority in Egypt and then, to counter that threat, legitimated the government's handling of religion over and against groups like the Muslim Brotherhood. The Islamists sought to gain authority in one of the few areas left to Sha'rawi: that of going straight to the people with a message of religious renewal. In return the Islamist groups in Egypt offered a critique of Sha'rawi's program by saying that it called attention away from social and political problems and the culpability of the government and thus that it allowed injustice to persist.[8]

Sha'rawi did not say that Islam was a private matter, only that it began with the relationship between the individual and God, which then resulted in the knowledge of how to live at every moment:

> Worshipping God means that religion is [always] present, but the relationship between the human being and the lord should be without influence on the country . . . Who said that religion is a relationship between the human being and the lord only? Truly it is a relationship between a human being with the lord so that the lord can clarify for him his relationship with the existence in which he lives.[9]

Sha'rawi was not stating that religion should remain between creator and creature but that it should not directly influence government policy. For Sha'rawi, religion was based on the notion of individual freedom; it was not reduced to belief but to the freedom to implement God's system in life in every interaction. He argued that God's system should be applied in every matter, even in the choices people made about political leadership. Thus his discomfort seems to have been limited to applying God's system to or for political influence. In this he was reacting to the strong influence of Islamism in Egypt in the late twentieth century, but he was also molding his rhetoric to fit his mutually beneficial relationship with the government and his nationalist beliefs. Consistency was not the issue; realigning society was.

Sha'rawi's attitude that enforcing religious laws subsumed God's will to human desire ran exactly counter to the attitude of the Muslim Brotherhood more generally. The goal of the Islamists in Sha'rawi's time was to live in a society ruled according to Islamic law that was enforced by political leaders.[10] In the early 1980s, the Muslim Brothers began running candidates in parliamentary elections. In 1987, their campaign slogan was "Give Your Vote to Allah, Give It to the Muslim Brotherhood."[11] Coming under attack for entangling themselves in a system that went against the shari'a, the Muslim Brotherhood engaged in a vigorous defense of their entrance into electoral politics. Umar al-Tilmisani, leader of the Muslim Brotherhood from 1972 to 1986, went as far as to say:

> When the Brotherhood talks of politics they don't speak as political men but as Islamic du'a [those who call to God, or engage in da'wa] . . . some think that when we speak on political matters that this has nothing to do with religion and that this is the talk of parties, but . . . we do not work for ourselves, we work for God.[12]

This defense was meant to affirm the Brotherhood's commitment to the ideology of ruling by the shari'a, which was exactly what Sha'rawi criticized them for. For him, the further entwined they became in the political system, the more threatening they became, both to his political views and to his assertions that religious authority rested with religious experts.

As the Muslim Brotherhood became more pragmatic, Islamists who were against their gradualist approach critiqued them for a different reason. These groups broke away from the Muslim Brotherhood; formed their own parties in the 1970s; and advocated the use of violence, which they called jihad, to bring about political change.[13] In many ways these groups resembled the Muslim Brotherhood on moral and social issues; for example, they all believed that the only good political system was one in which the ruler was pious and implemented the shari'a. But unlike the Muslim Brotherhood, they proclaimed that participation in the violent overthrow of the government was a duty for every Muslim.[14] They were inspired by the writings of Sayyid Qutb (1906–1966), a leading member of the Muslim Brotherhood and critic of the Egyptian government who was executed by the state in 1966. Qutb was well known for his position that tyrannical governments must be held accountable in this life by being overthrown through violent means because they will not give up power willingly.[15]

The most notorious group advocating violent jihad during Sha'rawi's time was the nebulous group known as al-Jihad (known in English as the Islamic Jihad), and specifically the division of the group that followed the teachings of Muhammad 'Abd al-Salam Farag. It was this group that was responsible for the assassination of President Sadat. Farag, born in 1954 and executed by the Egyptian government in 1982, was an engineer by training. He wrote the now infamous pamphlet "The Neglected Duty" (*Al-Farida al-Ghayba*), which inspired the men who were responsible for the assassination of Sadat in 1981. In "The Neglected Duty," Farag said that those who do not rule by Islamic principles are unbelievers (*kāfirūn*).[16] Because Muslims in Egypt do not live under a state that is governed by Islamic rules, they live in the realm of unbelief.[17] He directly attacked the Egyptian 'ulama' for not declaring jihad against rulers who did not institute the shari'a. Farag claimed that it was not the duty of the 'ulama' to spread knowledge (*'ilm*) but to lead the community in jihad. The true religious leaders of the community were responsible for leading the battle to install rightly guided leaders, not for educating the public (i.e., preaching) about knowledge.[18] Farag went a step further and said that, because the 'ulama' had failed in this duty, they themselves were not truly Muslim and that he was therefore sanctioned to replace them and to lead the jihad.[19] What made him qualified to do so? He seems to have felt qualified by his engineering degree and his ability to quote Ibn Taymiyya (1263–1328 C.E.) and other scholars extensively to support his views.[20]

Because of his infatuation with Ibn Taymiyya, who lived during Mongol rule, Farag did not compare the situation faced by Muslims in Egypt to what the early Muslim conquerors faced, as Qutb did. Instead he compared the Egyptian regime to the Mongols (al-Tatār), which allowed him to claim that, because the leaders of Egypt did not rule according to Islamic law, they were unbelievers by choice and therefore apostates.[21] It was well known, according to Farag, that apostates must suffer the punishment of death according to Islamic law. As for those who joined the Egyptian government, scholars, Sufis, or any other Muslims, they were worse than those who joined the Mongols (those whom Ibn Taymiyya said were the evilest of humanity), and they were also to be treated as unbelievers according to Farag.[22] Farag likewise extended the definition of apostasy to include those who publicly professed that they were Muslims but did not perform the five pillars or who refused to impose the *jizya* (tax) on Christians and Jews, or even those who refused to fight and kill other apostates.[23] In other words, he regarded anyone who did not follow any and every act he defined as an obligation, whether understood as an individual or communal obligation, as a willing apostate who therefore must be killed.

Sha'rawi responded to this new definition of apostasy directly in interviews and indirectly in his sermons, according to his usual habit. When he was asked in an interview if Sadat's assassins had a religious purpose, he answered:

Who said it was religious? Who was it that said it was religious?

The al-Jihad group? The jihadi groups [say so] because they are governed by their own judgments. Their ideas remain null and void with me because I do not want [change] to come for the sake of [changing the government] alone. I say to them [a new form of] governance will come with peace, with peace *ya ḥabībī*. The preference is [of course] for Islamic principles, but that is only permissible with allegiance to Islamic ideals. It is forbidden to force [the president] out. Because throwing him out will cause great chaos (*fitna*). I do not agree with these groups. What I have said is that they must wake up . . . If they were truly connected to the truth, they would not need to establish nine or ten organizations—where is the truth in that? The truth varies between them, how can we be with those who continue differing in their religion and are fractured [in their message]?[24]

Sha'rawi was referring to the fact that, even though the Egyptian groups advocating for violent jihad agreed that immediate action should be taken against the Egyptian government, they were splintered into different organizations during his time. Sha'rawi presented their knowledge of Islam as limited, which was evident because they lacked understanding of the full spectrum of Islamic ideas. Because these groups had no clear methodology for deriving their list of duties, Sha'rawi characterized their disagreements as a clear indication that they were subject to their own thoughts and desires. For Sha'rawi, God's system was unified; human systems were divisive.

But Sha'rawi clearly disliked Sadat's assassins for more than theological reasons. (For more on Sha'rawi's relationship with Sadat, see chapters 1 and 2.) Sha'rawi was concerned most of all with the attacks men like Farag made against the 'ulama'. In one sermon Sha'rawi indirectly responded to Farag's direct attack on the 'ulama' of al-Azhar and on those like himself who relied on preaching and the government. In the broadcast Sha'rawi appears very agitated, something uncharacteristic of his usual style. He said:

> Egypt is a protected land. The Prophet said that [Egypt's] people will be unified until the Day of Judgment. Who said Egypt is a nation (umma) of unbelievers (kuffār)? [If this is true] then who are the Muslims? Who are the believers? It is Egypt that has exported (ṣadr) the knowledge of Islam ('ilm al-Islam), even to the countries to which Islam was sent [loud agreement from audience]. Egypt has exported Islamic knowledge to every place in the world. What [do] we say about that [knowledge]? [We say] that the formulation (taḥfīn) of [Islamic] knowledge occurred at Egypt's noble al-Azhar. As for the defense of Islam, look at history. Who was it that fended off the savage Mongols (al-Tatār)? It was Egypt. Who fended off the Crusaders and their attacks against Islam and Muslims? It was Egypt. Egypt will always remain. In spite of the vengeful, or the envious, or the exploiters and exploited, [in spite of any] opponents of Islam, inside and outside of Egypt.[25]

This response directly counters the idea that Egyptians should be considered unbelievers because they are Egyptian or because they live under and accept the laws of the state. Sha'rawi defended Islam by defending the nation of Egypt, al-Azhar, and the people of Egypt. He called for national pride by saying that it was not war and arms that defeated and ultimately brought the Mongols to Islam but the learning and knowledge of the 'ulama' of al-Azhar. Because the 'ulama' focused on 'ilm and not on armed struggle, the Mongols were defeated. Sha'rawi also defended himself against the attack that the 'ulama' were concerned only about preaching Islam, which is not the true jihad.

For Sha'rawi, being Egyptian and an Azhari was the very definition of being Muslim. As he said elsewhere, the Egyptian government did not force
people not to adhere to the shari'a, so it was each individual's responsibility
to implement it in their lives. He therefore saw no reason for a violent overthrow of the Egyptian government.[26] He also affirmed the lasting power of
al-Azhar against the vengeful, envious, and exploited, what he called the true
enemies of Islam. These people remain unnamed in the sermon, but it is clear
from how he characterized them in the beginning of the passage (those who
call Egyptians unbelievers, and his references to the Mongols and the Cru-
saders) that he used these adjectives to characterize violent groups like
al-Jihad. In this sermon he presented his case about why those trained at
al-Azhar were the true defenders of Islam; it was their knowledge and
understanding but also their loyalty to Egypt as purveyors of the truth, not
as political actors. Sha'rawi derived all of these points as a discursive defense
against particular attacks; as part of this defense, he did not acknowledge that
the Azhari scholars in his time were politically entrenched.

Sha'rawi also fought the ideas of the groups calling for violent jihad more
generally by reverting to a more acceptable and established notion of the concept of jihad and violence. Sha'rawi's interpretation of Qur'anic verses 2:189
and 2:193–194[27] is indicative of his attitude:

> God instructed the *ummah* (community) of the Prophet Muhammad to be bal-
> anced and to protect the dignity of human beings. Human beings have the freedom
> to choose their religion; believing in God is not compulsory. Struggle for the sake
> of God (*jihad*) is ordered to protect this freedom [of choice], not to impose reli-
> gion. Struggle was enjoined to put an end to the tyranny of those who stop people
> from freely choosing their religion. . . . Some may think that Islam enjoined fight-
> ing on the basis of self-defense. In fact it defends the human being by struggling
> against what could have a negative effect on the freedom to choose religion. It is a
> defense of those who choose to believe, it protects against those who would harm
> the believers, but also against those who would force non-believers to become
> Muslims. We reject those who seek to impose religion on people and instead [we]
> engage in *da'wa*, calling others to faith. We will struggle against those who try to
> block us from this *da'wa* because they do not allow people to freely choose their
> faith. We do not force people to accept Islam; we struggle so that people will be
> free to choose. This is also a defense.[28]

Sha'rawi was making the argument that religion should be freely chosen, but
he is also re-appropriating the word jihad (for him, a struggle in the way of
God), removing it completely from its violent connotations and making it a

struggle against those who would force belief on people. It is a double enforcement of his position; first, as a more quietist interpretation of the word and
its association with knowledge, and second as an indirect attack on violent
ideals.

Sha'rawi took the idea of fighting or struggling (jihad) and turned it into
a battle not requiring physical force but of convincing through oration:

> Islam does not carry the sword in order to force people to believe in it . . . why
> would the raising of the sword be permitted? Surely [those who are] the best ex-
> ample and the best model and [who follow] the clearest way (uslūb) to God . . . they
> are the soldiers of Islam. Concerning this God has said: "Say: The truth is from
> your Lord: Let him who will believe, believe, and let him who will reject, reject.
> For the wrongdoers we have prepared a fire whose smoke and flame, like the walls
> and roof of a tent, will hem them in" (Qur'an 18: 29). . . . In this way God confirms
> his method. The truth is God's method, which leads to happiness in this life and
> the next. Falsehood leads to the fire, which will surround the one who disbelieves
> in God (al-kāfir bi al-haqq) from all directions.[29]

For Sha'rawi those involved in da'wa through speech and action were the
soldiers of Islam, defending God's method. He reversed the Islamist concerns about combining political action with da'wa, especially the groups
advocating violence, those who spoke of da'wa as if it meant a physical
struggle. Sha'rawi reclaimed the definition of jihad by using the language
of war to affirm nonviolent religious speech and exemplary pious behavior.
But he also stated that the unbeliever is judged and punished by God in the
next life, not by other human beings in this life. Truth leads to happiness in
this life and the next; falsehood leads to punishment in the next life. Sha'rawi
was not arguing that those who freely chose not to believe would not suffer for
their choices. That would have been a human judgment and against his main
point, which was that it was up to God to judge such people.

In another attempt to define the nature of pious acts, Sha'rawi taught that
religious actions performed by force do not count as acts performed for God
(see chapter 4). Sha'rawi concluded the statement above by saying that religious deeds begin in the heart and therefore rely on proper intention:

> God wants us to go to him obediently . . . even if those that call us [to faith] are
> from the weakest classes because this means that love is what pushes us to faith.
> We know how much trouble the Prophet Muhammad (peace and blessing upon
> him) had in the beginning of his religious life. He did not [even] have the ability
> to protect his companions. Maybe this is an allegory that God wants those who
> only have the power to love to [understand].[30]

Sha'rawi was here speaking to the majority of his audiences, those who were powerless in society. By emphasizing the power of love and worldly powerlessness, he was raising the "weakest classes" to a higher status, comparing their situation to that of Muhammad. He was offering a different reaction than the Islamists to the injustices he saw in society. But these types of interpretations left Sha'rawi open to the criticism that he attempted to quiet the masses and thus allowed injustices in his society to continue.

Sha'rawi clearly understood and defined Islam very differently than people like Farag did, and he made his definitions appealing to the people. Challengers forced him to defend his position, and it was that very challenge that he lamented. He was seeking to affirm what once, not so long before his time, had not needed defending. But he was not just defending his right to teach religion or even longing for the past; he was trying to bring back the ubiquitous symbol of the once dominant religious experts. He was living in a time of flux, when people were choosing between religious ideologies, and his discourse demonstrates how the ideology of al-Azhar and its mainstream scholars, even among so many hostile competitors, was still viable.

RELIGIOUS KNOWLEDGE AND SCIENTIFIC PROOFS

For Sha'rawi, once the threat of communism had passed, the two greatest threats to faith in Egypt were the Islamists who transformed the meaning of religious duty and scientific postulations that countered Qur'anic claims. Unlike Islamist truth claims, scientific claims were not a direct threat to Sha'rawi's authority; therefore, he did not dislike science or see it as a threat generally. Instead he sought to subjugate scientific thinking to his Qur'anic understanding. Yet he was less thorough in his attempts to affirm the Qur'an against science than he was in countering the Islamists and extremists in his society. Because Sha'rawi recognized the difference between the rational and religious (exegetical) sciences, he taught that what comes from the human mind is always secondary to what can be derived from the revealed texts and thus that science was not true unless his interpretations of the Qur'an proved it to be so. But his insistence on this knowledge hierarchy meant that he did not always take scientific claims seriously according to their own means of proof. As a result his argument that all scientific discoveries originated with God and not in the human mind were very inconsistent, sometimes even on theological grounds.

While Sha'rawi recognized the limitations of human thought when it was not grounded in the Qur'an, he did not always recognize the limitations of his own thought as human interpretation. Instead he presented his interpretations as subjugated to the divine. He did not say that his interpretations were the only possible true interpretations; his assertions were more subtle. He instead presented them as equivalent to God's meaning when other theories directly questioned what he considered the very basis of faith: belief in the inerrancy of the Qur'an. At these moments of defense, Sha'rawi did not present his interpretations as one among many possibilities; if they affirmed the veracity of the Qur'an against threats, they were the truth, which means that, in these instances, he remained blind to the possibility of his own fallibility. The necessity of defending the Qur'an in this manner also meant that he sometimes rejected ideas that relied on human capacities, or at the very least attested to their unreliability, without fully engaging them.

For Sha'rawi, God's knowledge could be accessed directly, through the Qur'an or through a combination of both, which reinforced his idea that the Qur'an needed to be constantly reinterpreted in order to assess new information. He believed that the Qur'an, unlike human thought, had no limitations, in time and through time:

> We have come to the things in which the Qur'an rends the veils that cover the unseen. For our first example we will take the war between the Persians and the Romans in which the Persians were victorious . . . This war was between the two most powerful countries of the time, but it did not concern Islam or its [Godly] method. Yet [through it] God proved a matter of truth in the universe, which is that God grants victory (*yanṣuru*) to those who have faith in their hearts against those whose hearts are filled with disbelief. . . . God sent down upon his messenger the following words: "Alif. Lām. Mīm. Defeated have been the Byzantines in the lands close-by; yet it is they who, notwithstanding this defeat, shall be victorious within a few years: [for] with God rests all power of decision, first and last. And on that day will the believers [too, have cause to] rejoice [for] He gives victory (*bi-naṣri Allah yanṣuru*) to whomever he wills, since he alone is almighty, a dispenser of grace" (Qur'an 30:1–5) . . . Here we must ask ourselves who is able to decide the outcome of a war that will not happen for another nine years?[31] Who is able to decide who will be victors and who will be defeated? This was revealed in the noble Qur'an in which worship through recital will not change or be altered until the Day of Judgment. . . . The Qur'an which is a scripture [sent to convey] God's method, speaks about this battle, even though this battle is far removed from matters pertaining to God's method.[32]

For Sha'rawi, God's knowledge was unlimited, but human knowledge was limited even in matters pertaining to human life. Some aspects of God's knowledge remained hidden and some were revealed, but God continues to disclose information, and the Qur'an continues to reveal information because God's knowledge is of all things that have happened, will happen or are happening. The Qur'an for him was the repository of that knowledge as it pertained to all matters of human life.

Sha'rawi further believed that scientific discoveries could not take place unless they were guided and directed by God, who reveals previously hidden information:

> Even human progress (irtiqā'āt) has a beginning. This is not a characteristic that applies to humanity alone, but everything in the universe has a beginning and an end. For example even scientific discoveries have a time when they begin to carry out their purposes in the universe. If a researcher during the course of his research encounters a discovery [after it has reached its time of beginning], God will uncover it for him. If that information is not encountered by a researcher, then God will reveal it to one who researches the signs of God in the universe, as we say, by accident. It often happens that you find a researcher researching one thing or theorizing about something and he ends up researching something completely different, something he did not know he would be looking for. But God guides him to it by what we humans call an accident. . . . Healing from sickness also has an appointed time and thus a beginning, which is when God authorizes the restoration of health. He guides the physician to the illness and reveals the cause of the illness to him so he [the physician] can treat it and restore the health of the patient by the permission of God.[33]

In Sha'rawi's epistemology, human beings never discover things autonomously; God appoints a time of beginning and then uncovers information, which is then discovered. Sha'rawi implied that research was not always necessary because God chooses when to reveal something, which will be discovered by what appears to be chance but is actually a result of God disclosing it. He affirmed that it takes some human effort to complete the uncovering, even if human beings are not involved in the initial bringing forth of knowledge. The process is: God initiates, humans search, God uncovers. (It is very much like Sha'rawi's theology of human action, which I explored in chapter 4.) By placing God firmly in control, Sha'rawi sought to support the primacy of God's knowledge in relation to the universe but also to restore belief in the living quality of God. In his account God intervenes in human history, often to aid discoveries that will benefit humanity. God's control is therefore not merely predetermined, it is also active.

Yet Sha'rawi also stated that what comes to be known through human endeavor alone is always limited. Human beings cannot even know all that can be discerned; things happen all over the world that, even with television and other media, are not known to all people.[34]

> If witnessed knowledge is the least of the least [type of knowledge], then general matters, whatever matters have been discovered through the careful study of researchers, are also the least of the least. Researchers come to know only some things while other things remain hidden from them. You will not find, since long ago, a worldly matter or a worldly law (*qānūnān dunyawiyyān*) except that it needs to be altered or modified after a short time (*fitra qalīla*). Why? Because those who studied the matter or established any law [were able to] learn some things but other things remained hidden from them. Yet as time passes (*marra*) the things that were hidden become manifest (*ṭahar*), necessitating amendments. This is as it is because every generation (*'aṣr*) uncovers things which were previously hidden from the generation that came before . . . God is the sole legislator, nothing remains hidden from him, he has knowledge of the uncreated, and everything in the universe is in his knowledge until he brings it forth (*yujidhu*). Nothing in the heavens or in the earth escapes God's knowledge.[35]

Sha'rawi offered a very distinctive critique of secular ways of knowing; they are incomplete in comparison to God's knowledge. Thus he categorized worldly knowledge as being unstable rather than necessarily wrong. But if all knowledge is revealed by God and God's knowledge is perfect, why would it need amending? Because human beings are not privy to the completeness of God's knowledge; thus partial information can be incorrectly understood. Even interpretations of God's words sometimes need revisiting because interpretations as human knowledge are also limited.

In terms of scientific data, Sha'rawi maintained that precedence should be given to understanding God's universe through God's words properly interpreted. He did not reject science; he merely sought to point to its epistemological limitations by vetting all discoveries through the revelation, which, of course, meant through his evaluations of scientific claims based on his readings of the Qur'an. If what he found in the Qur'an supported scientific findings, then he considered them verified. Sha'rawi stated that there were two possibilities for explaining what happens when the Qur'an and science conflict. The first is that the Qur'an is right and science is wrong, and the second is that the Qur'anic verses have been misunderstood and misinterpreted. The second answer reinforces the continual need for reinterpretation because wrong or incomplete understandings of verses need to be corrected.

In his interpretation of the following Qur'anic verse: "And the earth (*al-arḍ*), we have laid it out (*madadnāhā*)" (Qur'an 15:19), Sha'rawi said that some have misinterpreted it to mean that the Qur'an asserts that the earth is flat and thus that science is a lie. According to Sha'rawi, science in this case is not a lie, and those who believe the earth is flat based on this verse have misinterpreted it. His argument depended on his knowledge of the Arabic language because it was based on his understanding of the word *arḍ*, which can mean either "earth" or "land." Because Sha'rawi interpreted it as land, he was able to say that what the verse actually means is that when human beings walk the earth, what they see from any point on the earth is the *land* laid out in front of them. So when the verse says that the land is stretched out in front of human beings, this is according to what human beings see and does not mean that the earth itself is stretched out.[36] After dispelling the idea that there is a conflict between science and the Qur'an, Sha'rawi stated that what the Qur'an said when it was revealed reflected what humanity would only come to know later:

> When this noble verse was revealed there was no conflict between what the eye saw and what the noble Qur'an said. The human being saw the land stretched out (*mamdūda*) in from of him. Later God uncovered for his creatures something from the secrets of his universe, so that science could prove that the earth is spherical (*kurawiyya*). After that space exploration began and astronauts shot pictures of the earth from space showing that it is spherical. In retaliation some of the scholars of religion accused whoever said that the earth was spherical of being unbelievers. That is because these scholars did not understand the exact details of this Qur'anic verse. When God says: 'And the earth (*al-arḍ*), we have laid it out (*madadnāhā*),' . . . [this means] that when you go to any place on the land (*al-arḍ*) you will find it spread out in front of you (*mabsuṭa amāmak*). This could not happen except if the earth was spherical. If it was a hexagon, a square, a triangle or any other shape, then you would reach an edge [and in that case] you would not find the land out stretched in front of you.[37]

Sha'rawi showed linguistically how the Qur'anic verse supported the scientific finding that the earth is spherical. He also used science to explicate how God brought forth knowledge and how that knowledge was verified in the Qur'an. Knowledge, verified through pictures or other human means, was understood primarily as being brought forth by God and embedded in the Qur'an.

Sha'rawi also stipulated that, although in this case his reinterpretation of a previously misunderstood verse was needed to affirm faith in the Qur'an, it should not be used to prove the correctness or falsity of a scientific theory. It was when scientific information threatened to weaken an adherent's faith in God, as when the Qur'an could be interpreted to contradict what had become widely accepted fact, or when scientific knowledge seemed to replace God's knowledge, that the human sciences were subject to Qur'anic verification through proper interpretation. Thus, Sha'rawi appeared to remove himself from the problem of using the Qur'an to verify or falsify science by saying that he only did so when science threatened faith.

Sha'rawi runs into this contradiction again when he states that what contradicts Qur'anic knowledge is only a threat if the believer does not understand its theological purpose. To explain this idea Sha'rawi took the Qur'anic term al-muḍallīn (those who are astray) and applied it to those who rely on the material world or philosophical ideas to formulate their truth claims.

> Why does God say: "I do not take those who are led astray (al-muḍallīn) as helpers?" (Qur'an 18:51) This is a warning to the heedless (al-mutaghāfilīn) who use philosophical means to [explain] the particularities (kayfiyya) of creation. . . . God wants to place impediments (ḥijrān) in the mouths of every one of the misguided by setting up proofs [of what they cannot know] in the material universe. He does not silence those materialists. However, they are not able to speak about this [those things that God has hidden from them]. To those we say God's creation of man has been concealed (ghaybān) from before we have known ourselves. . . . God verified that there will exist a people who will try to lead God's creation (humanity) astray . . . at times even proclaiming that humanity originated as apes or fish. God has named them those who are led astray, but if they had not come, we would not know the details of the controversy surrounding the matter of creation. So the existence and the sayings of those who are led astray are proof of the truth of the Qur'an.[38]

Sha'rawi posited that God keeps some knowledge hidden from humanity and that anyone who claims to know or to have discovered through material or philosophical methods what God has kept hidden is misguided and is leading others astray. Yet such people serve a theological purpose by proving the veracity of the Qur'an's prediction of their doubt. Properly understood as those whom God spoke about centuries before they existed, the limitations of materialists even in their area of expertise is exposed.

Yet in making scientific judgments, Sha'rawi does not seem to be adhering to his own idea that different spheres of expertise should be separated from one another for purposes of evaluation. Sha'rawi's hierarchy of knowledge meant that only one who properly understood the Qur'an could evaluate rationally based judgments. In terms of countering political groups who used the Qur'an to gain religious authority, this line of defense made sense. But in terms of scientific knowledge, Sha'rawi did not acknowledge that those trained in the sciences depended on their own truth claims and procedures, which differed greatly from Sha'rawi's reliance on exegesis as truth. The following question still remains: If rational and religious knowledge should be kept separate, how can Qur'anic knowledge be used to judge scientific theories? From within Sha'rawi's knowledge hierarchy, it could be argued that because religious knowledge is the only certain truth, it is the only measure of truth. Yet his lack of in-depth engagement with scientific claims is one of the reasons that Sha'rawi and his followers have been labeled unsophisticated and even backward.

Sha'rawi sought to maintain a delicate balance between not rejecting science and affirming the absolute correctness of his interpretations. He did not always succeed, yet his ideas about knowledge did not reject the human intellect; he believed that human thought and reason were absolutely necessary for God's plans to become manifest. For Sha'rawi, human knowledge could never be right if it opposed his understanding of God's knowledge or if it had not been first disclosed by God. He also believed that human thought could cause corruption, which led to his own assessment of what posed a danger to proper religion in the modern era. He used exegetical methods not to dissolve the tension between different epistemological visions of the universe but to attempt to make Sunni theological belief preeminent in society once again. He simply tried to affirm that only the Qur'an could be trusted to have irrefutable knowledge about the universe.

> We accept God's method and then proceed to leave it behind. We enact the method with regards to material matters but we ignore it in matters concerning the universe. We are certain that God is the creator of the universe, that he created the human being, that he created a method for life in the universe, and that he conveyed that message to us. But we come to the method of God then we proceed to abandon it. We legislate ourselves by our own deficient minds (*bi-'uqūlinā*) and our limited understanding, believing we are improving ourselves (*nuṣliḥ*), but all the while we are engaging in corruption (*mufsidūn*). We abandon what our creator gave us and begin accepting new things from among ourselves, believing that we are more capable of producing (*al-ṣanā'*) what the creator has already made. About this God has said: "And when they are told, 'Do not spread corruption (*la tufsidū*) on earth,' they answer, 'We are but improving (*muṣliḥūn*) things!' Oh,

verily, it is they, they who are spreading corruption but they perceive it not (Qur'an 2:11–12)." Any activity (ḥaraka) undertaken for improvement that is removed from God's method spreads corruption in the earth because it is moved far from the knowing creator and closer to the creature who knows little. Nothing comes from God's creation that does not improve the universe, and that which comes from God cannot corrupt. The sun, as an example, has lit up the universe since the birth of time and since then has never caused the type of corruption like [the problems] that have been caused from factories or from the emissions of cars in only a few years.[39]

Advancement or improvement (in contemporary usage the term muṣliḥūn can also refer to reforming) based solely on human capacity or human proclivities will be corrupting. To prove his point Sha'rawi used the denigration of the environment as an example. For Sha'rawi, human use of technology caused trouble because it did not take into account God's truth; human beings forgot about the creator and believed that they could reform based on solely human knowledge. The correction to this problem is to act based on what God has revealed about his method and based on what God has created.

How human beings could know that factories would be corrupting (which is how Sha'rawi identifies people as being removed from God) until those factories actually caused damage is left unspecified in this example. If God provides human beings with all new information through disclosures, what is the nature of new technology that is not supplied by God? If the answer is that all new knowledge is supplied by God, then surely even technology that has not been previously disclosed is also revealed by God. If this is the case it implies that God discloses knowledge that can potentially harm human beings. While Sha'rawi did say that human knowledge is limited, even with God's disclosures, the question still remains: Why would God not disclose enough knowledge to prevent corruption such as environmental degradation? Because it was Sha'rawi's habit to focus only on the positive aspects of the God–human relationship (a focus that served him well in other contexts, especially in terms of the personal attachment his viewers felt for him), the larger implications of his point in this example are left unanswered. If, according to Sha'rawi, the sun is helpful because it is of God, and factories are corrupting because they are examples of human beings trying to compete with God by making what God has already made, why would God reveal the knowledge of how to build factories? To fully develop his point Sha'rawi needed to explain either how human beings could gain new knowledge without God's interference or why God would support and even help bring into being that which corrupts.

CONCLUSION

By discursively demonstrating and reiterating in his sermons that God was the source of all verifiable knowledge, Sha'rawi reasserted the primacy of the religious sciences above all other types of human endeavor. He sought to establish that knowledge was primarily a theological concept, the source from which all other knowledge springs. Embedded in this approach is not only an affirmation of the fact that all human knowledge must be viewed in light of its source in God's knowledge but also the necessity of Sha'rawi's own evaluation. Because of his expertise in Qur'anic language, he was needed as an intermediary to decipher God's knowledge as it was disclosed in the revelation and to verify or reject any human knowledge accordingly.

Sha'rawi's sermons are replete with the discursive methods of the 'ulama' and with the interpretive outcomes that resulted from centuries of their application. As the metaphor about the washing machine demonstrates, he wove together his exegetical skill with his assessment of what would result if the dividing line between the Islamic sciences and the natural and social sciences was not maintained. For Sha'rawi, blurring the lines between the sources of these distinctive sciences led experts in one field to discuss subjects that they were not trained to understand. But Sha'rawi did not recognize that he himself often blurred these lines, although in less obvious ways. He made judgments about science based on his Qur'anic interpretations and he directly worked for the Egyptian government. This obscuring of what was accepted in Islamic epistemological understanding as different spheres of knowledge came about in part because of the government usurpation of 'ulama' authority in modern Egypt and the resultant mixing of secular and religious education. Thus Sha'rawi's discursive displays of knowledge were influenced by historically determined constrictions and possibilities, which included not just the competition he faced but also the state of education in modern Egypt, loss of 'ulama' independence, and his inherited epistemological discourse. Yet he did not yearn for a past system; instead he sought to infuse the public talk of his nation with the ideas he inherited as an 'alim, especially as they concerned the relationship between truth, knowledge, and God. Nevertheless, his positioning of his own orientation toward the Qur'an presented his interpretations as representative of divine knowledge.

Sha'rawi was very effective at using powerful displays of historic claims and associations to convince through discourse, even though his defensive rationale was not always complete. The point was not to make the most rational argument; it was instead to reinforce his orientation by connecting to it to renderings of theological truth. Sha'rawi's orientation as a moderate, government-employed 'alim was familiar to his audience members, many of whom shared Sha'rawi's Egyptian pride in al-Azhar as an institution that has been training Sunni 'ulama' for centuries. He offered critiques of his competitors through his Qur'anic interpretations in order to assert his discursive dominance while displaying his attachment to the Qur'an, Egypt, and al-Azhar. Knowledge was therefore central to Sha'rawi's program of renewal because he used his hierarchy—with God's knowledge at the top, the religious sciences in the middle, and the secular sciences at the bottom—to affirm the primacy of his speech above that of his competitors and detractors.

CHAPTER 6

Sha'rawi and Sufism in Egypt

INTRODUCTION

In twentieth century Egypt, the rivalry between those seeking religious authority was directly related to the struggles taking place between different groups seeking definitive ideological dominance. Distinctive definitions of piety and godliness were taken directly to the people, who in turn solidified authority through their interactions with various forces. It was an era of upheaval and disruption, in which success became centered in reception. One major realm of contention in Egypt concerned Sufism, a term that signifies both Islamic mysticism generally and *ṭarīqa* Sufism, or Sufism associated with the organized Sufi orders. The struggle to define Sufism's relation to religion, society, and the nation began in Egypt in the late nineteenth century as an attack on Sufi beliefs and practices. Over the years, various forces in Egypt have sought either to reform Sufism or to eradicate it altogether. Those who sought to eliminate or curb the influence of Sufism in Egypt spoke against more than the Sufi orders; aspects of Sufi belief and practice were also part of the institutional orientation of al-Azhar and were associated with certain practices considered to be Egyptian more generally. In reaction to this threat, the Sufis remade Sufism by redefining what attachment to the esoteric entailed. Their reforms, which were grounded in the ethical strains of Sufism, helped many Egyptian Sufi leaders, both inside and outside of the orders, effectively compete in defining an Egyptian-Islamic identity. They centered this identity in mystical practices and beliefs as they related to the Qur'an and Muhammad as well as to common Egyptian activities.

In very general terms, what differentiates the Sufis is that while they believe that direct knowledge of God or unveiling (*kashf*) is derived from the Qur'an and practice of Muhammad (sunna); they also seek to perfect and complete "proper activity" and "correct beliefs" through "direct communion with God."[1] For the Sufis, direct communion is the only means of "actualiz[ing] the divine qualities latent in the soul and bring[ing] about the appropriate manifestation of these qualities in society and the world."[2] Sha'rawi's connection to Sufism as a mystical orientation was very subtly portrayed in his sermons, yet it was still recognizable. He emphasized that love and the quest for intimate knowledge of the creator were the goals of worship, and that ritual obligations were only a starting point. But he also explained these ideas in a more complicated manner by describing how God unveils knowledge, which results in a type of communion with God. He portrayed this communion in epistemological terms as sharing in God's knowledge removed from the realm of existence. Yet these verbal indications were not enough to definitively account for Sha'rawi's widespread designation as friend of God (*walī Allah*). Instead Sha'rawi's relationship to the esoteric as a distinctive aspect of his authority was solidified by those who portrayed him as a holy man, or friend of God. Picking up on his discursive and visual cues, they designated his saintly qualities and signified acceptance of his charisma, which in turn substantiated this authority among them. Transmitted mystical legitimacy, because it does not represent facts, is affirmed when narrations of saintliness are repeated. The saint is "remembered, perpetuated, and transmitted through the very recollection of these narratives" *as* a saint.[3]

Sha'rawi also defended the Sufi–Sunni orientation of al-Azhar as quintessentially Egyptian; as such, he defended al-Azhar not as an institution but as a doctrine, which he believed was, from its earliest days, accepted by the Egyptian nation.[4] For Sha'rawi this meant defending the Ash'arite theological school of thought and the main Sufi orders because defending them meant creating an identity that brought together "theological, doctrinal and behavioral choices" with affiliations of place.[5] As discussed in other chapters of this book, Sha'rawi preached basic Ash'ari creed, specifically the belief that God controls the universe and all human endeavor, although individuals are still responsible for their actions (see chapter 4). But he also believed that this theological orientation coincided with the complicated concepts of mystical thought, for example, the idea that in order to maintain control, God was everywhere, that is, present in all aspects of the universe including in the material world. He also preached this difficult combined ideology to the people. Once again it was through popularization that he sought to preserve al-Azhar's place in his society not only in its connection to knowledge and learning but also in its long-standing commitment to Sufism.

Three distinct groups contributed to the denigration of Sufism in Egypt. First, modernists like Muhammad 'Abduh said that Sufism kept Egyptians ignorant; second, the government sought to curb the influence of Sufi groups among the population by officially recognizing certain orders and practices; and third, groups like the Salafis attacked the Sufis as engaging in un-Islamic beliefs and practices. The rise and growing influence of various Egyptian Salafi groups who vehemently oppose Sufism in any form has led to the declining popularity of *tarīqa* Sufism in Egypt. But the Salafis go even further and have sought to redefine what it means to be Egyptian according to their own version of a true Islam, which excludes Sufi practices that are thoroughly embedded in Egyptian life.

SUFISM AND REFORM IN MODERN EGYPT

Sufism has been an important component of Muslim belief and practice for centuries, according to the Sufis since the time of Muhammad. Sufism had a major impact on Islamic history, theology, ethics, philosophy, and art and on the spread of the Islam throughout the world. Even so, condemnation of certain mystical practices appeared throughout the centuries. Yet it wasn't until the modern era that these practices were characterized as a threat to religion that needed to be systematically eradicated.[6] In the eighteenth and nineteenth centuries, Sufism came under attack by Muslims who claimed that Sufi practices were not sanctioned by the shari'a, and were corrupting to society overall. Critiques of Sufism were also prevalent in Egypt and are well illustrated in the writings of Muhammad 'Abduh and his disciple Rashid Rida, who carried on 'Abduh's critique in a more virulent way.

Besides his criticism of Sufism in general, 'Abduh criticized the Azhari 'ulama' for not being more vocal in their opposition to certain Sufi practices. Al-Azhar had officially sanctioned practices such as *ziyāra*, visiting the tombs of saints, and the public celebration of a saint's birthday (*mawlid*), signifying that such practices were Sunni and Egyptian as much as Sufi.[7] But 'Abduh characterized such practices as ignorant, against the shari'a, and hindering Egypt's rationally based progress. Overall his vision for standard religion in

Egypt was a reformulation of religious practice as he became more and more concerned with modern issues such as nationalism and "morality and community life."[8] 'Abduh also mildly appraised the negative effects of belief in *karāmāt* (that certain saints or friends of God can and do perform miracles), saying that it was absolutely unnecessary and even potentially harmful.[9] 'Abduh's disciple Rashid Rida (d. 1935) was harsher in his condemnation of the Sufis. He moved further from the reformist ideas of his mentor and grew closer to Muhammad Hamid al-Fiqqi, who in 1924 founded one of Egypt's earliest Salafi parties the Ansar al-Sunna al-Muhammadiyya.[10]

The second group seeking to reform Sufism was the government of Egypt, who in the nineteenth century sought to modernize Egypt according to European standards. They were susceptible to the critiques of Europeans who saw Egypt as backward, superstitious, and irrational.[11] As part of the rhetoric of Egyptian inferiority, Europeans denounced the prevalence of particular and very public Sufi *ṭarīqa* rituals, such as the swallowing of glass and the *dawsa*, a ritual where the leader of one Sufi order rode over his disciples on horseback.[12] The government response was to organize the Sufi orders and attempt to bring them under government control.[13] Even so, the rulers of Egypt were known to regularly attend the popular festival celebrating the birth of Muhammad (*mawlid al-nabī*) and even those of other saints.[14]

The third powerful and influential critique of Sufism began among Muslims worldwide but also affected the nature of modern Egyptian Sufism. Effective opposition began in earnest in the later latter part of the eighteenth century with Ibn 'Abd al-Wahhab (d. 1790) and his followers in Arabia. The Wahhabis were concerned with maintaining *tawḥīd*, or the absolute unity and uniqueness of God, which led them to condemn the Sufis as unbelievers equivalent to the Shi'a.[15] In particular they saw the Sufis as apostates because, among other things, they believe in the power of saints to intercede through their *barakāt*, special blessings bestowed on them from God. Sufis visit the tombs and graves of saints because they believe in the ability of saints to intercede by bestowing blessings, a talent that does not end when they die. According to the Wahhabis and those who agree with their ideology, such beliefs and practices are equivalent to *shirk*, associating others with God.

The idea that the Sufis are unbelievers whose practices are innovations and therefore not authentically part of Islam (*bid'a*), has been carried on by the Egyptian Salafis. While there is variation among Salafi groups in Egypt, the unifying thread tying them together is their insistence that the only true Islamic practices and beliefs are those in which Muhammad and earliest generations of his followers, the pious ancestors (al-salaf al-ṣāliḥ), engaged. Although the Sufis say that many of their practices originated with Muhammad, the Salafis categorize and define the actions of the early ancestors very differently and therefore universally condemn most Sufi practices, which they consider dreadful innovations. While researchers have recently shown that there is not an absolute divide between all Sufi and Salafi groups,[16] the relationship between them differs in different places, depending on circumstances. In Egypt the relationship has been generally contentious. In many ways the Salafis in Egypt were more successful at curbing Sufi influence than was the government and the early reformers because they gained increasing popularity in what had once been the strongholds of Sufism among the Egyptian people.[17] Thus the competition between the two groups is very much based on identity claims concerning which group represents the true Egyptian Islam and which group has introduced foreign elements into those presumably well-established practices.

Al-Azhar in many ways represents the struggle between Sufism and Salafism in Egypt. There is both a Salafi and a Sufi presence at al-Azhar, and there has been since Sha'rawi's time there. Even though numerous Egyptian Salafi scholars are trained in Saudi Arabia today, many of the founding and influential members of these groups have also been trained at al-Azhar.[18] There remains a fear among some Azharis, or hope among the Salafis, that al-Azhar is increasingly coming under the influence of the Salafis. The sermons and tapes of Salafi scholars now even receive al-Azhar's stamp of approval before they are sold.[19] In reaction to this tension within the institution, recent, highly placed officials of al-Azhar have been unfriendly to Azhari Salafis. Muhammad Sayyid Tantawi, who was Shaykh al-Azhar from 1996 to 2010; Ahmad al-Tayyib, who took his place and remains the head of al-Azhar until today; and 'Ali Gomaa, Grand Mufti of Egypt from 2003 to 2013, all sought to affirm al-Azhar's Sufi heritage over and against the Salafi perspective. Even the new Grand Mufti Shawqi Ibrahim 'Abd al-Karim Allam, the first Grand Mufti of Egypt not to be appointed by the state after the overthrow of Mubarak, is known for his Sufi affiliations.[20] Al-Tayyib is affiliated with ṭarīqa Sufism and with Mubarak's National Democratic Party, and he is particularly hostile to the Salafis, even claiming that they are "foreign to Egypt."[21] This attack of foreignness is partially due to Tayyib's Sufi affinities but also speaks to the struggle between the two groups as they each seek to claim credibility against the other. Tayyib has also argued that certain Sufi practices are Egyptian, an argument that has been used since the late nineteenth century against those who have criticized Sufism.

The Salafis, for their part, claim to be safeguarding true Egyptian values, which they present as Islamic values. Egyptian Salafis "endeavor to sacralize as much as possible secular society by basing [their] dress, grooming and daily behavior on examples set in those prophetic hadiths that have been verified by the Salafi."[22] They argue that their strict adherence to particular daily practices is what identifies them as Egyptian because it is that adherence that represents the true Islam, the Islam of Muhammad.[23]

In response to the reformist, government, and Salafi threats to Sufism in Egypt, Sufi leaders began to change their characterization of Sufi practice. In accordance with the type of Sufi revival that took place in many Muslim societies, Egyptian Sufi reformers focused on what was best for the whole Muslim community rather than emphasizing the importance of one particular Sufi order. They underscored the need to revive Sufism so that it could become a vehicle for the implementation of Islamic renewal more generally. They also began to portray themselves as "intellectual," and they became known for "giving advice" instead of for their role as intercessors.[24] The definition of the word *Sufism* itself now emphasizes aspects of Sufism that are consistent with these reforms. Egyptian Sufis today say that Sufism means the purification of the soul, downplaying the esoteric and miraculous, which critics have called backward and un-Islamic.[25]

As a result, a new brand of Sufism has emerged that supplements more conventional practices and beliefs.[26] Some Sufi reformers have gone as far as to condemn certain practices that take place during *mawlid* celebrations, such as the mixing of men and women and the use of music, although they stop short of entirely condemning these widespread Egyptian festivals. They also speak of tomb visitation as "renewing" the believer and as bringing together the "sacred" with "daily life."[27] In addition, tomb visitation has been presented as necessary for the protection of "faith, patriotism, nationalism, and high human values."[28] Egyptian Sufi revivalists also concerned themselves with social activity, as they have said, to increase both the welfare and the piety of the community as a whole.[29] These leaders were clearly aware of the vilification of Sufism that led to its rising unpopularity in Egypt, and they responded by attempting to incorporate and re-appropriate the language of critique.

A clear example of how reform has lead to diverse perceptions of Sufi practices in Egypt concerns the understanding of what is appropriate behavior when visiting the tombs of saints. The purpose of praying at tombs is now regarded by many as a means of showing respect to the memory of the saint and receiving the special blessings associated with such respect.[30] According to this view visitation is rendered as a purified Muslim practice, but one that is also quintessentially Egyptian because it remains popular even among those Egyptians who dislike Sufism. For these people, it is a practice no longer associated with its intercessory origins. Yet there are still many who stand at the tombs of saints and family members of the Prophet buried all over Cairo weeping and asking for help.[31] The significance of such rituals is different for different people and, as such, reflects the various critiques of Sufism, the changed Sufi rhetoric of self-presentation, but also the fact that many Egyptians continue doing what both the critics of Sufism and the leaders who have reformed its image do not condone. These customs have become complex and multilayered national activities, signifying a naturalized practice that reflects multiple possible identifications depending on how sainthood is understood.

SHA'RAWI AND THE UNITY OF EXISTENCE

Sha'rawi found himself in the middle of these contestations and changes, especially as they concerned the rising influence of the Salafis in Egypt. In response he carefully affirmed both elements of reform Sufism and his Azhari orientation while distancing himself from *tarīqa* Sufism. Even so he was criticized as a Sufi by the famous Salafi Muhammad Nasir al-Din al-Albani (d. 1999). Al-Albani is credited as being one of three most influential Salafi figures of the twentieth century because he introduced into the movement a near obsession with using sunna to define true religion.[32] Albani even thought that authenticating and using sunna alone could lead to proper understanding of the meaning of the Qur'an, and he was keen to label the creeds of many well-known Muslims of his time, including Sayyid Qutb, un-Islamic whenever they deviated from his own ideas.[33] He was particularly sensitive to what he identified as the wrong-minded creed of the Sufis. About Sha'rawi he said:

> The scholars of al-Azhar master the Arabic language, *tafsīr*, jurisprudence and other subjects. But they are as far from the sunna as anyone else. Although some of them are sincere, Sha'rawi was not one of those.[34]

Al-Albani went on to say that Sha'rawi was once asked by a Salafi to inter-pret the Qur'anic verse 20:5: "The Most Gracious is established on the throne of his almightiness." Sha'rawi responded by saying, "God does not have a [single] place, God does not exist in [only a moment] of time, God is in every place. God also does not just belong to the Muslims; God is everywhere." Al-Albani then decreed that Sha'rawi espoused a deviant creed ('aqida), one that proved he was a Sufi and an Ash'ari.[35] Although Albani's attack was superfi-cial, made according to his Salafi stance against Sufism, it was a theological illustration of his ideology. He reproached Sha'rawi not only for having an in-correct view of God but also for sharing the deviant view of so many Azhari scholars, specifically the Ash'ari-Sufi notion that "God is everywhere."

Sha'rawi was certainly a proponent of such views, although he thought they represented true Islam, which for him was the Islam espoused by the right-minded scholars of al-Azhar. While Sha'rawi did not add to the literature con-cerning the foundations of these beliefs, he was considered dangerous by men like Albani, who was a prolific lecturer and preacher, because he presented simplified versions of them to his vast audiences. Sha'rawi told his viewers that all things in the visible world correspond to something in the hidden world. Humans have limited capacity in both realms of knowledge, which contrasts with God's complete and unlimited knowledge of both. God knows everything because God created everything, an esoteric idea that would be acceptable even to scholars who do not espouse Sufi ideas in their expositions about knowledge. But Sha'rawi went further, saying that God's knowledge of all of creation coincided with the notion that there was unity in being because things existed with God before creation, which meant that existence was pre-eternally unified as part of God.

> In order for God to have created it its creation must have been a part of his knowl-edge as God has been the creator prior to the existence of anything he created, because he engendered (awjad) and created by his [divine] attributes (sifat). As the creator, [God's] attributes have existed pre-eternally after which the creation was engendered. In the same way all of God's attributes were pre-eternal. God has been compassionate (rahim) prior to the existence of one who deserves compassion (al-rahma). And [God has been] the provider prior to the existence of the one who needs provision. This is [the nature] of God's attributes.[36]

Sha'rawi's thought here resembles the concept of wahdat al-wujud, the unity of being or existence. Wahdat al-wujud is an idea that is associated with the famous Andalusian Sufi Muhyi al-Din ibn al-'Arabi (d. 1240), although it did not come into use until after his death. It seems that the first time this term was attributed to Ibn 'Arabi was in the writings of Ibn Taymiyya, the medieval scholar often cited by the Salafis to justify their opinions.[37] *Waḥdat al-wujūd* "postulates that God and his creation are one because all that is created preexisted in God's knowledge and will return to it, making mystical union with God possible."[38] This idea is very problematic for groups focused on defending a particular notion of the oneness of God (*tawḥīd*) such as the Wahhabis and the Salafis. Based on the writings of Ibn Taymiyya they consider the idea that all being is unified as antithetical to the notion of God's absolute uniqueness because it equates the creation and the creator.[39] The belief that the creation is one with God can lead believers to seek union with God through creation, which is equivalent to associating what is not God with God.

Ibn 'Arabi also believed that all beings in the universe were manifestations of the divine names and attributes,[40] resembling Sha'rawi's statement above that God "created by his [divine] attributes (*ṣifāt*)." Further, Ibn 'Arabi said that by creating "through the word *kun* (be) . . . Absolute Existence descended into the determined beings through various stages."[41] Similarly, Sha'rawi grounded his ideas about existence in the Qur'anic notion that, in order to create, God said "be" and things became. For Sha'rawi, the idea of the Qur'anic *kun* ("be") was that things in the disclosed world existed first in the invisible world, and therefore when God said, "be and it is," God said "be" to something that already existed in the esoteric realm as part of God's knowledge:

> God created the heavens and the fire of hell and the afterlife and the day of judgment. All that exists (*mawjūd*) [was first] in his knowledge . . . in precise details. Before God created, he devised delights for the people of paradise and [then] brought them into existence (*yūjid*). For the people of the fire [he devised] punishments and [then] brought them into existence (*yūjid*). God did not bring [all of this information] forth from the unseen world to our visible world (*ʿālamunā al-mashhūd*). It exists [only] with him in his knowledge with all of its details . . . We must contemplate the Qur'anic verse in which God says: "His being alone is such that when he wills a thing to be, he but says unto it, 'be' and it is (*Innamā amruhu idhā arāda shay'an an yaqūla lahu kun fayakūn*)" (Qur'an 36:82). We must think carefully about God saying: "he says unto it (*an yaqūla lahu*)" and the meaning of what he says is that it (*annahu*) pre-existed in God's knowledge and when God wants (*yurīd*) to bring it forth to human knowledge or to our visible world (*al-ʿālamunā al-mashhūd*) he says to it 'be' (*kun*). How? He says to something existing with him 'be' and thus he brings it forth from [his] unseen knowledge to the visible world.[42]

Equating how humans know to how creation occurs, Sha'rawi modified Ibn Arabi's idea about all of existence being manifestations of God. He used his linguistic skill to make it easier to understand and to make it seem less controversial. The idea that everything was unified in God was transformed into an epistemological concept grounded firmly in a Qur'anic verse, which according to Sha'rawi affirmed that all knowledge preexisted with God. Sha'rawi never went as far as to say that, as a result of creation being unified, all material existence was really different manifestations of God; such ideas were criticized even by Sufis. Instead he stopped at making epistemological claims about unity, which he then connected to ideas about God's absolute control. Sha'rawi maintained that God had knowledge about all that did or will happen and created the conditions for those events to occur:

> God is the sole legislator, nothing remains hidden from him, he has knowledge of the uncreated, and everything in the universe is in his knowledge until he brings it forth (*yujidhu*). Nothing in the heavens or in the earth escapes God's knowledge.[43]

Here Sha'rawi began to elucidate the connection between ideas associated with Ibn 'Arabi and those associated with Ash'ari thought. Because God had complete knowledge, which was unified with God, God had already determined what would occur, although this knowledge remained hidden until events came about. To elucidate what the hidden realm of knowledge consisted of and thus who had access to it, Sha'rawi explained that the unseen was comprised of an "absolute unseen" (*ghayb muṭlaq*) and a "relative unseen" (*ghayb nisbiy*).

> The relative unseen . . . is the unseen that humanity knows about. It is something that I do not know but someone else does. If, for example, something is stolen from me, then I do not know who the thief is, his [identity] is hidden from me. The police also do not know who the thief is, but the thief knows himself . . . Do I say he knows the unseen? Of course not! . . . It is possible for any human being to know these types of events. They are that for which imposters and others ask help from Satan. They try to convince the people that they are familiar with the unseen realms, but the truth is that they do not know [anything] about the unseen. Because the unseen is truly the absolute unseen about which no one knows except God.[44]

The relative unseen was therefore among that which existed, and the absolute unseen remained with God as other than existence. According to Sha'rawi, the absolute unseen could be witnessed by certain human beings, but when they did so, that knowledge, unlike what is in the realm of the relative unseen, remained with God.

Sha'rawi again devised his ideas about the esoteric aspects of knowledge by framing them according to elements associated with the thought of Ibn 'Arabi. Ibn 'Arabi said that because God is unified, God is without limits or is *muṭlaq*, "infinite and absolute." In contrast he used the term *mawjūd* to refer to existent things that are "limited and defined."[45] Sha'rawi combined Ibn 'Arabi's concept of God's absolute being without limits with the idea that the absolute unseen was related to aspects of God's knowledge by saying that what God knows is unlimited (*muṭlaq*). Ibn 'Arabi's notion of God's unlimited being, or even of the hidden (*al-ghayb al-muṭlaq*), was that all of existence was otherwise limited, which for Sha'rawi meant that all other knowledge was limited. Sha'rawi's views about the relationship between the known and unseen can therefore be seen as a simplified epistemological presentation of Ibn 'Arabi's ideas.

While it is a Qur'anic notion that there are two realms of knowledge, seen and unseen, for Ibn 'Arabi the absolute unseen was "absent from the realm of human perception" but present with God and could be known only through God's self-disclosures.[46] Belief in the idea that when one witnesses those disclosures, one comes into the presence of God and becomes absent to creation through the unveiling is what identifies the Sufis as Sufis.[47] For the Sufi, this state of absence is "eminent and praiseworthy . . . since only here does it demand a presence with God."[48] Sha'rawi's view of knowledge implicitly identifies the presence with God through God's self-disclosures as signifying absence from what is created or existent because it is part of the absolute unseen. One can know the relative unseen because this is fully in the realm of existence, but knowledge of the absolute unseen must be disclosed by God. This does not mean that such knowledge has entered the realm of the existence; instead it remains with God.[49]

God must reveal the absolute unseen for it to be known, but this does not mean that God has brought the information forth from the unseen to the world of dominion; it does mean that this type of perception was given only to a select few who through that knowledge partake in what belongs to God and not the world. Sha'rawi gave the example of when God revealed future events to Muhammad to verify his mission but also ordered him to say that he did not have knowledge of those events; the information Muhammad received in order to verify his mission did not belong to Muhammad.[50] Muhammad knew this aspect of the absolute unseen, but he was not meant to share the information because it still remained with God as part of God's self-disclosures and was absent from the realm of human knowledge.[51] God's knowledge was associated with both realms, but for Sha'rawi, when the absolute unseen was revealed by God, it did not become part of the disclosed world but remained in the realm of the absolute unseen. This epistemic formulation is roughly equivalent to the idea that when one shares in God's unlimited qualities, creation is absent, although God, as absolute, is never absent from either.

Sha'rawi further elucidated these ideas in his exegesis of *Surat al-Kahf* (The Cave).

> What is a cave? A cave is a place inside of a mountain. Is it possible for you to know what is inside a hole without entering it? The answer is no, of course! God has created caves so that we can find out what is inside them for ourselves; we must discover the impression they make on our senses. We cannot know a cave unless we see it and witness it.[52]

For Sha'rawi, the secrets of God, like the cave, had to be experienced directly, as witnessed through sensory impressions or feelings. Using the language of the Sufis, Sha'rawi further explained that it was not possible to know even a little bit about the cave or for its secrets to be unveiled (*iktishāf*) until one arrived at the entrance. Coming into the cave meant coming to the truest, highest levels of knowledge (*ma'rifat ḥaqīqiyya*).[53] The term *ma'rifa* ("gnosis") signifies the level of knowledge that can only be accessed through God, which opens one to the divine through removal from the mundane world.[54] The Sufis identified gnosis as "knowledge allied with (religious) practice and feeling (*ḥāl*)."[55] *Ḥāl* refers to a focus on feeling as a spiritual state centered not in the intellect but in the heart. *Ma'rifat ḥaqīqiyya* refers to knowledge of the truth, the absolute, knowledge that God transcends the world but also that God "mysteriously penetrates all things."[56] For Sha'rawi, the cave and the knowledge gained in it were an allegory for how the mystic leaves the world and enters into God's self-disclosure by witnessing the highest levels of knowledge.

While Sha'rawi shared Ibn 'Arabi's perspective (which was so influential on the Sufis that came after him) that with unveiling one can come into the presence of God, he affirmed that position very carefully. Sha'rawi's teaching was based on the premise that everything in creation existed first in God's absolute unseen knowledge, but he also taught that, in the Qur'an, God gave every unseen thing a perceptible image in order to elucidate it for the mind.[57] Thus he connected the idea of the unity of existence with the Ash'arite idea that the Qur'an was not created but preexisted with God. It is striking that Sha'rawi preached about such complicated and controversial Sufi ideas on television. Even in a less complicated form, these ideas were still very complex for a weekly broadcast transmitted to the nation. He popularized the theoretical by blurring the lines between Sufism philosophy and his well-liked television presentations[58] in order to preserve certain concepts among his audiences.

But in these national television events, Sha'rawi was doing much more than defending theological positions; he was affirming a particular Azhari view concerning the correctness of Ibn 'Arabi's ideas by presenting them directly to the people. As such, he was commenting indirectly on the social and political situation in Egypt. In 1979, the Egyptian People's Assembly tried to ban the publication and distribution of Ibn 'Arabi's books on the premise that he was an "extremist Sufi" and that his ideas caused confusion among Muslims.[59] One of the rectors of al-Azhar 'Abd al-Halim Mahmud had died one year earlier, in 1978. Mahmud had encouraged the reading of Ibn 'Arabi in the institution and even wrote a book defending Ibn 'Arabi's notion of *waḥdat al-wujūd*.[60] With his death the anti-Sufi opponents of Ibn 'Arabi saw an opportunity to reverse Mahmud's influence with their proposed ban. But many Azhari scholars criticized the interference of a political body in decisions about religious material, insisting that even in medieval history diversity of opinion was allowed and that powerful sultans had been censored by the 'ulama' when they attempted similar bans.[61] The incident gave these scholars the opportunity to affirm their right to decide which religious literature should be read and to affirm the Sufi heritage of al-Azhar among its many critics. Within a decade of this incident, Sha'rawi was presenting a version of Ibn 'Arabi's ideas through a medium much more likely to reach the public than print material. Despite the controversy over Ibn 'Arabi's ideas, Sha'rawi was still able to present a version of those ideas on state-run television while becoming the most popular religious authority in late-twentieth-century Egypt, which attests to both his cleverness with words and his commitment to making certain Sufi concepts salient in his society. But it also demonstrates how alliances were made between different forces in Egypt during Sha'rawi's time. In this case the alliance between those who had something to gain by reinforcing the notion that true Egyptian Islam was the Ash'ari-Sufi orientation of al-Azhar.

PERCEPTIONS OF SHA'RAWI: *KARĀMĀT*

In the same way that Sha'rawi grounded his esoteric ideas in language about knowledge and the Qur'an, his disciple represented his mystical orientation as tied to normative Qur'anic notions, specifically about behavior. In a lecture given to a small audience on a Thursday night in July 2008, 'Abd al-Ra'uf said that Sha'rawi was a Sufi if Sufism is defined by the last verses of *Surat al-Furqān* (The Criteria, Qur'an 25:72–75),[62] which primarily describes the behavior of the servants of God. He also said that Sufis should love God as if they see God, not out of their own desires but because God deserves such a love (*ḥubb Allah ka-Allah*). This, he said, means uncovering one's love until one sees God, which is precisely what Sha'rawi did. Why did 'Abd al-Ra'uf connect Sha'rawi to Sufism through these Qur'anic verses? Like the idea that Sufism is the purification of the soul, he grounded Sha'rawi's connections to esotericism in norms derived from the Qur'an. The rest of his lecture that evening focused on the idea that those who practice proper *adab* (etiquette or morals) receive blessings from God as a reward for applying the shari'a to the best of their ability.

The way people like 'Abd al-Ra'uf presented Sha'rawi's connection to the esoteric fits Sufism's well-developed ethical strain, which describes good behavior as essential to gaining intimacy with the divine and which began long before the modern era.[63] Reaching God through ethical behavior means that the mystic is considered a "moral guide," someone who demonstrates perfect *adab* and has in-depth religious knowledge.[64] Saints who achieve this level of intimacy with God can be found both inside and outside Sufi organizations, and many receive gifts without practicing as Sufis or acknowledging that they travel the Sufi path in any form.[65]

It is significant that Sha'rawi never referred to himself as a Sufi or even as one favored by God with insight into the realms of the unseen. He indirectly affirmed his commitment to a literary presentation of mystical principles through his expositions about knowledge, but it was his disciples and followers who affirmed him as a holy man and ultimately communicated his mystical legitimacy. Because hagiographies are written after the death of their subjects, they are removed from the very lives they recount and therefore are effective in helping shape the response of "the hagiographic community" that grows up around a saint.[66] Thus biographical communications can create both the lasting impression of the saint and of the community that reveres him or her.

Hagiographies are embedded in and therefore reflect social worlds; through presentations of saintliness they offer a notion of religiosity that affirms particular values.[67] The telling of sacred stories presents the actions contained within them as "complex religious symbols, (which) could synthesize a multi-layered ethos with less ambiguity than an argument."[68] The trust that people place in those they consider holy therefore relies on shared conceptions of saintly qualities. Because they recount these qualities, hagiographies confirm them as manifest in a particular person, thereby bestowing an elevated status on the saint. They elevate the legacy of the saint in comparison with others without any need for direct confrontation, affirming not only the saint but also his or her perspective.[69] Hagiographies testify to that superiority within the community, which helps preserve it for posterity.

Hagiographies are therefore a "rechanneling" of notions of piety, an appropriation and creation of a text in a particular time.[70] The making of a saint through biographical accounts tells the history of neither the saint nor the biographer; instead it reflects a particular social milieu. Yet those accounts can say something about the way that milieu is structured and possibly contested because they reflect a desire to see social context restructured in a particular manner, often in distinction to other teleological visions. Sacred biographies therefore do not connect the mundane and holy through a person; they are not interpretations "of signs . . . pointing to an association of the person and the sacred,"[71] but a way of telling how expressions of mystical values are formulated as an engagement in historical and contemporary struggles between various religious modalities.

Just as hagiographies are not signs pointing to the sacred or factual accounts, they are also not universal. Even within societies, different accounts of holiness can express different notions of social value and the place of the holy within them.[72] People vest others with sainthood in order to access something that seems unattainable without help. They retell stories to engage holiness because stories "have had instructive meaning for those who engage them."[73] As stories are passed on, they confirm and instill in individuals a particular formulation of holiness. Individuals make these commitments as part of groups, and in the case of the wrangling over definitions of piety in twentieth-century Egypt, as a confirmation of one presentation of true religion over other presentations.

This expansion of the notion of holiness as a discrete territory within a larger social context in which different conceptions of holiness compete with one another can be further stretched to include the notion of time. The sacred biography relies on past notions of holiness, making them newly relevant in the present while pointing to the future. The attempt to make a particular understanding viable in all times works because holiness is affirmed by its timeless quality.[74] Present threats therefore can be contrasted with hagiographic accounts as presentations of eternal qualities because hagiographies are a (re)telling or a vision of what previous exemplars were and what future ones will be.

In the case of Muslim hagiographies, precedence begins with biographies of Muhammad and continues through the *tabaqāt* literature (biographical compilations). The biographical accounts of Muhammad's life that are used as mystical prototypes do not come from his "quasi-historical biographies" but from the *qiṣaṣ al-anbiyā* (stories of the prophets), popular literary renderings in which both the miracles associated with Muhammad and his particular character traits are emphasized.[75] For the mystic, Muhammad's example brings together the everyday, ethical imperatives of imitating his conduct with the absolutely extraordinary. Because the *qiṣaṣ* were not canonical, this extraordinariness was sometimes read back into the Prophet's life for the sake of creating him as a dual exemplary.[76] Still the spiritual lineage created through biographical similarities, as mundane conduct and as supernatural powers, was a means of establishing the authority of the saint in comparison to Muhammad.

The *tabaqāt* literature that developed to record the lives of Muslims after Muhammad's death is vast and has continued to be written generation after generation.[77] It is divided by subgenres of association (Sufis, 'ulama', legal scholars, etc.) in which biographical accounts relate information about individuals, their communities, and their place in the literary history of the genre and subgenre.[78] But like hagiographic literature generally, biographical dictionaries, no matter which subgenre they belong to, cannot be read as accurate depictions of history.[79] They cannot be considered historically accurate precisely because they present a viewpoint as legitimate based on connections to the past for the sake of posterity.

Some of the most commonly retold accounts from Sha'rawi's life fit descriptions of holy men that are extant even in early Sufi accounts of saintliness, for example, the idea that the friend of God can be recognized as having gained direct insight or favor from God because he or she is "upright, refined, educated, purified, cleansed" and has "developed a friendship with God [and] is brought to perfection for him."[80] Other "external signs" of the friends of God include that "they are endowed with clairvoyance . . . receive divine inspiration . . . all tongues agree in praising them, except those who are afflicted with jealousy . . . they are manifestly capable of miracles such as traveling distances over the earth and walking on water."[81] In this eighth-century account of what sainthood looks like, the Sufi al-Tirmidhi also recounted the many nonvisible signs of the friends of God. Dreams of Muhammad and of saints are also presented as common to the friends of God.[82] But accounts of the nonvisible signs of the saint are meant as instruction reserved for those who travel the Sufi path and seek knowledge about how to progress.

These excerpts of al-Tirmidhi's text concerning the observable signs of the saint are reflected in the narrative retelling of Sha'rawi's life, even if in modified form. Characteristics I repeatedly heard about Sha'rawi included the notion of him as educated, pure, refined in behavior, and even perfected. I was also often told about the widespread praise of him among the elites of his society and about his miracles, clairvoyance, and special dreams and visions. Although the miracles I heard about and recount below do not have to do with traveling distances or walking on water, a connection running through these types of miracles and the ones Sha'rawi was known for can be discerned in how he was presented as able to defy the laws of time and space. Sha'rawi's disciples did not recount his life as the life of a Sufi or as instruction on how to progress as a Sufi.

This selectivity also applies to how Sha'rawi's biography can be compared to Sufi biographies more generally. Many Sufi biographies helped institutionalize a saint and that saint's teachings; as such, they can be read according to how that process unfolded.[83] Hagiographies were also written to attract followers to a saint in order to develop a Sufi order around a singular personality in a particular historical milieu.[84] While the specific purpose of these hagiographies as they relate to Sufism cannot be applied to Sha'rawi, their more general uses can. Stories about Sha'rawi were not told to establish a Sufi order, but Sha'rawi's followers certainly hoped to distinguish his saintliness in order to attract followers to his methods in a competitive environment. For this purpose they also told about his miracles in order to demonstrate his "physical and spiritual care for the welfare of disciples, combining teaching with authority," in the hopes of validating his saintly prestige.[85]

Sha'rawi was also said to have exhibited many of the characteristics of the saintly conduct expected of the friends of God in medieval Sufism, traits that academics have seen as contradictory, including:

A reputation for strict orthodoxy . . . meticulous performance of Islamic duties . . . austerities of a more or less orthodox character . . . the working of miracles (karāmāt), together with a careful avoidance of the vulgar display of them . . . a reputation for inaccessibility and dislike of human society, often combined with care for disciples.[86]

Yet Sha'rawi's exhibition of many of these characteristics was anything but contradictory. Instead stories about him were repeated in order to establish his closeness to God as a "homogeneity . . . present[ed] . . . in terms accepted by universal Muslim standards."[87] Many Sufi saints have been known to believe in miracles and to have recounted the miracles of others, but more often than not they downplay their own importance and rarely recount their own miracles.[88] The importance of proper action and care of others in Sufi biographies means that accounts of Sufi miracles are intertwined with accounts of piety and correct behavior as particular presentations of virtue.[89]

The biographical retellings of Sha'rawi's life both resemble typical medieval Sufi hagiographies and differ from them. Those who told stories about him used common hagiographic tropes especially as they relate to barakāt, karāmāt, visions and dreams of Muhammad, wisdom, and behavior. Yet it is precisely the centering of Sha'rawi's mystical legacy in the words of his followers that makes his hagiography, like most of his legacy, different. These aspects of his biography were transmitted among the people and on television, so they reflect the expectations more of these people than of those engaged in recording mystical lives in the literary genre of ṭabaqāt. While the ṭabaqāt literature of the past was written by elites for elites, the recognition of illustriousness no longer depends on elites. Thus, Sha'rawi's biographical retellings cannot be examined according to literary structure.[90] They can be examined, however, according to how the perception of his holiness served as general religious instruction for those who recorded and repeated hagiographic stories about him. They can also be interpreted "in terms of genre, audience patronage and literary convention," or in this case verbal and mediated articulations taken on their "own terms."[91]

Whether Muslim saints are remembered as such and the longevity of the legacy of their holiness depends on more than what is said about them after death. It also relies on two other elements. First, the major events of their lives need to be recognized and praised in their time as conforming to "attitudes, activities, and allegiances esteemed by the various groups compromising the elite" of the era.[92] Second, longevity relies on how families and followers care for the memory of the saint by disseminating his or her teachings and building a shrine-tomb that can be visited in the future.[93] These criteria, while meant to describe why some Sufi saints in medieval South Asia were remembered and others were not, can be used to discuss the possibility that Sha'rawi will be remembered as a charismatic.

The longevity of Sha'rawi's mystical legacy no longer depends only on the ability and willingness of his followers to carry on his teachings. They have been carried through his own media transmissions, not only through reruns on television but also as clips on the Internet. Even his supporters have kept the miraculous aspects of his life alive by telling about his miracles on Egyptian television after his death. Such stories have also been rerun and repurposed on the Internet. One such example is a clip taken from an interview and posted on YouTube of the well-known Egyptian preacher 'Umar 'Abd al-Kafi (b. 1951) in which he told of his affection for Sha'rawi. He also, upon prodding, related a story in which he witnessed Sha'rawi's *karāmāt* when Sha'rawi demonstrated that he was able to read al-Kafi's thoughts.[94] Although his family and followers did build Sha'rawi a large shrine-tomb in his home village of Daqadous, his tomb, like the other buildings Sha'rawi himself built in Daqadous, including a mosque, library, and affordable housing, were paid for by the revenue gained from his television shows. Thus, with Sha'rawi's *karāmāt* and the building of his shrine-tomb, the lasting influence of Sha'rawi's saintly legacy is being propelled by media, from his days in television to the Internet today.

Sha'rawi's family and disciples have sought to keep this aspect of his authority alive by planning and executing a yearly *mawlid* in Daqadous on the date of Sha'rawi's death.[95] When, a year after his death, Sha'rawi's son 'Abd al-Rahim, announced in a prominent newspaper that the first yearly *mawlid* would take place in Daqadous, controversy ensued.[96] Many claimed that Sha'rawi was against *mawlid* celebrations, but in fact he had defended them, saying,

> As long as there is no immorality and transgression . . . it's all about dhikr and blessing, and the Prophet, it is okay. Some Arab countries do not recognize that; they have even been saying that the mawlids that we celebrate have no base [in religion]. I say to them: We do not . . . judge the idea of the mawlid, but what

happens at the mawlid. If nothing happens except obedience to God, then what is the proof that obedience to God should be forbidden?[97]

Despite the controversy, the festival remains a popular event. Every year in June, people come to Daqadous for a couple of days and celebrate day and night around Sha'rawi's grave with special food, carnival rides, and other events. When I asked 'Abd al-Rahim al-Sha'rawi and 'Abd al-Ra'uf, about the mawlid in Daqadous, I was told that it wasn't really a mawlid but a dhikr, a commemoration. 'Abd al-Ra'uf said that Sha'rawi had specifically asked that no mawlid take place at his grave, which is probably why it occurs on the date of his death and not on his date of birth, the usual day for such a celebration. But Engineer 'Abd al-Rahman, who represents Sha'rawi in the village of Daqadous, told me that the festival benefits the people of Daqadous economically, which is a great help to them, and for that reason Sha'rawi would have approved of it.[98]

'Abd al-Rahim al-Sha'rawi has been very careful to keep activities associated with Sha'rawi's tomb free of controversy. The tomb does not stand near the mosque Sha'rawi built in Daqadous. Near the entrance to the shrine-tomb, a sign tells visitors to pray to God and to behave properly in the shrine. A printout of some of Sha'rawi's poems are made readily available for people to read while they are visiting. In terms of the mawlid—gambling, dancing, and alcohol are not found.[99] Instead, during the commemoration, people come from all over Egypt, and scholars and Sufi leaders give lectures about Sha'rawi and the important aspects of his teachings in order to provide guidance to the people who attend the celebration. Engineer 'Abd al-Rahman said that, although Sha'rawi did not belong to one particular Sufi order, he loved and respected all of the Sufi leaders in Egypt, and they continue to love and respect him in return.[100] Because of this love, each of the three days of Sha'rawi's mawlid in Daqadous is organized by a different Sufi order, and the representative of each gives an edifying talk.[101]

The festival keeps people visiting Sha'rawi's shrine, making the yearly celebration into a respectable Egyptian mawlid. Besides the good behavior exhibited by the event's attendees, the event is organized to downplay the connection between this commemoration and traditional ideas of barakāt associated with the Egyptian mawlid. It demonstrates that those in charge of Sha'rawi's legacy devised that legacy and his "hagiographic community" as national, Islamic, non-ṭarīqa, and Sufi. But Engineer 'Abd al-Rahman was also keen to relate this event to Sha'rawi's care for his community.

Another example of how his friends and disciples helped construct Sha'rawi's saintliness was when they discussed his *karāmāt* on a television series that ran in the summer of 2008. I was also repeatedly told by his friends, family members, and even people who did not follow him about the miraculous occurrences that took place during Sha'rawi's life.[102] When I visited the Sha'rawi Center in his home village of Daqadous, I spoke to Engineer 'Abd al-Rahman about the miracles associated with Sha'rawi. At first he was reluctant to talk about them, saying that Sha'rawi did not talk about these things because they were very personal; when Sha'rawi saw something, he kept it to himself. As an example, Engineer 'Abd al-Rahman shared with me something that happened while he was at Sha'rawi's house. One evening, while he and Sha'rawi were sitting together, Sha'rawi said that he saw paradise and all of the small angels of paradise. As he started to explain this to Engineer 'Abd al-Rahman, someone came into the room and interrupted. Every time after that, when Engineer 'Abd al-Rahman asked him to explain this vision of paradise, Sha'rawi would forget. Finally, Sha'rawi told Engineer 'Abd al-Rahman that he was not meant to speak about this vision but to keep it to himself.

In the story, Sha'rawi's refusal to relate his experience exemplifies important qualities related to the proper behavior of a saint; he did not share his gifts for the purposes of notoriety but instead downplayed them. Engineer 'Abd al-Rahman emphasized this behavior more than the fact that Sha'rawi had seen, in the course of an average day, something miraculous. He did not explain how these visions came about, what they could mean, or even why Sha'rawi would have had them. He instead sought to demonstrate to me that Sha'rawi's actions verified that he had actually seen the unseen in the course of an average day. The event also corresponds to Sha'rawi's notion explored earlier in this chapter that knowledge or insight that is disclosed by God remains in the unseen and should not be shared with others.

Another story I was told concerns Sha'rawi's ability to heal the sick. According to the story, once when Sha'rawi was traveling and had just disembarked from his plane, he was approached by a man who worked at the airport. The man told Sha'rawi that he knew who he was and asked Sha'rawi if he could help him with a serious problem. Sha'rawi took him to dinner, at which time the man told Sha'rawi that he could not sleep and that he had not slept in a very long time. He had been to many doctors, but no one could help him. When the man was finished talking, Sha'rawi wrapped his arms around him, whispered some verses of the Qur'an in his ear, and then breathed out on the side of his ear. The man then went home and slept for three days. Sha'rawi never shared this story; it was only after his death that his disciples learned about it. They met the healed man and heard the story when he came to Daqadous to plant trees at the grave of Sha'rawi. This story again strongly connects behavior to sanctity by suggesting that Sha'rawi was concerned for people and could heal the sick. He used the Qur'an to fortify his miraculous abilities, signifying that God had purified him as an intermediary, and again he downplayed his miraculous abilities. It also demonstrates how his shrine, as the location of his legacy, made the man's visit and thus the spreading of the story possible.

The last story I will explore was told during a lecture given by 'Abd al-Ra'uf after Thursday evening prayers in an apartment across the street from the Husayni Mosque in Cairo. The story is connected to a long-debated issue among Muslims about the throne of God. The debate concerns whether, when the Qur'an references the throne of God (for example, in verses 2:255, 13:2, 25:59, 32:4, and 57:4, among others), it is a reference to a physical throne. If God actually has a throne, it implies that God would be able to sit, which according to some anthropomorphizes God. On the other hand, some early scholars, like Ahmad ibn al-Hanbal (d. 855 C.E.), argued that if one did not accept the way God is described in the Qur'an, that person would doubt the veracity of the Qur'an. These debates continued among the 'ulama', although some of the questions that animated the debate changed over time. Among the new questions that arose were those concerning the nature of God's physical attributes. As a part of this debate, scholars asked about the attributes of the throne of God, which became the subject of the lecture given that summer evening in 2009.

During the lecture, 'Abd al-Ra'uf said that many 'ulama' before Sha'rawi's time were in agreement that human beings can know *that* the throne of God remains stable, but they cannot know *how* it does. Sha'rawi, on the other hand, said that not only is it known that the throne of God remains stable but it is also known how, so asking and answering this question is not an innovation. How do we know how the throne of God remains stable? Because any king who has the power to master all things can stabilize all things. Therefore, God has subdued the throne because its stability is commanded and thus it has been subordinated to the command.

What is most interesting about this story is how Sha'rawi came to this new understanding; he did not receive it through Qur'anic interpretation but through his dreams. 'Abd al-Ra'uf told his audience that night that Sha'rawi dreamt of someone who asked the Prophet Muhammad, "What is your God doing right now? If everything that is written is enclosed [cannot be changed] (ḥāfa al-āqlām)?" According to 'Abd al-Ra'uf, this demonstrated to Sha'rawi that God creates things beforehand and only later makes them known to people. "God makes some people high and others low; he is in control. He constricts and releases."[103]

'Abd al-Ra'uf's story of the dream does not seem to explain how Sha'rawi connected his interpretation and the dream itself. But if the point of the story is considered, the connection is clarified, as is the connection to the Ash'ari theological position. Although God predetermines (encloses what is written), God still intervenes in history (makes people high and low). So while there seems to be instability, there is constriction and release because what is pre-destined cannot change; it remains stable. As I discussed earlier in this chap-ter, for Sha'rawi, everything preexisted with God, who wrote it all and then substantiated it in worldly creation. This idea here reinforced the notion that God's throne remains stable because it is subordinated to God's eternal command. To doubt this stability, one has to doubt the power of God over creation.

The idea that humanity can gain constant insight into God's truth even while God remains all powerful was demonstrated when the person in the dream asked Muhammad how, even though God has decided everything, God is still active ("What is he doing now?"). The dream is affirmed because in it Sha'rawi saw Muhammad. Dreams of Muhammad are always considered true according to the hadith in which Muhammad stated that anyone who sees him during sleep has seen the truth because the devil cannot take his form.[104] Besides the connection it makes to Sufi hagiographies and how they present dreams of Muhammad or direct disclosures from God as signs of the saint, the story 'Abd al-Ra'uf told also relates back to Albani's complaint about Sha'rawi. Its telling therefore had many repercussions in terms of affirming Sha'rawi's place among the scholars and mystics of his time and of the past and future.

CONCLUSION

Many Sufi authors have connected the "knowledge granted directly from God to the ethics and spiritual practice of the individual seekers of knowledge."[105]

In this way the stories about Sha'rawi's esoteric gifts offer a "paradigm of behavior," but not just as the "supernatural intervening in daily life."[106] This connection between Sufi and shari'a perspectives was always emphasized when Sha'rawi's disciples spoke of him and his connection to Sufism in an attempt to distance him from *ṭarīqa* Sufism. These attempts also reflected how critiques of Sufism had entered the language even of the mystically oriented.

Government attempts to control the Egyptian Sufi Orders began in 1812 when Muhammad 'Ali, the then ruler of Egypt, chose one Sufi leader and gave him authority over all the Sufi orders in Egypt.[107] Today this attempt at control is realized through the Supreme Council of Sufi Orders. While the council is supposed to protect the interests of Egyptian Sufis, besides certain leaders of Sufi orders, the ministry of the interior, local authorities, and representatives from al-Azhar are all responsible for appointing the members of the council, some of who are affiliated with the National Democratic Party. The council does not recognize all Sufi orders, and those that are not recognized are not given government permission for public activities, such as holding *mawlid* celebrations.[108]

Even more than government intervention, Egyptian Salafism has strongly influenced the way Sufism has been re-formed in modern Egypt since the early twentieth century. The anti-Sufi polemic of the Salafis, which combined with their success in attracting members to their movement, has been damaging to Egyptian Sufism. The connection between al-Azhar and Sufism, and the desire the Salafis have to become more instrumental in al-Azhar, has meant that the struggle between these two groups has also played out within that institution. And yet the traditions associated with being Egyptian, which are also grounded in Sufi hagiographies, are still actively and creatively engaged in by the fans of Sha'rawi, a government-sponsored television personality. The acceptance of him as a holy man has relied mostly on how his disciples, family members, friends, and followers retell his life story, creating him as a man that was loved and purified by God because he perfected his piety. He is presented according to the notion that Sufism is concerned with both shari'a (following God's legislation) and *ḥaqīqa* (developing intimacy with God).

CHAPTER 7

Relevance through Language Use

INTRODUCTION

Popular preachers like Sha'rawi include their values and perspectives in their sermons, but they also must use their words to attract crowds. Often this means that they have a more expansive view of what can be included in their public articulations even when they are seeking to reinforce normative expectations. Through the practice of preaching, agents choose certain possibilities inherent in social or religious structures and exclude others. By selecting certain structures and excluding others, they try to "bring about changes in . . . knowledge . . . beliefs . . . attitudes, values, experience, and so forth."[1] This attempt to change attitudes through language is what makes sermons ideological—as a social practice these articulations can both support and counter arguments through language, but always in negotiation with audiences and the environment in which sermons are devised and delivered. When sermons display the outright affirmation of particular theological stances, they are a means for preachers to assert their dominance.

Sha'rawi used language to convey his ideology—he expressed his values in language, in his ideas about language, and in his attempt to regulate language. All three types of expressions helped distinguish Sha'rawi from other prominent figures of his time because they were bound to his context, goals, and orientation. To fully examine how Sha'rawi expressed his ideology, however, the definition of the word *context* must include more than just the situation of modern Egypt. It must also consider language communities, contestations over meaning, modes of delivery, and displays of authority.

While Sha'rawi tried to bring neglected and threatened foundational con-cepts to the public for the purposes of renewing faith and revitalizing his pro-fession, he could not have been as successful as he was, and still remains, if his sermons did not include the shared language used to express views about religion in late-twentieth-century Egypt. A major aspect of this shared language pertained to contestations over authority, which came to the fore because of historical contingencies and which are observable as multiple responses put forth in discourse. Sha'rawi made a case for his own viability through terms, declarations, and explanations that reflected an ultimate concern—that of the God–human relationship. Beyond demonstrating the ascendancy of his type of knowledge, Sha'rawi tried to convince those who sought guidance elsewhere, or who may not have accepted his entrenched theological premises, that his God-centered approach to the universe, which was based on his interpretations of God's speech in the Qur'an, was the only legitimate truth. Whether in his epistemological, theological, or political talk, Sha'rawi's language was always presented in a specific revelatory context ac-cording to his distinct goals. Because Sha'rawi extracted his epistemological theology from revelation, his language was saturated with ideology.[2] He used language as discourse—as a structure that supported and created particular institutional definitions of correct Islamic belief and practice. But his mean-ing was inextricably informed by his context because it gave him relevance and because communication, especially television communication, is an interac-tive exchange between presenter and audience.[3]

For language to be effective, speakers must do more than understand gram-mar correctly; they primarily have to convey orientations through signs, which inscribe even the form of language with particular ideologies. Language use can affect form by expressing social functions and institutions, such as those of the nation and religion, through statements that are concerned with "identity . . . aesthetics . . . morality, and . . . epistemology."[4] Sha'rawi's ser-mons demonstrate how forms of language can succumb to context because his words communicated ideas about institutions prevalent in his society. In devising concrete linguistic instantiations of identity, morality, and epistemol-ogy, he related divine language to existing political and religious institutions. Through explications on the nature of knowledge in connection to religious identity, he reinforced a relation between society and a particular vision of religious behavior, one that downplayed direct action and was instead quietist. Sha'rawi focused on instructing people how to develop a personal relationship with God, which helped him distance himself from the official functions of al-Azhar while remaining valuable to the government that employed him.

The ideology expressed by Sha'rawi exemplifies the idea that language always varies in context and that, as a result, texts do not have autonomy. Whether a text can be used in different contexts depends on how entrenched it is in its environment.[5] Anyone seeking religious authority in contemporary Egypt has to repurpose revelation, but every text that is oriented toward a particular goal or toward particular audiences must vary in some way from those geared toward other ends.[6] Thus the same sacred language is rarely equivocal; it can signify difference in distinct instances. Sha'rawi was one of many actors competing for religious legitimacy in Egypt, and his speech, as text, marked him as both a member of a group and distinguished him from others in that group according to his assessment of the good. His sermons demonstrated social, political, and religious interests based on his view of Qur'anic language, often in conversation with other perspectives present in his society. These conversations and expressions of difference reflected and also helped institute change through linguistic expression.

How language is used within particular communities can shed light on how value systems are expressed. Thus, the postulation, "There is a standard denotative language," becomes problematic. The practice of labeling language systems as denotative assumes that the meanings of words remain stable, which is itself an ideological construct used to judge the worthiness of different types of language uses.[7] Even when unity in language is postulated, that unity is ideological more than real because such a postulation privileges one form and therefore one set of values over others. Any example of language instantiation references a unique view of the good, even if the same words or sentence structures have been used elsewhere. Therefore, when speakers, events, social conditions, or communities of receivers change, so does the signification of words in context.[8] Variation occurs through interaction, through changes in setting, and because of multiple possibilities in use.

Part of the context of Sha'rawi's sermons was political, situated as he was in the overall national context as well as in his role within the state as a national preacher. While arguments continue over Sha'rawi's involvement with the political leaders of his time, particularly whether he did or didn't capitulate to them, this very controversy reflects the greater conversation about religion and society within Egypt, especially with regard to reform and how it should be accomplished. Discussing the relationship between political and religious institutions in terms of how ideas about that relationship are instantiated in words leads to important questions about formations of national and religious identity through language. By dissecting speech, prominent voices and positions within society can be discussed in terms of how they intersect through usage. Discussing only the denotational use of language, as if a word, even when used in varying contexts, always has the same meaning, can lead to distortion or—worse—misrepresentation of the linguistic expressions of those who share rules or ways of speaking.[9]

Sha'rawi's language was embedded in a speech community that used Qur'anic references in the context of time, place, actors, receivers, and goals along with various intonations, enunciations, and tones to accumulate religious authority.[10] Considering Qur'anic terms that are commonly used yet contested in contemporary Egypt means engaging in a different type of evaluation: adding diachronic to synchronic context. Even past meanings of certain Qur'anic terms did not remain stable, and this instability helps explicate how meanings fluctuate in the present in terms of how past conversations are included in present uses of words. "At any moment in the development of dialogue there are immense, boundless masses of forgotten contextual meanings, but at certain moments of the dialogue's subsequent development . . . they are recalled and invigorated in renewed form."[11] The history of usage of Qur'anic terms helps link epistemological expressions to religious institutions and in current times helps to distinguish different goals within linguistic communities.

In the next section of this chapter, I will examine the ideological considerations that remain prominent in the contemporary use of Arabic in Egypt and explore what sort of ideologies are implied in the use of certain forms of Arabic compared to others, particularly how authority is displayed through form, or how form is used to express authority. To fully explore this point, I will examine how these contestations eventuate in the attempt to control the meaning of terms, specifically, how Sha'rawi used Qur'anic verses to metapragmatically regulate language use according to his own views.

Next, I will discuss how values are conveyed through language, specifically how Qur'anic language is transformed in speech communities for particular ends, assuming that speech communities exist "in the intersection of different socio-political interests around . . . far-from-neutral ideological portrayal[s]."[12] This indeterminacy and the presence of multiple voices in single language use (heteroglossia) can be deciphered in how Qur'anic terms are explained in contestation. But multiple voices can also be presented in terms of time, especially in religious discourse that accepts that authenticity and truth are evidenced in language that originated in the past. In the last section of the chapter, I delve further into the concept of heteroglossia by considering how the television text privileges the presence of the receiving community while allowing for further contestations among claimants through language and other signs. I will stretch the idea of mode by looking at language as more than speech, but also as a media text.

PUBIC INFLUENCE ON LANGUAGE USE IN MODERN EGYPT

The struggle to control Arabic in the context of the diglossic situation in Egypt gives cultural specificity to the broad ideas about language and ideology.[13] Classical Arabic (*fuṣḥā*) has an inextricable link to Qur'anic Arabic, which means that it is considered pure. This elevated status stands in contrast to how the local Egyptian dialect (*'āmiyya*) is viewed, which is as a corrupted, low form of speech, even though it is the language Egyptians use for social communication. This situation has been further linked to ideology in modern Egypt because the government chose Classical Arabic (CA) as the official state language to build both the state apparatus and the nation. The government has attempted to control "the modernization of CA by overseeing institutions of learning, publishing, and social affairs since the middle of the nineteenth century."[14] Through this control, the state presented itself as the gatekeeper of language for the good of the nation.[15] Thus the "form" and "meaning" of Qur'anic Arabic (here in contrast to Saussure's structuralist idea that the relationship between form and meaning is arbitrary) are related.[16] In Egypt, Classical Arabic was enmeshed in discourses of power, authority, and control, and therefore it could not be neutral. Control of a language believed to come from a divine source and to be stable in structure deliberately privileged a specific view of history and a sense of identity.[17]

Because the structure of Arabic as it appears in the Qur'an is itself considered holy, its repetition can transfer that sense of holiness to the one who memorizes or recites it just as it was delivered to Muhammad. But in interpretation or use, the form of that divine communication is influenced by contingent considerations. The interpreter or the one who repeats divine speech in context can instantiate judgments about religion, society, or politics for the purposes of assessing those institutions. Thus the function of language is superimposed on the form through use in speech and can legitimate a particular stance in context.

Because Arabic associated with the Qur'an is considered perfect, people who memorize and interpret the Qur'an are often considered closer to the divine. Through the repetition of God's speech, a type of authority is bestowed. The power and authority that comes merely from the knowledge of Qur'anic language (here even as it undergirds Classical Arabic) cannot be underestimated. Usage itself can become a type of discourse of power; beyond a mere labeling of good or bad speech, it inextricably links the user to God through sound.

Because all the figures and movements I consider in this chapter sought to control aspects of religious discourse and by extension religious sentiment, each had to ground their discourse in Qur'anic language no matter what their perspectives or specialties. Sha'rawi carved out a niche for himself through his skills with language, allowing him to infuse his interpretations seamlessly with a sense of divine mandate. He constantly interjected Qur'anic terms into his sermons as explanations of everyday interaction and as theological reflection. As has been demonstrated throughout this book, Sha'rawi never spoke about religion or human emotions, actions, or ideas except in reference to the Qur'an. His opinions were stated before and after he quoted the Qur'an, and those opinions carried the wording of the verse in the context of his interpretation.

Along with repetition of the Qur'an, Sha'rawi's opinions were often peppered with phrases and stories spoken in *'āmiyya*, reflecting his understanding of the purpose of revelation as God's instructions for humanity. His sermons personalized Qur'anic language and justified the spoken by demonstrating his sermons' compatibility in the context of divine speech. His expressions were popularized because of this exchange in both directions: Common "low" language expressed the divine objective, and the theological infused Egyptian dialect. This deliberate exchange was a display of his worldview. He was both marking his connection to an ultimate authority and defining his identity as belonging to the community to which he spoke, signifying different voices in each textualized site, including God, the community, the man himself and his interlocutors.

Sha'rawi's sermons were later written down in Classical Arabic, and putting them in writing distinguished them significantly from the moment they were delivered, which is also what makes the popularity of his sermons on YouTube so interesting. Even in repetition, Sha'rawi's spoken words include the language of his audience, the language of divinity, and the language of the state. Sha'rawi was hired as a language gatekeeper by a state that expected his speech to bolster a national identity. The state therefore sought to impose its agenda on religious language in the hope that this imposition would authoritatively unify meaning, which proved to be impossible. Even if the state succeeded in silencing opposing views, Sha'rawi's sermons themselves contained various voices—authoritative, personal, and otherwise—within each text.

DA'WA IN TWENTIETH-CENTURY EGYPT

The first consideration of speech in context concerns the present use of the term *da'wa* (preaching, calling, mission, or inviting or summoning one to God's way). *Da'wa* is a Qur'anic term, one that has been discussed by Muslims throughout time. After Muhammad's death, *da'wa* entered different discourses. For example, in political discourse, especially during the Abbasid era, it came to mean inviting one to accept the right of a particular religious and political leader to rule.[18] Although *da'wa* was also conceived of as an invitation to follow Muhammad's way for Muslims and non-Muslims, it was never equivalent to the Christian notion of mission. After the initial Arab conquests following Muhammad's death, Islam was often spread by Sufis who were traders and merchants and who served as "holy" guides and examples for those who wanted to accept Islam. But their work was not referred to as *da'wa*. Organized mission work did not begin among Muslims until the late nineteenth century, after Muslims came into contact with Christian missionaries.[19] Yet because Muslims had contact with Christian missionaries before this time, it seems probable that this shift in usage was because of the context in which these missionaries entered their lives—as part of the colonial presence.

Da'wa has found a novel place in Egypt today, where it has become synonymous with preaching as exhortation, "commanding the right, and forbidding the wrong"[20] for both 'ulama' and non-'ulama' *dā'iyāt/da'iyyīn* (callers or inviters). The increased dynamism and spiritualization of *da'wa* has led to the popularization of the concept and to the inclusion of good works as a major aspect of its meaning. It is also associated with national and international movements that are led by those who are not religiously trained, which is an indication that the concept has been removed from its juridical connections.[21] But in Egypt the institutionalization of these movements has not lead to a focus outside the greater Muslim community (umma). Da'wa movements in Egypt are usually focused on rectifying improper belief and practice among Egyptian Muslims. Da'wa has also become central to the call for the revival of religion in Egypt, which means that it has become part of the contemporary Egyptian Muslim identity.

Although da'wa is still thoroughly steeped in past usage, it has also taken on a decidedly contemporary modification. The fact that da'wa can come from any Egyptian perceived to be pious shifts the focus of responsibility for correcting those who are led astray from the community at large and the religious scholars to individual Muslims, a trend begun by Rashid Rida. Other, newer meanings of da'wa include social activism, mosque building, and educational practices.[22] In addition, even though the movement is based on religion, it is centered on the necessity of living correctly according to certain prescriptions or established rules, which are repeated by the dā'iya. The meaning of the term da'wa within these movements signifies an objectification of what constitutes true Islam, which in turn signifies that individuals are no longer subject to the authoritative constructions of an intermediary class.

By offering their own normative vision of what it means to be a good Muslim, Egyptian da'wa movements have developed ideological postulations of particular interpretations as a standard. The propagation of rules concerning belief and behavior depend on members adhering to a vision of normativity, which in turn is the qualification one needs to teach that vision to others. Thus it bolsters a particular notion of religious authority because it postulates that every Muslim who agrees with this ideological positioning is responsible for "commanding the right and forbidding the wrong" of others.[23]

Saba Mahmood discusses the da'wa movement in Egypt in the context of group meetings where women teach one another the right and wrong ways to behave for the sake of cultivating virtue.[24] She goes as far as to say that dā'iyāt in modern Egypt have as much authority as was previously reserved for the 'ulama' and that secular universities have been producing the most prominent *dāʿiyāt* of the last century.[25] What is perhaps more accurate is that the ʿulamaʾ have used this term in a different context to express different ideological purposes. Part of how this term became so ubiquitous in modern Egypt is through subtle contestations over meaning. Although these changes in meaning are subtle, they also mean that a lot is at stake, especially as they concern the future of religious discourse and authority.

Because the term is Qurʾanic and once had juridical import, the rules of *daʿwa* were discussed extensively, and often rhetorically, by the ʿulamaʾ.[26] At the same time the reason some ʿulamaʾ have become effective summoners is because they have adapted the language of modern *daʿwa* movements. These ʿulamaʾ are known as masters of *daʿwa*, which implies not a community of believers helping one another but an authoritative construction where the learned teach the unlearned proper methodologies. In fact the only way to get a clear idea of what separates lay *dāʿiyāt* and ʿulamaʾ preachers and media personalities like Shaʿrawi is to distinguish Shaʿrawi according to the purposes, tone, and setting of his discourse.

SHAʿRAWI AND DAʿWA

Shaʿrawi was often introduced in his television interviews and labeled on the cover of his books as *imām al-duʿā*, "the leader of those who summon to Allah." He used the term *duʿā ilā Allah* (call to God), linking summoning directly to God and reflecting his role as intermediary and popular preacher. This term has the added implication of supplication, referring to an intermediary role for the one who not only calls but can also lead individuals to God through some capacity.

In his own speech about summoning, Shaʿrawi, like many ʿulamaʾ before him, tried to regulate the use of the term in a metapragmatic way. The term *metapragmatics* concerns how language is used to correct or regulate conditions of usage. By "giving the 'essence' of the social category" metapragmatics mark the "valued versus devalued forms of language because they are in keeping with tradition of the way of the ancestors or not."[27]

Shaʿrawi was involved in such metapragmatics. When he spoke about *daʿwa* in his sermons, he defined the word *summoning* according to certain notions of ethics, and he defined who could be a summoner and why. He enforced the notion that the *dāʿiya* must be soft and gentle in his interpretation of the Qurʾanic verse 16:125:

Call to your lord's path (*ud'u ilā sabīli rabbik*) with wisdom and a goodly exhortation, and argue with them in the best manner (**bi al-ḥikmat wa al-maw'iẓat al-ḥasana wa jādilhum bi-llatī hiya aḥsan**) for, behold, your lord knows best who strays from his path and who are the rightly-guided.

[Note that here and in other quotations in this chapter, I have placed in bold the Arabic transliterated words from the Qur'anic verse that are repeated in some form in Sha'rawi's sermon.]

About this verse, Sha'rawi said:

> To be convincing the case of Islam must be built on: the magnanimity of the presentation, softness of speech, the wisdom of the exhortation (**ḥikma al-maw'iẓa**) and the best argument (**aḥsan al-jadal**). For if the case made does not convince it will at least demonstrate that the one who calls to Islam is someone who is well mannered in the way of God's method (*bi-uslūb minhaj Allah*). Indeed, it is not possible for the one who calls to Islam to succeed if he proposes that people leave what they are used to, which will make them hate Islam. The person who calls to guidance knows that calling by a hated way causes people two hardships. The first hardship comes when the people are exhausted because they must leave what they are accustomed to. The second hardship is exhausting the way (*sabīl*) [to God's method], which will lead to a harsh way of convincing through rudeness and bad manners and [displaying] a lack of wisdom in the exhortation (*al-ḥikma fī al-maw'iẓa*). The Arabs of old used to say: 'Advice is heavy so do not send it as a mountain or make it an argument. Make the advice something that is simple and clear.' If we ask 'why is advice heavy?' we must know that advice pushes the one who is being advised to leave what he loves, in which case he might find that advice a burden. The advised might only love the one who embellishes his desire; he might not want to think about his own reform. For this reason we find that the Qur'anic method (*minhaj al-Qur'an*) is one of high manners.[28]

Sha'rawi here used language to define the manners of the summoner in ethical terms when he specified that the Qur'anic statement "in the best manner" (*bi-llatī hiya aḥsan*) meant "the magnanimity of the presentation, softness of speech" in addition to the "wisdom of the exhortation (**ḥikma al-maw'iẓa**) and the best argument (**aḥsan al-jadal**)."[29] He presented this ethical way of summoning as an important part of God's method and even as a purpose of summoning. For additional support of his qualification of this part of the verse, he repeats the Qur'anic Arabic in his sermon but uses a slightly different form (*bi al-ḥikmat wa al-maw'iẓat al-ḥasan* becomes *ḥikmat al-maw'iẓa* and *jādilhum bi-llatī hiya aḥsan* becomes *aḥsan al-jadal*). Thus his speech was an explanation, but in that explanation he appropriated Qur'anic terms, a tactic that enabled him to seamlessly add ethical specification to the task of summoning.

The Qur'anic words *ilā sabīl rabbik* (to the path of your lord) became in Sha'rawi's speech *bi-uslūb minhaj Allah* (to the way of God's method), which is connected to *minhaj al-Qur'an* (the Qur'anic method) later in the sermon. The term *minhaj* as a site of authoritative contestation is discussed in depth later in this chapter, but in this setting it transferred Qur'anic terms into common Egyptian understandings. Here its connection to God's path helps define it as Sha'rawi expressed it and therefore according to how he molded its signification as *minhaj Allah* (God's way), moving *minhaj* away from any other definition.

Sha'rawi's language also positioned him as a regulator of the purposes and manner of summoning because he offered exegetical instruction to those who call others to religion. His shift of focus on behavioral specifics was carried through to the end of the part of the sermon related to this verse. But why was Sha'rawi's language focused on softness and generosity? Precisely because that was how he used his method to distinguish his discourse from other, more forceful understandings of Qur'anic language. Sha'rawi's authority rested on the notion that people have to choose their religion freely, and he maintained this position partly because he sought to disparage what he perceived as political interpretations of scripture (see chapter 5). Indirect reference was therefore made to how use of the Qur'an to enforce values different from his own were mistaken. To demonstrate the authority of his view further, Sha'rawi connected his call for softness to the practices of Muhammad, the Prophet of Islam, who is the ultimate prototype of Muslim behavior:

> The Prophet (may God's blessings and peace be upon him) received instructions from his Lord [concerning what] to say to his opponents: 'Say: You shall not be questioned about our sins and we will not be questioned about what you do' (*qul lā tus'alūna 'ammā ajramnā wa-lā nus'alu 'ammā ta'malūn*) (Qur'an 34:25). Truly [with these words] Muhammad was speaking to his adversaries (*khuṣūmih*) by saying that each human is accountable [according to] his deeds. So [the words] 'you, the opponents (*khuṣūm*), you shall not be questioned about the sins (*lā tus'alūna 'an al-ajrām*)' are related to the sins of the believers, because in the beginning the opponents of Islam looked upon the faith as a sin. However, when Muhammad wanted to describe the behavior of the opponents he spoke with the tongue of God (*al-Ḥaqq*). . . . 'We will not be questioned about what you do' (*lā nus'alu 'ammā ta'malūn*). If the words were [equally] measured in this verse the Prophet would have said . . . 'We will not be questioned about your sins' (*lā nus'alu 'ammā tajramūn*). But God taught his Prophet manners in arguing. Their crimes were not mentioned even though their crimes were against those who were confirmed

by God. In spite of that the Prophet did not confront them with their sins. Here we have an example of a proper method of argumentation. God teaches us to be lofty in arguing. We do not sting the opponent with the whip; instead we raise ourselves above the human desire to be superior. We argue with the logic of God (*manṭiq al-Ḥaqq*) in heaven. This must be the condition of the one who summons to God. This must be the way all opponents receive Islam.[30]

Sha'rawi's language solidifies a method of summoning, treating it as timelessly connected to divinely inspired prophetic behavior as rules of speech. His sermon was not an instance of calling others to faith; instead it focused on the regulation of summoning. He defined how it should be done by defining the conditions and proper use of religious language. But his instruction was also placed within a reconstruction of a Qur'anic verse. He repeated terms in different forms and filled in interpretive gaps, such as the idea that Muhammad was talking to his enemies. It was a well-demonstrated linguistic skill that made his logic tenable. The enemies of Muhammad were referred to in the Qur'an in better terms than Muhammad's community were, which is a positive value judgment. But according to Sha'rawi, these value judgments were not evidenced in the Qur'an itself. The Qur'an references the sins of believers with the words, "You shall not be questioned about our **sins** (*lā tus'alūna 'an ajrāminā*)," but did not reference the sins of the enemies of Muhammad. If the Qur'anic language had been "We will not be questioned about your **sins** (*lā nus'alu 'ammā **tajramūn***)," then a judgment would have been implied. But instead the Qur'anic statement was "about what you do" (*ta'malūn*), which is neutral. This verse has been interpreted according to this historical understanding within the tradition of Muslim exegesis for centuries. Sha'rawi insisted on it as a category of essence, as exegetes had done in the past. He monitored the use of language through effective authoritative association.[31]

But his method of linking truth to tradition was not always obvious. Here Sha'rawi was also using a gradualist approach to the historic understanding of language by pointing out that the faults of one's enemies or arguing about right and wrong or focusing on possible hardships involved with a new kind of life can stand in the way of the attempt to win the hearts of those summoned. This definition of manners seems deceptive, but because it supports not speaking the full truth until a particular result is achieved, it is a gradualist approach that reflects how Muslim scholars have thought about revelation for centuries. It is salient in the theory of how the Qur'an itself was revealed and why. As Sha'rawi said about Qur'anic verse 16:126:

"Hence, if you have to respond to an attack, respond only to the extent of the attack leveled against you; but to bear yourselves with patience is indeed far better for you, since God is with those who are patient in adversity." These divine directions were revealed to the Messenger in the context of the events that occurred during the battle of Uhud. Later on, God made it known that this verse was general and that it applied to times of peace as well as to times of war. In this way he [Muhammad] could be a guide to people as they ascended into certainty.[32]

According to this interpretation, God's speech gradually introduced the full extent of rules, abrogating earlier senses and only revealing the full extent of them once the early followers of Muhammad were ready to accept them. As with Sha'rawi's own theory concerning knowledge, this view privileges the idea that language is stable in revelatory speech as essence and also that the human endeavor to regulate how that language is understood is not; therefore, such language needs constant revision.

Gradualism, and not force or harshness, was also Sha'rawi's method of *da'wa*. He finished his lesson about manners in summoning by saying that if opponents cannot be won over, then they must be left alone to live in peace as long as they do not engage in sedition.[33] Thus he reformulated the goals of summoning according to situations that were bound to arise in late-twentieth-century Egypt.

Sha'rawi did not try to reserve the role of inviting to religion only for recognized religious authorities because the practice of *da'wa* had already been removed from its previous institutional associations. Instead he said that even those who themselves do not follow God's prescriptions can call others to God. The benefit of such a call can occur in two ways. First, if the one advised is reformed by the advice, God may make the caller also follow the advice. Second, if everyone is involved in the call, even sinners, then all tongues will be summoning to God's way and no one will be without God's blessing.

All human beings are sinners. Does your sin prevent you from summoning people to God (*al-da'wa ilā Allah*)? When you summon to God, the one you summon may heed your call. You may not, but the other person might. Maybe God will cause you to heed your own words because you have caused someone else to heed them. Once there was a man who was circling the Ka'ba and another man heard him say: 'My God, you know that I have sinned . . . but I love those who are obedient to you. May that love intercede on my behalf because of my own disobedience' . . . Ok, but what about those who do not pray? Can they summon others to God? . . . They must summon others to God . . . if all tongues call to God and all ears hear the call, then none of God's creation will be without . . . what? None will be without the blessings of God. Thus anyone can summon others to God. There is [even] a kind of summoning without speech. For example, [when] people are in the market and the call to prayer is heard 'God is great, God is great,' . . . some of the people go to pray. There may be some who do not usually pray but one time they may join those who go to the mosque. This is a type of summoning. God wants believers to [persist in] their good deeds. They must know how to behave and they must be able to convey (*yanqul*) that to others. When they convey their good deed to others, they will receive compensation.[34]

The language in this sermon is meant to instruct common believers, telling them what they can do to help spread Islam. Any human being can serve as an example, and all believers have an ethical responsibility to speak to others about the norms of ritual behavior not just because it is what God commands but also because it is part of one's duty toward others. So summoning can be done by anyone who is familiar with correct behavior. Sha'rawi here set the terms of *da'wa* by defining who could summon and by attempting to regulate the practice of summoning. He was a new type of regulating *'alim*, someone who, through popular media, was given the voice to directly set standards among the people whether they were followed or not.

Talk of love as an intercessor, which was a common theme in Sha'rawi's discourse, elucidates how, in the midst of normative teachings about summoning to God, a particular orientation was inserted. This option was not formulated in relation to duty and behavior but instead in relation to what Sha'rawi called the inner condition of the heart. These words were meant to reinforce not only a gentle orientation but a personal relationship with God, as distinct from knowledge about rules. This was Sha'rawi's moderate or moderating stance, which characterized his overall program and was meant to distinguish him from others.[35] By preaching about God's intervention, Sha'rawi merged the modern notion of *da'wa* with his own mystical and knowledge-based views.

MINHAJ: GOD'S PRESCRIBED METHOD

In this section, I will be looking less at language forms and how they are used to express different values and more at how a plurality of values can be detected in word usage. I examine in particular how different voices within a text reveal authoritative contestation through dialogue, which is enhanced when those contestations concern the definition and use of Qur'anic words. But individual words as historically situated can also be used in particular language communities in different instances to reflect heterglossia in a way less related to a text and related more closely to the social perspectives apparent in the way individuals within the group seek to define and present those words. Language is not neutral and therefore does not belong to an individual user; it contains the inclinations of others, past and present.

> As a living, socio-ideological concrete thing, as heteroglot opinion, language, for the individual consciousness, lies on the borderline between oneself and the other . . . The word in language is half someone else's. It becomes one's "own" only when the speaker populates it with his own intentions, his own accent, when he appropriates the word, adapting it to his own semantic and expressive intention. Prior to this moment of appropriation, the word does not exist in a neutral and impersonal language . . . but rather it exists in other people's mouths, in other people's contexts, serving other people's intentions.[36]

The concept of heteroglossia can help expose different layers of authoritative constructions as different voices heard in the overall discourse about the meaning of Qur'anic language. The use of the term *minhaj* by Sha'rawi presents the opportunity to begin to understand these layers.

Minhaj means "a frequently traveled path, method, or procedure," but it can also mean "a manifest, plainly apparent, or open road or way,"[37] and it is used according to all of these definitions today. When considering how Sha'rawi sought to define this term, it is important to take into account the time period in which he spoke. Sha'rawi was initially appointed by President Sadat, but not long after his appointment, an extremist offshoot of the Muslim Brotherhood, inspired by the writings of Sayyid Qutb, assassinated the president. These facts are telling for two reasons. First, in themselves they demonstrate different affiliations—Sha'rawi toward stability and the state, Qutb and those who followed him toward changing the government, even through violence. Second, Qutb was a religious authority in his own right; by the time Sha'rawi began to preach on television, Qutb's thoughts had gained influence inside and outside Egypt. As Sha'rawi gained popularity he found himself in a struggle to realign values. Both this contestation and the values represented by different parties can be evaluated through the use of the term *minhaj*, which has many meanings and is therefore variable in regard to its denotation. This variability is a result of the different ways the term was used in the past, which allowed Qutb and Sha'rawi to insert their respective positions more easily into their elaborations on the meaning of the term. In

Sha'rawi's case he often spoke about *minhaj Allah*, presenting the term as eternal, even while contested.

Minhaj has its roots in the Qur'an, but its importance as a term is closely connected to the processes of modernization, especially in Egypt. The word entered the discourse of twentieth-century Egyptian 'ulama' initially through Rashid Rida and his teacher Muhammad 'Abduh. It came to even greater prominence through its use by Sayyid Qutb to signify a complete and objective system for living life, one comparable to other ideological or political systems, a definition that is a direct result of the "objectification" of religion in modern Egypt.[38]

Sayyid Qutb was born in 1906 in the Egyptian village of Musha. He came to prominence as a leader of the Muslim Brotherhood in the 1950s, a role that continued until his death in 1966. In 1954, he was imprisoned for the first time by the Egyptian government and tortured. Later he was allowed to write while in prison, where he wrote his manifesto of political Islam, *Milestones* (*ma'ālim fi al-tarīqa*). The influence of Qutb's thought was extensive, and *Milestones* proved to be the most influential book in the development of radical Islamist ideology. Although Qutb was in the highest branch of the Muslim Brotherhood during his lifetime, the organization distanced itself from his political thought after his execution by hanging in 1966.

Qutb's ideas about *minhaj* help mark his ideological bent toward presenting Islam as a system, one that could and must be instituted in any Muslim society. For Qutb, God's method was the system of Islam:

> *Jāhiliyya* [ignorance leading to unbelief] . . . desires to turn Muslims away from the work of establishing a divinely ordained way of life by ensuring that they do not move beyond the stage of belief to the stage of movement . . . in which the details of the Islamic system develop through practical striving . . . This method (*minhaj*) [of movement] is the source of power for this religion . . . and the method of the revival of Islam is equally important; there is no difference between them . . . Other methods work for the establishment of manmade systems, but are incapable of establishing our system. Thus it is as necessary to follow this particular method for the establishment of Islam as it is to obey the way of life it outlines and to believe in its articles of faith. 'Indeed, this Qur'an leads to a way which is straight' (Qur'an 17:9).[39]

Before I discuss the term *minhaj* specifically I want point out some of the other differences in language use between Sha'rawi and Qutb. Qutb spoke against theological postulations that were formulated by the religious scholars, and instead focused on how belief in the one God and following the laws of

Islam are all that is needed. Sha'rawi's program of renewal for the general population was formulated through theological postulations. Freedom of movement for Qutb referred to the movement of the group toward a goal, that of establishing an Islamic society. For Sha'rawi, freedom of movement was what God gave humanity as a relational gift: Human beings were free to follow or reject God's method, which God gave as a gift to humanity. (Of course this explanation itself depends on theological postulations; see chapter 4.) Qutb also did not ground his argument in Qur'anic language but in the ideas of the Qur'an as he presented them. He used the Qur'an as justification for his definition of *minhaj* inserting a small excerpt at the end of the quote.

The above quote expresses *minhaj* as the system of Islam, which is the establishment of belief and then action, or group movement. Islam is also presented as a system among systems (here in contrast to *jāhiliyya*) embedded in the Qur'an in reference to the first years of Muhammad's mission. For Qutb, it was a complete system for all times, one that could be easily repeated if obstacles were removed. Qutb presented history as a static consideration; for him, reform meant instituting a timeless model. This model could easily be applied in any historical situation, as witnessed by the fact that he said that Islam and Islamic reform were accomplished by the same system. The system also gives religion power.

For Qutb, divine authority was referenced by the Qur'an, which also defined how that authority functioned in the perfect society once belief was established.[40] But Qutb's idea of the divine rested on his notion of *minhaj* as a "divinely ordained science through which society can be constructed."[41] He uses the concept of the systemization of religion to insist that it is necessary for Muslims to act.[42] If the purpose of life is to live according to Islam's system, then one must, like Muhammad, be actively engaged in making sure that that system is instituted.

Qutb's concept of God's system was ideological because it mixed religious and secular (philosophical and political) knowledge to produce something concrete that could then be applied to different situations. This metapragmatic moderating of language concerning the meaning and use of the terms *minhaj* and *Islam* presented Islam as a system that does not fully exist until it is realized in social action.[43] Thus the system of Islam must be followed as a complete system or else society becomes *kāfir* and not truly Islamic.[44]

Qutb's language exposed a particular definition of a living Islam, which was limited to following a system. He also formulated a definition of Muslim identity, separating those who followed that system from those who didn't and removing the second group from the community of believers. The dependence on human intellectual and worldly activity places a sociopolitical burden on individual Muslims in terms of their sense of belonging in distinction to those who are considered unbelieving and a straightforward solution to rectifying the problem of unbelief. Qutb's ideas have thus been the inspiration for many types of reform-oriented activity among Muslims in the late twentieth and early twenty-first centuries, including violent activity.

At the same time, Qutb's words very clearly include the voice of an authoritative 'ulama' discourse (theological) only to show how it was unnecessary and even misleading because it was not part of the system of Islam. Like Sha'rawi, he sought authority by regulating the meaning of important terms like *Islam* and *minhaj*. Even though they used the same words and insisted on a timeless sense of those words according to their own definitions, their definitions varied and even referenced the flaws of other definitions because they sought to use their authority for very different purposes.

In his sermons, Sha'rawi always emphasized that living life according to Islam meant following the precepts of God's way (*minhaj Allah*), which assumed belief and was not focused on action, especially not on social action, as an end unto itself or as a tool to create a perfect society. Sha'rawi stated:

> God's method (*minhaj Allah*), assigned the positive command "do" in order for creation to prosper . . . and "don't do" so that creation would not be corrupted.[45]

Here the term *minhaj* inextricably links human behavior to all of creation (not to society or politics but to a metalevel of existence) as a definition of God's method. Sha'rawi's system does not offer solutions to real societal problems. The idea that what can be humanly achieved by following positive and negative commands is to bring about a general notion of prosperity would otherwise not differ much from the idea of following a system to institute social change. It is the quietist assertion that theological purposes are gradually exposed and not fully revealed in a specific time or text or action that distinguished Sha'rawi from someone like Qutb.

For this reason, Sha'rawi did not teach that human beings needed to enact God's method in order for God to stay in control of society. Although Sha'rawi related human action to God's system, he was clear in his Ash'ari orientation: God's will was not dependent on the actions of human beings. Sha'rawi also reversed Qutb's idea that God's system becomes effective first on a societal level and then on an individual level (except for the select few who are responsible for instituting that system). Sha'rawi insisted that religion was an individual choice and that only when each individual chose to follow God's system could society, and by extension the entire universe, become perfected:

> When we praise God we express many feelings that together form love (*ḥubb*), gratitude (*shukr*), remembrance (*dhikr*), and recognition of God, all of which fill the soul . . . They come from the soul but remain in the heart, which overflows from the senses to the entire universe . . . Thus praise of God is not merely uttered by the tongue it goes through the mind . . . to settle in the heart.[46]

This sermon connects worship to human emotion, and proper orientation in worship to the benefit of the universe. It also centers worship in the individual heart, which sees action as a first step and perfection of the individual as the goal. Through language, Sha'rawi was rejecting the notion that group action toward any outcome in society is the ultimate goal. Reacting to extremist views, he warned about the danger of focusing on political outcomes instead of on perfecting the individual.[47] Thus the voices of others of his society were included in his language, subtly and indirectly. Because he lived in a particular context, that context found its way into his sermons and not always as agreement but often as contestation.

SHA'RAWI, LANGUAGE, POWER, AND THE STATE

The heteroglossic view of language can also be extended to the television text. Television is a medium that includes many voices as viewers enter into a dialogue with the television text in order to create meaning. According to Bakhtin, in any act of language creation and delivery, speakers always anticipate "an actively responsive understanding." They do not think that their speech will be transported exactly, as is, to the mind of someone else. Instead they expect "response, agreement, sympathy, objection, execution, and so forth."[48]

In the television text, this expectation of active response is also present because television depends on popularity for its success. What creates popularity is the presence of many voices, which counteract the attempt to put forth a uniform message in order to eliminate contradiction.

> Heteroglossia, polysemy, and contradictions are interconnected concepts for they are all ways in which social differences and inequalities are represented textually. As society consists of a structured system of different, unequal, and often con-

flicting groups, so its popular texts will exhibit a similar structured multiplicity of voices and meanings often in conflict with each other. It is the heteroglossia of television that allows its texts to engage in dialogic relationships with its viewers . . . Language, and that includes television, cannot be a one-way medium.[49]

Sha'rawi maintained his influence by embracing the opportunity that the Egyptian government gave him to become a television spokesperson. He represented a particular view of religion for the sake of the nation, but in turn his television appearances greatly increased his popularity with the people. As a television star, government employee, and 'alim, his texts were, by nature, heteroglossic. The state sought to control religious discourse by bringing Sha'rawi under its control, but Sha'rawi used television to attempt to dominate the conversation about religious authority. Both attempts to control were present in Sha'rawi's television appearances. Sha'rawi had to anticipate "response, agreement, sympathy, objection, execution, and so forth"[50] in regard to his viewers, whom he knew were diverse in their religious orientations.

Some Egyptians saw the dual vocation of national preacher and religious guide as a strength, but others did not. Sha'rawi was often criticized for putting forth a vision of Islam that helped the state's project of forming citizens instead of deflecting these attempts and offering an alternative, as other, less official preachers have done.[51] A closer look at his discourse reveals, however, that the assumed gap between official and counterpublics[52] postulates its own sense of stability and binary contestation, even though language always includes many voices within a single instance. Contestation is not only extra-textual; it is apparent in the text itself. The full implications of the interplay of culturally devised language and how it is saturated with distinct ideologies that can disrupt similar forms, yields information about the importance of language, in this case, religious language, in demonstrating diversity of thought in any given society.

Here I examine one event in context by considering the people involved, the goals of speech, and the mode of speech delivery (in this case, the semiotics of television watching) to demonstrate the heteroglossic nature of one of Sha'rawi's televised appearances. After a failed assassination attempt in Addis Ababa in 1995, former Egyptian president Husni Mubarak and his government orchestrated an event meant to celebrate Mubarak's safe return to Egypt; it included speeches made to Mubarak by the most popular religious leaders of the day, including Sha'rawi. The event was broadcast on national television and until today remains one of the most popular YouTube videos of Sha'rawi, attracting millions of views.

In the broadcast of the event, one can see Sha'rawi standing on stage beside Mubarak as well as other 'ulama' and then-leader of the Coptic Christian community, Baba Shenouda. The scene was carefully orchestrated as a display of religious authority in an attempt to bestow sanctification on Mubarak, whose life was in danger because he was perceived as an ungodly ruler. It was also meant to signify a sense of national unity regardless of religious affiliation, predicated on a positive identification with Mubarak.

When it came time for Sha'rawi to address the president, he stood close and said directly to Mubarak:

> Mr. President, I have reached the end of my life. I am [ready] to receive my death as appointed by God. I do not want to end my life in hypocrisy (*nifāq*). Instead I will say a brief word from my entire nation. Our government is [comprised of] parties and oppositions and men and [ordinary] people, all of whom, I am afraid to say, are inactive (*salbī*). I want them to know that dominion (*al-mulk*) is in the hands of God. He gives it to whomever he wills. The people cannot conspire to attain it, and it cannot be achieved (*wuṣūl*) by deception.
>
> God, blessed and most high, narrates (in the Qur'an) a dialogue between Abraham and Nimrod[53] and during this conversation, what did Nimrod say to Abraham? He disputed with Abraham over their differences concerning God [saying]: If dominion comes from God and I am an unbeliever (*kāfir*), then (why) did God give me dominion? Abraham said: 'He gives dominion to whomever he wills.' No one can conspire against God to receive possessions. No one can conspire against God to rule. No one will ever rule in the dominion of God unless God desires (*murād*) it. If the ruler is just, surely he will benefit (himself and the people) with his justice. If he is unfair—unjust—he spreads injustice and makes it repulsive in the souls of all the people. They hate all unjust people even those who are not the ruler himself. Therefore I say to the people. . . . We, praise God, assure ourselves of the truthfulness of God's words [when he speaks] about what results from misdeeds (*aḥdāth*).
>
> How shall we interpret it when God says: "They plotted (*yamkurūn*) and God plotted" (Qur'an 3:54)? And how shall we interpret "They conspire against God and we conspire against them" (Qur'an 86:15)? God wants to prove his self-sufficiency to his creatures. I advise anyone whose inheritance it is to be a ruler, not to pursue it (rule), it must pursue him. For as the Prophet said: "Whoever is pursued by something, he will be supported by God. Whoever pursues a thing, will not be able to manage what he pursued."
>
> Oh Mr. President, the last thing I would like to say to you, as this might be our last meeting: if you are our destiny, then may God lead you to the right path. If we are your destiny, then may God help you bear your burden.[54]

At one point in the speech (right before he said "Oh Mr. President"), Sha'rawi put his hand on Mubarak's shoulder. When Sha'rawi was finished speaking, he turned away from Mubarak and then lost his balance and almost fainted. Clearly the event was emotionally charged.

Sha'rawi used references to the Qur'an for specific purposes in this speech; he wanted to maintain his authority as a religious leader, expert in the Qur'an, and representative of his exegetical tradition. His speech again reflects the famous phrase "chaos is worse than tyranny" as a demonstration of his own values. He sought to reinforce a particular identity not in contrast to but in conversation with the government. In one sense, his speech reinforced the government's visual significations, speaking to and for his community, and he discouraged direct action against the government. At the same time, demonstrating a different perspective, he specifically removed religious sanctification from Mubarak's rule by comparing him to Nimrod and implying that Mubarak conspired against God.

Sha'rawi, as usual, spoke most directly in his sermons to those who accepted his theological premises that God is actively in control of human life and that human understanding and action, removed from a proper understanding of God's system, was potentially harmful. But he was also aware of his critics. For many, using the Qur'an to remove religious legitimacy by comparing Mubarak to Nimrod was not enough. But the language of Sha'rawi's text even addresses those people. Certain parts of the speech referenced the views of both the action-oriented religious authorities, like the followers of Qutb, and the government because Sha'rawi often said that both views were comprised of "human thought against other human thought." In Sha'rawi's terms, neither accepted that, although they plot, God plots, and while they conspire, God conspires, and therefore human action is always secondary to God's plans. It would not have brought agreement from his critics, but it is clear that Sha'rawi's expected their contestation. Sha'rawi was trying to impose his own stability in his speech through the different voices he represented. Even if he had fully supported the government's purposes in his speech, he could not have done away with contradiction in his language because of that multiplicity of voices: the people who shared his view of the nation, his followers, his critics, the government, and those who sought to kill the president (of course, there would have been some overlap between these groups), by which I mean his audiences.

If his speech is analyzed by comparing it to similar speeches or seeing it as representative of only one of the many voices included therein, variance will be read as stable singular intent. Instead Sha'rawi signified open contestation even while trying to remove contradiction. Precisely because the speech included different types of viewers and thus allowed them to enter into "a conversation" with his perspective, it has remained one of the most popular clips of Sha'rawi currently available on YouTube. It surged in popularity after the overthrow of Mubarak, demonstrating heteroglossic possibility through time. It is also the one event people in Egypt referred to most when I told them I was writing about Sha'rawi. Some of those people insisted that in his speech Sha'rawi spoke truth to power. Those people were usually his followers and they often eagerly showed me the YouTube video of this event on their cell phones and computers. Others insisted that Sha'rawi was obviously capitulating to Mubarak because of his quietist stance. Still others admired his use of language and subtly of exhortation. After 2012 it came to be read as a prediction of the overthrow of Mubarak and of Sha'rawi as a kind of national visionary.

Viewing stability in language as intent in usage hides how language can be used by those who share elements of discourse, or similar ways of speaking, but do not necessarily share values. Sha'rawi's popularity as a television preacher was not important merely because of his relationship to the leaders of Egypt; instead language helped him reshape public discourse and gain autonomy through the state[55] in order to attempt to transform institutions according to his own values. In his language delivered as television text, Sha'rawi found a way to influence directly how Egyptian Muslims practice and think about the meaning of religion in their lives.

CONCLUSION

I have treated Sha'rawi's theological language as the primary context, and the communities that received his words, and the conversations he was involved in, as secondary, which has helped demonstrate how multiple voices help disrupt stability. Terms that have come down through traditions of interpretation from the Qur'an to the present day are crucial to fully understanding the ideological content and import of language use. But even Qur'anic terms need to be constantly defined and redefined; they are authoritative symbols that allow speakers to position their perspectives linguistically. This view allows for distinctions to be made through the connection of form and meaning, as similarities and differences. It is a perspective that aids the understanding of

Sha'rawi as an individual speaker within various speech communities, including those seeking the right to interpret the Qur'an and those seeking to control the politics of Egypt.

Different voices, heteroglossia, within a text can represent different authoritative structures, which makes space for input as readers and spectators work within possibilities. Heteroglossia can occur in a singular event, or text, or in a body of repeated language when the desire to control key terms or to orient a community toward a certain goal is recorded. These struggles can be categorized metapragmatically as a struggle to establish one indexical expression over another through comments or rules concerning language use. Contestations and authoritative competition can become more pronounced over time as different communities experience the same text or references as part of varying contexts, which means further transformation through usage and understanding. More transformation or variation can lead to greater significations. With the heteroglossic nature of the television text, I also introduced the notion of the choice of the receiver as present in the text and the idea that television depends on the presence of many voices to ensure its popularity. The idea that viewers are present in the television text, and therefore that they have greater control over the meaning that those texts signify, leads to the following question: How much can receivers of television texts actually do with those texts?

CHAPTER 8

Television and the Extension of Authority

INTRODUCTION

Every Friday afternoon from 1980 until shortly before his death in 1998, Shaykh Muhammad Mitwalli Sha'rawi interpreted the Qur'an on state run television for millions of Egyptians. His show—Light upon Light (*Nur 'ala nur*)—was simple and did not vary much in content. In each broadcast Sha'rawi sat in the front of a mosque in a chair, wearing his signature white hat, with his live audience on the floor in front of him. He always began his sermons with a typical opening for a Muslim religious authority. For example: "In the name of God, the merciful, the compassionate. All praise belongs to God, lord of the universe. And peace and blessings on the most noble messenger and seal of the prophets, and the mercy of God be on the Prophet Muhammad and on all of his family and companions." After the opening he would say: "And now . . ." and then he would read verses from the Qur'an and begin to explain them according to his thoughts (*khawāṭir*). Sha'rawi made very distinctive gestures during his sermons. He would move his hands, make different facial expressions and often sway his body back and forth. He also spoke directly to his live audience—leaning his whole body in their direction. That audience, comprised of Egyptian men of various ages, sat side-by-side, listening with rapt attention. Although his television audience saw him in the mosque, usually near the *minbar* (the preacher's pulpit), delivering sermons comprised of sacred words, Sha'rawi never spoke directly into the television cameras. While his gaze remained on his live audience, Sha'rawi was also often filmed with microphones in front of him, signifying that each sermon was also a television event.

Sha'rawi's televised sermons involved mixed configurations of time. They captured the initial community ritual of listening to a sermon on Friday afternoon in the mosque but were then transmitted to the television viewer, which created a new secondary moment that remained linked to the first. The secondary television event opened the possibility for viewers to participate not just in how they received messages but also in how they integrated what they saw. Sha'rawi's sermons were received as a new practice that highlighted a reciprocal type of alteration in which viewers were no longer tied to the original space and time of delivery. Instead they now participated in a ritual that was both separate from the ordinary and embedded in its environment. Television texts are easily absorbed into the everyday because viewers simultaneously negotiate between sanctioned codes (elements of an authoritative past, language cues, or a television structure), and visual and auditory codes (present, sensory reality). Thus, during the secondary reception of Sha'rawi's Friday sermons, viewers, within their own worlds, helped create an event that came to them already formed.[1] Furthermore, because television engages the senses, audiences become involved in creating sensory meaning, but always within their own social reality and historical moments.[2]

Sha'rawi's television appearances did more than transmit language that reacted to social change, reaffirmed Sunni beliefs, defended theological and epistemological positions, or even made difficult postulations easy to understand. As a religious scholar in twentieth-century Egypt, Sha'rawi acquired a fluctuating yet resilient type of authority through television, from his ability to perform in speech and movement to his visual charm, to the reach his performances had, and to how his viewers participated in creating the phenomenon of Sha'rawi. He became a television text, one that reached people through affect, which in the case of media is how technology is transmitted—it "enters the human subject foremost through the human body."[3] Viewers connect to television through bodily affects as "the embodied perceptual present."[4] Besides his words, those who followed Sha'rawi knew him as what they saw and heard of him as a televised presence. The combination of characteristics that gave Sha'rawi his edge relied on how his presence encountered viewers and how those viewers encountered him as "swells of intensities that pass between bodies . . . able to reciprocate or co-participate."[5] As such televised religion changes the working of authority by influencing the reception of attempts at discursive dominance, and by changing the definition of success, both of which make religious speech secondary to the way television as a medium, engages viewers.

MEDIA AND RELIGIOUS AUTHORITY

As a charismatic preacher able to inspire awe in his audiences Sha'rawi resembled popular preachers before the advent of mass media,[6] although in many ways his authority was anything but rigidly tied to the past. Televising religious content at ritually significant moments is one example of how, thanks to media, messages were dispersed through new modes of delivery to multiple sites of reception. Because new media can include many voices in public discussion (also referred to by the much-debated term *public sphere*), this dispersion has been seen as helping discourse and therefore authority proliferate and democratize.[7] New media-centered publics are also said to be responsible for ushering modernity into many societies[8] because they challenge state and entrenched religious authorities.[9] Yet this picture of authority continues long debunked theories about how society can progress, or even change, only if the forces of firmly established religion are dislodged. In this vein the contemporary binding of Islam, media, and authority has been presented by terms like *fragmentation, the marketplace of religious ideas,* and even *blurred boundaries,* which are used to focus on what authorities like Sha'rawi have lost and what other, oppositional players now possess and exercise very effectively. As a result much work on media and religious authority in the Muslim majority world has been focused on how those who are not credentialed religious scholars have used media to contest centralized authority.[10] Yet Sha'rawi's career and influence prove that the opposite is also true: Through media, Sha'rawi—who in fact was an old, provincial, Azhari-trained government shaykh—claimed his authority, and it was through media that the public substantiated and furthered it. The phenomenon of Sha'rawi can therefore be explained by focusing less on discovering the gains and losses of particular groups and more on overall media effects. Equally important is examining how media introduced enactment and other non-knowledge-based perceptions to the overall picture of legitimated authority. Public interaction with televised performances is reciprocal and includes the interchange between actor and viewer, utterances and viewer, and also between what screens project and the environment into which they project it.

When considering the history of Muslim preachers and the diversity they brought to notions of authority throughout that history, it is inaccurate to say that media is responsible for introducing fragmentation and dissention into public discussions concerning religion and society (see chapter 3). What mass media, coupled with changes in political structures and education, did was to make religious messages more readily available and accessible, which expanded the field of contenders and the level of discontentment expressed. This mixing caused a shift in which characteristics and forces, recognized and unrecognized, became determinative, thereby transforming the relationship between those giving religious instruction, no matter who they were, and those receiving it. As the acknowledged qualities of authority were transformed by the contemporary context, certain qualities became preferred, enhanced, combined, lived, performed, and—in the case of media—transmitted to and received by the public.

Because of the concern for appeal, televised religious programs, like all television programs, make viewers partially responsible for content. Call-in shows are obvious examples of religious content becoming viewer-driven content,[11] but the television text is influenced by viewers in more subtle ways. It is opened to indecision because it contains "fissures and excesses," which allow multiple readings.[12] Television's polysemic nature, its multiple signs, are not completely open to every type of reading, however; there still exists a power struggle of sorts between the encoding of messages and the openness of television programs to signal various content-based meanings related to the identity of individual viewers.[13] The entire system of give and take survives and thrives as a system in which the power of writers, producers, censors, and in some cases performers limits viewer choice in deriving sense from content. Religious actors seeking legitimation through the embodied reception of their television appearances are therefore offered an opportunity for dominance both in how they attempt to limit possibilities and in how viewer choice within those limits can affirm their unique qualifications.

Sha'rawi's television career therefore offers the opportunity to rethink the notion that religious authority is always noncoercive. In Sha'rawi's case, his authority was tied to institutions that impacted how he was able to convince people of his authority.[14] Sha'rawi was connected to the government of Egypt and to al-Azhar, and both helped strengthen his prestige among the people through television. He used television to normalize his theological opinions, which represented a particular strain of thought at al-Azhar, and his role as spokesman, advocate, and defender of that institution was an important part of his discourse. Furthermore, nationalized, government controlled television fortified Sha'rawi's standing among Egyptians, as millions of them watched his show week after week. The Egyptian Radio and Television Union (ERTU), which broadcast Sha'rawi, was controlled by the state who used Sha'rawi as part of their program to present a reified view of Islam in order to create ideal citizens.[15] Sadat broadcast Sha'rawi in the hopes that his definition of Islam would counter the rise of Islamist rhetoric, which increasingly concerned him as president.[16]

Although states and other interested parties sponsor and partially control the content of religious messages, individuals do react differently to those messages. Viewers interpret and appropriate words and images in particular ways and according to their own situations because shared television reception is also an individualized experience.[17] In terms of Egyptian government programming, there was no guarantee that the push for uniformity in transmitted messages would be effective once received by viewers.[18] Part of the concern of those who control state media is how to communicate a particular vision and also how to engage viewers, which results in the transmission of mixed desires, competing voices, and diverse content, although even that possible variation is still limited in range in reception.

Yet television, like other media, gives viewers opportunities to create meaning not primarily from what is said or from any other figuration that is meant to engage listeners consciously, but from what television transfers as content that is seen and heard. Sha'rawi's legacy as a televised religious guide was based primarily on elements of appeal and expectation, or seeing and feeling, that were enhanced through television as a visual medium. It was through *feeling* that the limits set in place by producers and actors were ruptured. By removing enclosed language to a novel space in which senses and emotions are engaged prior to and not always in concert with language, television becomes more than a self-enclosed system.

TELEVISION STRUCTURES

Not everyone who writes about media effects agrees that viewers can create meaning, even through sensory interaction. According to Pierre Bourdieu, for example, television exemplifies the workings of "symbolic violence," in which both producers and viewers are complicit, "in so far as both remain unconscious of submitting or wielding to it."[19] Symbolic violence is therefore hidden—people are complicit precisely because they are not aware of it. For Bourdieu, symbolic violence also diverts attention from the fact that television is beholden to market forces. In order to achieve this diversion television texts offer content that is generally agreed on—programs that call attention to what interests everyone, and shocks no one; and at the same monopolizes people's thoughts.[20] Images aid monopolization of thought because they produce a "reality effect," making people believe what they see.[21] Since television messages augmented by the visual affirm what is already accepted, the people who appear on television can dominate when they make content easy through their visual or auditory appeal.[22] Thus, for Bourdieu, television texts can not cause a "symbolic revolution ... affect[ing] ... mental structures [to] change the way we see and think."[23]

Although in the last quote Bourdieu denies that television can cause a symbolic revolution, that is precisely what it does in the realm of religion. Televised religious programs influence how people see and think about religion. Sha'rawi dominated the field of religious programming in his time, but as a trained religious scholar he was also made and remade *by* television precisely because it is geared towards market forces, nationalist sentiment and visual and auditory appeal. Successful television programs are guided by concerns and processes that were not of primary importance to the workings of religion up until Sha'rawi's time.

Bourdieu's ideas about television and symbolic violence can therefore be adjusted to fit the example of Sha'rawi's religious broadcasts. He did seek viewer compliance with his perspective because the arena of religious authority had been increasingly diversified during his time and this once dominant view no longer guaranteed complicity. To say that his program operated merely at the level of subconscious compliance would be to simplify a very complex society and the changes in religious authority that were taking place at the time, partially because of media.

Additionally, religious programming geared towards viewer expectations introduced something novel, as audiences influenced discourse and other content in ways they could not have in the past. Sha'rawi did gain a following, but he did so through appeal, through his personal charisma, and through the attachment many felt towards him as a result of viewing him on television. Even if Bourdieu's notion of symbolic violence and television was applicable in Sha'rawi's case, once television production became the primary focus of religious programming, the complicit elements of religious discourse were remade through media presentations. Although television may monopolize what people think, the "reality effect" of the visual image does not always confirm what is being said. By stating that television monopolizes thought

Bourdieu implied that viewers' ideas are easily confirmed, but another way to understand it is to say that viewers are engaged through their senses, before, as a replacement for, and sometimes in spite of their thoughts. It is in *this* sense that television does not "record reality" but "creates reality"[24] in reception as much as production.

Televised religious content influences how people receive religion through affect. Viewers often imbibe content through their senses only to reconstitute it. Faith based programs change how people *see* and thereafter how they *feel* about religion. Newness comes in the form of viewer interaction with the sights and sounds of television, and this engagement with the senses can help create visual piety. The visual transmission of piety entails what adherents see and the images they experience, which help shape the practices, concepts and institutions associated with visuality.[25] But visual practices also influence presenters—how they use the visual and thus how they come into contact with audiences.

Many viewers came to see Sha'rawi as a saint because the transmission of his piety came through his image. While this was not an unprecedented means of designating someone a saint, because television highlighted the visual experience of viewers, it helped them determine meaning through praxis; the practice of continual visual engagement.[26] Television helped viewers focus on Sha'rawi's charismatic tendencies, which is how they came to read his person, including the creation of him as a saintly character. Imbuing him with saintly qualities was only secondarily connected to the linguistic content of his sermons. He did not affirm any controversial Sufi ideas, such as the power of saintly intercession, on his television show, yet that was the very power his ardent followers came to believe he had. Popular media as religious broadcasting was an important site that helped create new sensibilities in the contemporary world.[27]

AFFECT, TELEVISION AND PIETY

Pictures of Muhammad Mitwalli Sha'rawi can still be seen in many places throughout Cairo. Sometimes his image is displayed to entice customers into stores, but other times it is hung for personal reasons. In fact people often told me that they kept his picture close by because the visual image of Sha'rawi brought them blessings (*barakāt*).[28] This idea both goes against the discomfort many Egyptian Muslims feel towards displaying human images that are imbued with religious significance and seems a natural outcome of the increased visual presence of a preacher who became embedded in people's every day lives through television. The visual engagement with Sha'rawi during his life has had both intended and unintended effects after his death. The unintended effects have done more than create his posthumous legacy; they have also highlighted and enhanced certain attachments and practices, as viewers helped recreate a sense of Sha'rawi's piety and capacity through their visual engagement with him.[29]

On television, Sha'rawi was on display, which connected him to the esoteric elements of charisma beyond the ineffable draw of the charismatic. Some members of his audience saw him as someone who had an intimate relationship to God, which was a circular enforcement, beginning and ending in the everyday impressions of people that, by the nature of their being presupposed, exerted their influence on how Sha'rawi was presented, how he performed, what he said, and how he acted. But television also offered release from these circulating presuppositions because it was an intervening force of affect.

Sha'rawi's sermons were television performances, but he performed by engaging in dramatic renderings and by delivering his speech. Performativity today signifies two distinctive notions: that of speech or discourse ("ontologically dislinked from the world or introversively non-referential") and that of theatricality.[30] Television viewers receive both types of performances—language that is introversive and theatrics that are extroversive—but the two can sometimes be disjointed, moving in different directions.[31] In the first case, Sha'rawi did use speech to enforce very particular religious norms for very particular reasons, as linguistic meaning. But he also engaged in dramatic renderings directed at his audiences[32] through a novel medium that displayed his visual appeal. His performances were transmissions of typical even normative religious speech into unfamiliar contexts; they were living instances of language that, even when trying to "regulate" and "form" bodies, were innovatively mediated. According to Judith Butler: "Indeed, the efforts of performative discourse exceed and confound the authorizing contexts from which they emerge."[33] In other words, speech (re)uttered or (re)performed in a context other than that in which it originates can shift and take on different meanings (as "excess"), allowing it to break through conventional social norms and convey the unintended.[34] In the above quote, Butler means performance as discourse, but I will apply this idea to Sha'rawi's television performances as extraverted theater and not to his discourse. In this case the changed context included how audiences saw and heard all the elements of the television text simultaneously—Sha'rawi's voice and character, and also everyday noises, sights and smells, the screen on which he was portrayed, and the room where that screen was located. This sensory combination disrupted aspects of religious belief and practice, the very discourse that Sha'rawi put forth, and yet structured the lives of those who watched him. It created a reciprocal engagement between speaker (watched) and spoken to (watcher), an affect that arose between acting and being acted upon.[35]

> Affect . . . is found in those intensities that pass from body to body (human, non-human, part-body and otherwise), in those resonances that circulate about, between and sometimes stick to bodies and worlds, *and* in the very passages and variations between these intensities and resonances themselves.[36]

The passing of forces that are "other than conscious knowing"[37] between humans and between human and non-human bodies is an apt description of the world of the television environment. Viewers are engaged through their senses; acts of reception are imprints of hearing and seeing coming from and through the screen, which sometimes stick. Bodies that view television are bodies as "activities" and not as "substances" because within their environments they perform actions.[38] "One's bodily sense is formed in and through one's interaction with the world" because it cannot be formed through language. But it is precisely this formation through interaction that one's affect, or body as action, becomes "informative, powerful and helpful."[39] This is a definition of bodies as "transactional" or as "patterned activities that come to have complex and multiple meanings."[40] Understanding bodies as *transactional* also means understanding that communication is "a transactional circle in which all parties involved in a situation jointly constitute its meaning."[41] Because all are active in the world of the environment prior to engaging bodily meaning, that meaning can be imprinted differently on different bodies and thus cannot be considered homogeneous; it is instead complex and variable.

Physically unconscious bodily responses, or affect, can be transferred from one body to another without recourse to language or content as something called affective resonance.[42] Media can also transmit *affective resonances* by transmitting the source of the message, which can be received unconsciously and can be embodied before the message because, like music, it "moves people" before they move themselves.[43] Media are means of communication that, like music, determine meaning not always as consciously appropriated. But this unconscious appropriation is not completely undetermined. The "ideo-affective posture," as a loose organization of emotions, is "the result of the systematic differences in the socialization of effects."[44] In other words, certain resonances stick to certain people because they have already been socialized to certain ideological postures, which then come forth in affect when they are influenced by the transmission of bodily stances and residues.[45] Affect is not ideology imprinted on the body and it is not transferred visually as a means of passing on ideology; it is merely bodily response or intensification that occurs outside and prior to thinking. But this is not unthinking as an automatic response within a larger system; it is an individualized response on and through the body. Ideological formation is also possible. When it is separately formed, it can interact with bodily imprints by becoming entwined by further separating from those imprints.

Sha'rawi was turned into a saint when his resonance stuck, or when his bodily portrayals became transactional through television. As he was transmitted through media, individual viewers' reactions came originally as unthinking bodily imprints through intensities, but they did not guarantee stickiness. Sha'rawi's popular performances as affective communication involved different parties constituting meaning through interaction with each other and with the environment (or as part of it). Television, for its part, popularized religious norms while transmitting Sha'rawi's performances into a new context.

Transactional bodies have also been presented as bodies that "signify an affect, praxis and imaginative landscape informed by a relationship to the necessarily unseen, invisible and unrepresentable—a transcendent God."[46] According to this account, television watchers can feel what an actor is feeling and go where an actor goes; they see inward dispositions made outward and experience feelings, which for them become proof of the authenticity of what they witness on their screens.[47] While it is helpful to understand how affect and media help inculcate a sense of transcendence, this description makes emotion the primary site of affect. Yet bodies do not always mean what actors or anyone else intends, especially on television, because bodily acts are acts in motion. Affects are not feelings precisely because "an affect is a non-conscious experience of intensity; it is a moment of unformed and unstructured potential . . . it cannot be fully realized in language . . . because . . . it is always prior to and/or outside of consciousness."[48] The devotion many felt for Sha'rawi was an active response to seeing the projection of a living body, images, and performances of movements and sounds that, together with their own acts, helped his audiences create meaning. Although that meaning was later felt as piousness or later resulted in seeing the unseen, those feelings and perceptions were aftereffects. Affect gives our feelings intensity; for example, when we are injured, we would not actually feel pain without our bodily responses. Once we feel pain, we are also perceiving those responses. Our feelings and perceptions in turn aid the process of "rational decision-making."[49] Affect was transmitted bodily between Sha'rawi and his viewers and gave intensity to the feelings and perceptions people had when they saw his picture as aftereffects. These aftereffects in turn gave rise to new "rational" practices. Signification, like feeling, is secondary; affective bodies are bodies that act; they are not bodies as substance. One sees a closed system, the other possibilities because the primary site of affect is through exchange not signification.

Media does not exclude one from being pious, and being pious does not necessarily exclude media. A new kind of piety is made possible precisely because there is no one-way cause and effect, only moments of "unstructured potential," which are made possible by the simultaneity of sensing all at once. Through the act of seeing, bodies are formed and re-forming; the new context of television is mingled with bodies, which influences how meaning is imprinted, and how media becomes the site of intensities. The act of seeing can result in objects becoming "forces of intensity." These forces can be transmitted through television as a "form of communication where facial expressions, respiration, tone of voice, and posture are perceptible."[50] In the television environment, feeling piety takes shape in a new space.

The practices that arose based on the way Sha'rawi's projected piety resonated with and stuck to certain bodies were models of "new effectivities,"[51] or the creation of new bodily meanings that organized the *"lived-ness of life."*[52] This "lived-ness of life" allowed practices, movements, and interactions to be expressed,[53] which in Sha'rawi's case included watching him deliver the Friday sermon on television, telling stories of his *karāmat* (miracles), celebrating a *mawlid* at his grave site, and seeing the unseen in his likeness. As a new site for normalizing Sunni language, televised language stood outside and secondary to the bodily appropriation of the person of Sha'rawi.

SHA'RAWI, AFFECT, AND PIETY

I now want to use affect theory to try to understand how the practice of hanging Sha'rawi's image in order to receive blessings from his presence came about as an activity focused on the speaker and not on the spoken. This analysis means separating that practice from other forces that contributed to Sha'rawi's television success: namely, television production, the Egyptian government, and more specifically Sha'rawi's own attempts at ideological linguistic dominance. The last is interesting because the practice of visual *barakāt* seems to have arisen despite his language use; it was given primary impetus as a combination of seeing and being disposed to the resonances of his pietistic displays.

First, I will argue that television created the space for practices that were not new, but were enhanced and became more common among the public. It captured visual images, but the objects of those images were removed from their living context, which allowed practiced meaning as excess to arise when viewed.[54] But that practice did not arise because the image was imposing a structured meaning, as authoritative language does; instead, it arose through a transfer of intensities between bodies, one affecting, exuding externally to the other who affected, actively resonated with that image. "Sensory flow" can unconsciously envelop the body and add intensity to it, and the recollection of such intensity, although it is also not conscious, can be stored in the body.[55] In television, affective resonance flowed between the viewer and Sha'rawi, as the source of the spoken word, a resonance that, when it stuck, intensified the experience of the viewer. Thus television was the site of new types of interchanges that opened and closed possibilities for both action and language content.

The practice of hanging Sha'rawi's picture was not an expected outcome of his media celebrity, nor would he have encouraged it. By connecting the viewing (or presence) of the image of a perceived saint to special blessings, Sha'rawi's followers ascribed powers to him. Television enabled the intensification of the visual experience of his projected charisma, which then bypassed the normative rejection of using the human image as a sacred object. Many Muslim religious leaders have recognized the power of the image to portray actions as real and as contagious, which is why hanging certain pictures has been rejected by them, even if it has not always been rejected in practice. Sha'rawi's audiences viewed his image as a meaning, and because response mimics what it is responding to, that sensing "amplified awareness" of Sha'rawi's own projection, resulting in the linking of capacity with his image based on that mimicry.[56]

As I have discussed throughout this book, Sha'rawi's authority as an 'alim preacher was not limited to the exoteric realms associated with knowledge. He did impart an affirmation of his piety and the veracity of his knowledge visually, and many of his followers accepted that he had knowledge and that he received special gifts from God. Yet Sha'rawi's closeness to God could not be proven or signified primarily by his actions. It didn't need to be. People either accepted elements of his teachings that relied on the claim that he received special gifts bestowed on him by God, or they didn't. By this, I do not mean to imply some notion of faith, but that acceptance happened in a moment that cannot be pinned down, as a flow that occurred somewhere in the domain in which viewers witnessed Sha'rawi's externalizing affect visually.

Even the idea of *karāmāt* incorporates ideas about the saint's behavior, but is not visible through it. Behavior may be a signifier of miracles, but believing in them must originate in reciprocal action transferred through affects and between them. In the case of Sha'rawi's image, this interaction happened when the visible became unseen, outer movements were seen and then imitated in affect, and finally given meaning as inner states. The visible was primary; the unseen seen was formulated after the meeting of eye and image. When his visible affectations stuck, they gave intensity to feelings about him. This led to the perception of the visible unseen as part of the aftereffect of seeing, which led to the notion that Sha'rawi's image contained blessings; both perception and notion were possibilities made manifest.

But outside this circle, or perhaps prior to it, the affected body encountered the affecting body that projected closeness to God through affect. Many Muslim mystics have written about how the signs of one's life, including piety and sincerity, are visible on the face. But these signs are not limited to a person's past; the fate of people, what will eventually unfold in their lives but is unseen until that time, can also be read on their foreheads.[57] The visible is the primary mode for encountering the invisible; through encounter and suspension of thought, the image of the forehead sticks to one who can then perceive it as unseen. In the same way, *karāmāt* is understood as a gift for one's faithfulness and dedication to God that works through the body. But it is meant to remain a secret between God and the friend of God. *Secret* in this instance means not speaking, not explaining in words, but miracles are still

witnessed. *Karāmāt* can't help but be visibly witnessed or, in the case of heal-
ing, transferred to those who see it or feel its physical effects. Thus visuality
is an essential aspect of witnessing, which is about transference and aftereffect, not knowledge. According to this understanding, seeing images creates
new dispositions built on or removed from the old.

Viewing therefore can power the feeling of piousness, but the viewing of
the human image has not been normatively accepted in Islamic tradition precisely because of the recognition of the power of acts of seeing to lead to a
religiosity that should not *be*. While depicting the human form was never
widely practiced in Islam, the discomfort seems to have come from two particular concerns. First, human beings should not attempt to create what God
has already created, usurping God's sole creative power; second, it is possible
that people might turn images into idols. In either case, the spiritual is believed to exceed and emanate not from the material but as an aftereffect of
seeing the material. (How can human beings possibly create what God has created? How can idols possibly have efficacy?) To treat an image as if it has
power is cautioned against because of the risk of turning someone's likeness
into a type of divinity where "presence and blessing are indistinguishable."[58]

Yet somehow the visual aspects of television have not been widely condemned by the 'ulama' (although there are some exceptions). Part of the reason Sha'rawi did not oppose television as a method for delivering his sermons
was because he saw it as a way of getting religious information to people. He
began broadcasting on television once it had already become a normal part of
the everyday life of Egyptians; he argued that, as long as people were careful
about what they watched, television was not forbidden. He was not concerned
with the portrayal of the human image on the screen but with the linguistic
content of the broadcast as a whole. He did not anticipate what could happen in the moments when people see without thinking about the meaning of
discourse.

In the same vein, some 'ulama' today have argued that the creation of the
photograph, and by extension, the television image, is not the same as using
the human hand to depict the human form, which can be seen as imitating
God's act of creation. The famous television personality Yusuf Qaradawi's
opinions about television watching are well known because he is an expert in
Islamic law (mufti). Qaradawi has stated that a photograph is unlike a painting
or other drawn representation of a person because it represents what is actually present. Thus taking a picture with a camera does not create something

that is not actually there, that is, something only God can create.[59] Even though a photograph is still a depiction of, or still causes God's creation to appear on paper, Qaradawi does not voice his concern about idolatry until he speaks about uses of the photo. For Qaradawi, as for Sha'rawi, photos and television used for the right purpose should not be prohibited; thus it is proper use of the filmed image that becomes the paramount consideration. When considering the question of representation, Qaradawi seems concerned only with the creation of the photo and not with the fact that, once the photo is created, it is as susceptible to the same aftereffects of seeing as is a painting. In other words Qaradawi is unconcerned with what happens outside formed creed as meaning, but outside or besides is precisely where the deviation he worries about actually begins to take shape.

Qaradawi is not completely blind to the power of pictures to prompt action. He believes that images that depict human involvement in a particular activity are imbued with more than a visual presence; they also represent deeds and actions visually, which in a sense spill out of the frame. For example, Qaradawi clearly states that polytheistic rituals are prohibited from being visually depicted because they are depictions of reprehensible acts. Thus he assumes that photos are more than images frozen in time; in such a case the image is dangerous because it can, through affect, lead to the act one sees in it. Hanging a picture of a polytheistic ritual in the home can bring that reprehensible act into the home if the image of something absent becomes present as a result of the image being seen. According to Qaradawi, the image is therefore extended through time and has effective moral repercussions. The concern about how photography and television are used goes against more than mere discomfort with possible idolatry; it extends the understanding of what is prohibited to the object depicted, as if can be made to exist outside of the picture but through the picture, because it becomes effective through viewing.

Even though 'ulama' like Qaradawi assume that images of certain objects should not be represented, that does not mean they think that the ineffable should never be viewed in an image. The written word of the Qur'an is assumed to contain a certain power, not just as book or word but also as calligraphic image. The words of the Qur'an are for Muslims the words of God, and each one of God's words has particular significance and power. As Sha'rawi said, no sound or letter in the Qur'an is unintended because each is imbued with its divine origin. Hence the propensity to mistrust images (or the "attitude" against creating human forms[60]) did not mean that Muslims rejected the potential power of the visual; once written, Qur'anic words were considered by some to contain *barakāt*,[61] which flowed from the page to the world. Calligraphic writing of the Qur'an, according to this view, is infused with the divine and serves as a means for the divine to enter the life of the viewer because it is the visible embodiment of the divine word. Access to the blessings of the calligraphic Qur'anic word is passed from page to sight and, as an aftereffect, can be felt to bestow blessings. It can eventuate in sensing the divine presence in the image, allowing the viewer access to that presence through sight.[62] This means that, when one sees the unseen on the page and then touches the page, something physical can be intensely felt or perceived as an effective consequence.

The inclination to distrust images that can be used for the wrong purpose is thus counterbalanced with the acceptance of the visual representation of God's speech, and these competing (although not contradictory) elements have a counterpart in the world of the televised sermon. Sha'rawi did not foresee the potential receptive effects of transmitting the words of God and their exoteric and esoteric interpretations simultaneously with his visual presence. Because the 'ulama' could not stop its dissemination, television watching was infrequently constrained by religious opinion in Egypt. Thus in justifying television, the argument Sha'rawi made resembled the justification for the use of the visual image of God's words, but as oral content—it could bring one closer to God. Yet like the Qur'anic image, once intensity is passed to the receiver, that intensity can turn the one pictured into an assumed means for directly accessing God, and that assumption is mediated by the feelings that arise after reciprocation. The notion of the visual enabling access to the friend of God combined with constant visual engagement viewers had with Sha'rawi gave rise to the practice of keeping Sha'rawi's image close by so that, by touching it and seeing it, one could receive blessings. This practice reflected both agreement with the notion that one can receive blessings by seeing, touching, and reciting the Qur'an, and disagreement with the notion of attributing the same power to a human image. Television's acceptance as a site for forming affects bridged the gap between the two.

When watching a sermon on television, absent preachers are visually transferred by being captured on film and then transmitted into present time. As a consequence, some have said that preachers like Sha'rawi represent a type of transcendence.[63] But *transcendence* is a misleading term because it ignores the body. The visual, when incorporated with the notion of absence strong enough to appear, is anything but transcendent. Television enables reciprocal relationships between pious preachers and watchers who see them and feel them, and in this sense it resembles the connection an individual may have with a living saint. Mystical devotion is often later described as that which cannot be explained in words because, as a bodily experience, it is passed on and then felt often without or besides consciousness.

CONCLUSION

Television may seem disconnected from the description of how *barakāt* can be seen in images and then felt as new meaning in the world. The description of television as giving viewers the opportunity to become part of a "collective potential open to anyone"[64] is more commonly accepted. This idea posits that television extends the meaning of the message as it "transform(s) ideas of publicness, of religious affiliation and authority, as recitation and commentary move from face-to-face to the mediated event."[65] From this description, focused as it is on meaning as content, it hardly seems possible that televised religious figures can touch viewers. Television may have the power to transform the significance of the sacred image and of religious authority, but according to this view, it does so as connected to public notions of authority. Yet according to my description of religious programming, transformation takes place not in conscious, democratic choice. Religious programming also does not result in the kind of unthinking that makes people accept without question what they are given through television. The contact between religion and media does illustrate a different side of authority, however, seen as a fluid conception that is secondarily moved among and between interacting figures, with the key being the presence of a new context, which can give rise to original formations of authority and ideas about sanctity. In a preconscious interaction in a secondary location, authority turns into an interplay, one that is preceded by an exchange not primarily of thoughts but of affected and affective intermediated by television. Pushing this even further, it is the presence of "effectivity" or the power to affect that makes any site of interaction possibly a site of contestation. This effectivity enables and transforms, and today it occurs as part of popular media. Feelings and eventually thoughts and words can later signify or ignore, in concert or against those primary interstices.

In my office, I have a photo of a reed mat being sold in one of the outdoor markets in Cairo. The mat, which stands about six feet tall, is hung in a small stall among other mats and reed baskets used by people all over Egypt. On the mat is a very colorful, airbrushed painting of Sha'rawi. He is pictured sitting cross-legged on a cushion wearing his white cap, looking down at what is presumed to be the Qur'an. Minarets and a pink sunset are pictured behind him. He is depicted on the mat as a knowledgeable preacher of the people whose proper behavior included his humility and his detachment from worldly goods. I don't know if the person who made the mat believed that Sha'rawi's image was extraordinary, but he or she reproduced Sha'rawi's own projected image of himself as a pious man of God.

The mat also signifies many of the elements I have discussed in this chapter, for example, the loosening of past standards of visual piety coupled with an increased attachment to the person of Sha'rawi. But the mat depicts more than Sha'rawi; it depicts the interaction of forces that function without words. It also speaks to the popularity of Sha'rawi's image, which has become a commodity, one that is airbrushed onto a common household item. Through the mat, the power of the human image was being sold.

Sha'rawi offered a particular state-approved version of religion, but by presenting himself as a television text to be received in domestic space, neither he—nor the government—understood how outcomes would be partially determined not by what was said but by moments of transferences among or even prior to words. Sha'rawi relied on sensory cues and displays of emotionality to capture the attention and devotion of his audiences, and because of the involvement of the senses of hearing and seeing, television audiences became active bodily participants. Visual cues can display standards of proper religious actions that, when engaged as such by viewers according to their expectations, elicit unthinking but embodied responses. Sha'rawi consciously displayed a visual model of piety as a cue that he embodied his own message, which was important to him in his quest for religious authority. For those who engaged Sha'rawi and whose socialized effective postures made it likely that they would read piousness into his image, it was only a short step to turning interaction with his televised personality into interaction with what it projected—proximity to God. In this case, affect was bodily movement through reception but also a means of becoming, of intensifying feelings and taking them into the world. The perfect example of this is how the public made Sha'rawi a saint whose visual image was believed to bestow blessings. The concept of Sha'rawi's saintliness was devised through retellings of his life posthumously, but during his life television already set this possibility in motion by involving the nonlinguistic in the construction of his abilities as *barakāt*. Even the signs of the saints as told in sacred biographies concern their bodily contact with the divine or from the divine to others. Through the visual reception of his image, viewers were able to see those bodily signs and take them in a less well-established, somewhat unprecedented direction.

Because of media attachment to the person of Sha'rawi, the unconscious appropriation of him, he was later read as a pious friend of God and was brought ever closer to his audiences until he was intermingled with them through sight and sound in the everyday. The imprint or affect, which became meaning and came through media, then increased the participation of viewers later, when this imprint of visual piety became the practice of viewing Sha'rawi's picture to receive *barakāt*. Even though Sha'rawi's television appearances were meant to be a controlling religious symbol, as bodies meeting bodies in a popular medium, his appearances helped the formation of devotion that his followers felt toward him when watching.

Preaching Islamic Renewal: Religious Authority and Media in Contemporary Egypt has focused on the implications and lasting influences of Sha'rawi's life in order to help explain the workings of religious authority in twentieth-century Egypt. In a period when the boundaries of authority were rapidly shifting, Sha'rawi's talk about renewal, theology, epistemology, and even esotericism helped keep Azhari traditions of discourse viable. Television made Sha'rawi the phenomenon that he was and continues to be, but as such it reflects the changing nature of the criteria used to judge religious authority in Egypt because it depends on and affirms qualities not previously considered essential. Sha'rawi defended his Sufi-Ash'ari perspective, which he saw as representing Egyptian Islam, but proclaiming his perspective on public media distinguished him from his competitors and helped him gain a following of millions. While television furthered Sha'rawi's goal of asserting his discursive dominance, it also rewarded anyone, including Sha'rawi, who could attract a large audience, ultimately expanding the sites and workings of authority by making it more porous and relying further on its flexibility.

Sha'rawi's importance did not result from his rethinking or rejection of classic Sunni positions in light of contemporary ideas, as an intellectual. The supposition that only this sort of ingenuity can be truly innovative assumes that breaking free from tradition is the most viable stance. What made Sha'rawi innovative in his time was his reinvigoration of linguistic methods of exegesis through popularization. By preaching on television, he helped blur the lines between official presentations of religion, whether Azhari or governmental, and what regular folk practiced. What is most surprising from an academic perspective, although not from the perspective of the many who followed and continue to follow Sha'rawi, is the effectiveness of his media discourse. Sha'rawi used the exact methods and assumptions considered by different groups to be relics of the past or to be backward, or even mistaken, and he did so through new media. Through his affirmation that God controls the universe (a stance that brought him criticism from politicians, secularists, and Salafis), his struggle to maintain the primacy of 'ulama' methods, and even his simplification of mystical concepts, Sha'rawi attempted to set the boundaries of religious talk in his nation.

Sha'rawi reinvigorated the "Sunni-Shari'a-Sufi synthesis"[1] by bringing it to the present and making it digestible and important to his large following. Popularization of what was once part of specialized discourse was in keeping with the changes taking place in his society since the late nineteenth century. Tasks once relegated to those with high levels of training in the religious sciences, such as making independent judgments by returning to the Qur'an and hadith (*ijtihād*), were now claimed by many who disregarded the very methods that defined those tasks in the past. As a preacher who received his degree in Arabic language studies, Sha'rawi also would not have been considered capable of performing *ijtihād* according to juridical standards. Instead, his rejuvenation of religion meant converting theology, epistemology, and esotericism into unspecialized language or, as his disciples explained it, it meant speaking on different levels for people with different capabilities. He repeated the opinions of some of the most influential religious scholars of the past while also distancing himself from that past. Thus he was relevant as someone who used speech and modes of delivery to take advantage of both the fluidity of discourse and the unique history of modern Egypt.

How was a man who grounded all notions of truth in a well-worn Qur'anic worldview, who used Qur'anic language in his speech to signal his superior status, and who believed in the intercession of saints able to become so effective in a nation comprised of many who were trying to move away from those very elements? It was not, as some of his critics claimed, because he appealed to the "lowest common denominator" or because he reinforced backwardness and superstition as a way of rejecting progress. In fact, what made Sha'rawi relevant was how he used his skill with language to define what was acceptable in the present as something that affirmed the beliefs he was committed to. He read present contingents in terms of what was, for him, not the past but the eternal present. When he sought to affirm this belief in contradiction to scientific principles, his ideas were not always able to pass scrutiny. This made him all the more infuriating to his critics, especially when he disagreed with things like organ transplantation. But, once Sha'rawi had become famous, even when he disagreed with official positions, those working for the government still sought to sway Sha'rawi to their side if they needed him politically; it was never a simple matter of rejecting a stagnant past in order to realize a brighter future. Instead Sha'rawi reinforced a different worldview that identified threats as false and fleeting because they contradicted a particular reading of the revelation. When this reading showed that religious leaders should not be politicians, and the other way around, Sha'rawi's thought seemed dynamic. When it showed that human beings could not have evolved from monkeys, it seemed out of date and regressive. What was true for him was what was part of God's ever-unfolding, living system of human meaning as he interpreted it from the Qur'an. But this stance also sometimes made him blind to how he added to injustices in his society.

Sha'rawi's authority was gained through different realms—exoteric expertise, esoteric insight, charismatic presence, and apposite speech—and those realms were signified through different aspects of his public persona. To elicit the authoritative backing of the people in his particular time and place, Sha'rawi had to be more than a scholar. He had to signify through his connection to and ability with God's words something of his status, giving a particular meaning to the idea that language can exert power. He also had to navigate the political situation by carefully cultivating his persona during his lifetime (a task that was taken up by his family and disciples after his death) as conforming to the notion that piety can preserve in the face of political power, which accorded him an air of righteousness. But ultimately Sha'rawi's voice became ubiquitous throughout Egyptian society because he innovated the Friday sermon (khutba), making it a nationally televised weekly event. All of these subtle accommodations demonstrate that Sha'rawi worked through the educational and political shifts of his time, even those that threatened his authority. In fact, he accepted some elements, like media, that in turn influenced religious authority in ways that he did not foresee. The increased insertion of media into religious ritual means that authority now relies more on adherent opinion, which was not important to most of the learned elite of the past.

I have presented authority as interactive and blended among many factors: the field of actors, shifts in the everyday, the past, and media, to name a few.

Yet as an agreement among various and overlapping subgroups in a society, religious authority is not determined by any singular external tool. I also showed that what is usually said about authority, and authority and media in contemporary Muslim societies, is not always helpful or accurate. Many writing about contestation and change, for example, often give precedence to disruptive forces instead of recognizing how synchronic and diachronic qualities—stability and change in and through time—are blended. In the historical practice of preaching, public and private were always blurred, and authority was divided among distinct and dissenting voices. Therefore media is not responsible for introducing variation into public discussions concerning religion and society. Instead media, politics, and educational change disrupted the agreed-upon qualities of authority and how those qualities were lived, which amplified dissention. Authority by this account is dependent on application, and can manifest differently among individuals or groups within populations. Even though the shared linguistic descriptions of authority that define legitimation may seem solid, in practice authority is anything but stable. In contemporary Egypt this instability was exacerbated by historic events. Throughout this book, I looked at authority and its diversity on multiple levels within Egyptian society instead of discussing newness in isolation, which is not always the best way to understand complexity.

Sha'rawi's authority was enabled when it was accepted and assimilated by practitioners. He brought the texts to life by moving through time, but he also moved between how meaning is presented as stable through language and how it is destabilized in individual reception. Authority also depends on the movement of meaning because intermediaries like Sha'rawi present a rendering of what is eternal in conversation with circumstances, both societal and individual. To be an intermediary between the people and the words of God is to play a specific role through a particular vocation. Authority figures can become texts, which is especially evident in Sha'rawi's case because he relied on his charisma and visual appearance. He centralized and popularized the sermon, but also himself. The reading of him, the meaning with which viewers imbued his presence, helps explain his overall influence, or more accurately the overall influence of media on religion and authority. Sometimes the substantiation of authority through reception affirms authority in unanticipated ways, as was the case with the influence of affect on Sha'rawi's legacy.

By tracing the institution of 'ulama' preaching, one can argue that the autonomy that preachers enjoyed in the past because of their direct access to the people translated, in the modern era, into strength in a time of threat. Many Egyptian 'ulama' have been able to take advantage of this vocation in order to maintain an influence among the people. Preacher independence and noninstitutional influence also fit well with the changes brought by new technologies, new forms of government, and new competition among authoritative contenders. Preaching, specifically as *da'wa*, is successfully practiced by many actors, which has increased competition for the 'ulama', but has also meant that preachers remain at the forefront of public talk about religion. Thus it has become a way for 'ulama' preachers to compete successfully but also to reclaim some of what they lost when their institutions and functions were taken over by the Egyptian state. Public competition meant adaptation, which in turn meant that some aspects of the preacher past were sacrificed in order to ensure continued relevance. For example, in the past, the Friday sermon was delivered in the mosque and usually by those officially appointed by the state. Sha'rawi's televised preaching was always aired on Friday afternoon, so it took the significance of the Friday sermon from its sacred place in the mosque and situated it primarily in the home. It did not replace the mosque sermon; instead, Sha'rawi created a new type of ritual, one that depended on a continuous, inviolable practice but also now made available to individuals in a different time and space.

Although the content of Sha'rawi's sermons were based on his textualist orientation, that textualism inhered flexibility, which was apparent in his use of technology but also in his theory of renewal. Sha'rawi did not have a literalist understanding of the meaning of *tajdīd*; for him renewal did not mean bypassing the literary traditions of 'ulama' exegesis in order to return directly to a seemingly unmediated reading of the revelation. Instead, he used *tajdīd* as a way to mark his special type of authority. Although there is no doubt that renewal has been folded into the more general discourse of reform in the modern era, *tajdīd* as Sha'rawi understood it was the responsibility of credentialed scholars. Sha'rawi's version was not the same as discourses of reform that call for erasing generations of secondary literature built by the 'ulama' and the methods they used to compose them. This difference helps distinguish Sha'rawi's textualism from that of the Salafis and many Islamists. At the same time, Sha'rawi's *tajdīd* maintained notions of theology and divine justice but applied them within the context of the nation-state. He did not see reform as political; he opposed the idea that, in order for renewal to take place among the people, society had to be governed by a particular method. This stance also distinguished him from the Islamists of his time.

Although for Sha'rawi, as for others seeking religious authority in modern Egypt, the Qur'an as God's speech was eternally giving and relevant, he did not understand that perpetuity as extending to human interpretations of the Qur'an. For him *tajdīd* meant that what one generation or individual interpreted from the Qur'an could be contested. He believed that, as new historical and political situations and knowledge arose they needed to be vetted through the Qur'an, and therefore past and even present interpretations were not always relevant and correct. Still he confirmed 'ulama' methods of exegesis, especially linguistic methods, for accepting differences of opinion, reaffirming past opinions, and updating the message of the revelation. When Sha'rawi did find fault with interpretations or understandings of the texts, he always assigned blame to the human mind and never to the revelation. The concept of the deficits of human thought helped differentiate his ideas from that of rationalists and also helped him build his knowledge hierarchy. Sha'rawi's knowledge hierarchy relied on the understanding of knowledge as both hidden (*al-ghayb*) and disclosed (*al-shahāda*), an understanding long salient in Islamic epistemology. But he explained those divisions in his sermons in order to defend against threats posed to revelatory truth by scientific and political thought, and to defend his Sufi beliefs from those Salafis, and others, who attacked his positions.

Sha'rawi posited that divine knowledge was the pinnacle of knowledge and that it encompassed both what was disclosed and what was hidden. Disclosed knowledge was comprised of what God allowed human beings to know by releasing it from the divine mind (because all things were with God before they were created). Hidden knowledge was what remains hidden until God allows it to be known. Some hidden knowledge remains hidden to some but not to others (i.e., because of time and space); some remains hidden with God until the end of times. This last category is what Sha'rawi called the absolute unseen. Some aspects of the absolute unseen are revealed to a chosen few (prophets and the friends of God), but they remain in the realm of God, which is where they are encountered. Through an explanation of both exoteric and esoteric knowledge, Sha'rawi posited that God is in control of all knowledge, even human knowledge.

Sha'rawi said that even scientific discoveries are not the result of the human intellect alone. God first discloses something and only then can it be discovered. But it was only the exegetical mediator, someone versed in the religious sciences, who could vet discoveries through the revelation in order to discern the truth or falsity of rational claims. This meant that Sha'rawi did not engage scientific knowledge on its own terms—through its own methods of proof—which resulted in him making less than convincing arguments against science that contradicted the Qur'an.

At the pinnacle of Sha'rawi's knowledge hierarchy was God's knowledge, which controls everything and depends on nothing. Next is the knowledge of religious experts, which depends on the interpretation of God's knowledge as it is revealed. At the bottom of the hierarchy is rational knowledge, which depends both on God's knowledge and the knowledge of religious experts for verification. But the language Sha'rawi used to expound his knowledge hierarchy assumed the correctness of his own interpretations based on very particular theological and epistemological grounds that often made his arguments tautological. This tautology was necessary because he was consistently in a defensive position, defending what he believed was true in the face of real threats to the ascendancy of that truth. He was not concerned about logical inconsistencies, but with using language to try to keep traditional concepts concerning God, the universe, and the revelation dominant by bridging the gap between those sometimes very difficult concepts and the everyday lives of practitioners. He did so through the use of traditional preacher methods like repetition, metaphor, and the use of stories, but his use of technology also made his messages accessible by making them part of everyday, sensing life. Sha'rawi also used methods particular to Muslim preachers and exegetes, methods like explaining the revelation through intratextual interpretation and in terms of the historical occasions of revelation (asbāb al-nuzūl). Most of all, Sha'rawi relied heavily on his skill with the Arabic language.

In modern Egypt, Sha'rawi's interpretation of the Qur'an helped reinforce his particular worldview by signifying a connection between his speech and the divine origins of what he interpreted. But Sha'rawi's reuse of epistemological, theological, revelatory, and esoteric words and concepts to express his perspective also demonstrates their instability. Although similar words and phrases can be understood by people living centuries apart, they become viable through understanding, which is determined by context. While notions of God's control of the universe may maintain traces of the past, especially if texts and interpretations are shared in different eras, the situation and ideologies of users (producers and receivers) help determine meaning. This is partially because the conversations in which those ideas are embedded always differ. Religious language is both shared with the past and unique in the present. It must be both; otherwise such language would neither come forth nor be understood. In a similar manner, shared language can signify both similarity and distinction in time because the speech of individuals must include the voices of those with whom they share conversations. It is precisely a word's inability to exist as "neutral and impersonal" but instead "in other people's mouths, in other people's contexts, serving other people's intentions"[2] that makes it understandable and therefore usable both diachronically and synchronically.

The importance of religious talk in modern Egyptian politics further exemplifies the connection between language and context. Sha'rawi was not the only religious scholar in Egypt in the twentieth century to understand that his responsibility included concern for his nation. Although he thought that the 'ulama' should remain independent from direct political activity, he sought to maintain the right of the 'ulama' to subject human thought to divine thought. Sha'rawi did not devise new political systems; he used and was used by the government because both he and the government wanted his brand of Islam to dominate over his competitors. Sha'rawi wanted the credentialed religious scholars to have the authority to legitimize or delegitimize other authoritative claimants. Even though the role of the 'ulama' as regulators of Islamic society had been lost to them in Egypt, Sha'rawi sought to reassert some aspects of that responsibility within the bounds currently available to him.

The Egyptian government recognized that Sha'rawi had the ability to bestow or remove its religious legitimacy; that was why President Sadat hired him as a national television preacher and why Mubarak grew weary of his influence once Sha'rawi had gained enough fame to oppose him. At this stage Sha'rawi also revisited decisions he made early in his career, before his popularity gave him autonomy. But even when he was able to, Sha'rawi rarely criticized the government. When it came to politics Sha'rawi's idea that properly trained religious scholars were the only ones capable of knowing the truth contradicted his idea that those same scholars should never make direct political statements. His critics saw these stances as quietist capitulations to political power. But the agreement between the government and Sha'rawi was mutually beneficial. It represented the reciprocal dependency that developed between al-Azhar and the Egyptian government in late-twentieth-century Egypt.

Sha'rawi never spoke about re-creating the caliphate or a worldwide umma because he was thoroughly a nationalist. He sought to institute his ideals within the Egyptian nation. His view of the nation was yet another example of his Azhari perspective. The 'ulama' of modern Egypt took part in nationalist revolts—in 1919 they protested the British presence in Egypt and demanded a nationalist government. Sha'rawi, like many Egyptians in the 1930s and 1940s, also flirted with different political alternatives. He settled on the view of an inclusive nation, but he also decided that he would not involve himself directly in politics or in trying to force political change. Thus, he did not join the Muslim Brotherhood, as some of his 'ulama' contemporaries did. Instead he tried to be a guide for political leaders while remaining separate from politics, which was in reality an impossibility.

By the end of Sha'rawi's life, lines were clearly drawn in Egypt between pro- and anti-government groups. These lines are still visible in Egypt today, although those groups and the government itself have changed. Even after the 2011 overthrow of Husni Mubarak by popular revolution and the 2013 military ousting of the first freely elected president of Egypt, Muhammad Morsi (who was also a member of the Muslim Brotherhood), the idea that one is either for the nation of Egypt or against it remains prevalent.

While visiting Egypt in the summer of 2013, I heard nationalist rhetoric everywhere. On June 28, 2013, two days before planned demonstrations against Muhammad Morsi and five days before the Egyptian military ousted him from power, the Christian television station al-Hayat ran a clip of one of Sha'rawi's sermons, the one that I discussed in chapter 5. Part of what Sha'rawi said was:

> Egypt is a protected land. The Prophet said that [Egypt's] people will be unified until the Day of Judgment . . . the formulation (tahfeen) of [Islamic] knowledge occurred at Egypt's noble al-Azhar. Egypt will always remain. In spite of the vengeful, or the envious, or the exploiters and exploited; [in spite of any] opponents of Islam, inside and outside of Egypt.[3]

Why were these statements of Sha'rawi played at that moment in the summer of 2013? Because it was a moment in Egyptian history when nationalist rhetoric was being used by those who wanted to overthrow Morsi and define true Egyptians as those who seek the good of all Egyptians. In contrast they asserted that traitors, like members of the Muslim Brotherhood, could be identified because they were only interested in benefiting people, inside and outside Egypt, who were affiliated with their own group. The Muslim Brotherhood were identified as those who defined belonging not based on the nation, but on a particular religio-political point of view. Sha'rawi's sermon was therefore used to imply that the Muslim Brotherhood were the hypocrites he was referring to and that their associates were the paid enemies of Islam. It also equated the Muslim Brotherhood with the harshest Islamists, those who advocated for violent overthrow of the Egyptian government. Those who disliked Muhammad Morsi and his government were using Sha'rawi's popularity as a religious authority among the Egyptian masses for legitimacy. It is also interesting that, even during the brief period when Morsi was in power in Egypt (June 2012–June 2013), Sha'rawi's sermons were replayed on national radio and again on Friday afternoon on television.

The use of Sha'rawi's words to support various, sometimes even opposing, political positions points to the fact that his legacy is also very much technological. Technology has allowed those in power to select particular excerpts of his speeches and repeat them to the nation as often as they want. But the appropriation of Sha'rawi's words by opposing political groups also means that Sha'rawi's speech contains a kind of indeterminacy, and technology helps further that variance. Sha'rawi's televised sermons were therefore not a direct transmission of ideas from him to users and receivers. Instead the reception of his sermons ultimately molded their long-term significance. His viewers affirmed, and continue to affirm, his importance, and anyone who uses his television recordings can take advantage of that continued affirmation.

Sha'rawi probably did not anticipate the full extent to which television would change religious transmission and reception. Because television is neither neutral in the way it depends on nonreligious actors and messages nor in the way it is received, it does amend the way believers relate to the structures of religion as a whole. Religious teachings received through televised broadcasts leave the question of religion's role in the public and private lives of individuals in flux. Sha'rawi's use of media therefore changed the nature of the religious text for the future. Today on cable television many young non-'ulama' preachers have become media superstars by preaching about and exemplifying what it means to be young and pious in the twenty-first century. They teach lessons from the Qur'an and rely on many of the same elements that Sha'rawi did, most especially charisma, but also relatability and perceived piety, to help listeners assimilate the message. Historical circumstances dictated that the 'ulama' share their claims to religious authority with non-'ulama' actors, but television neutralized that claim even further through its modes of transmission.

For example, *wasatiyya* (moderation) was an important part of Sha'rawi's message of renewal, and his emphasis on moderation was necessitated by the plethora of extreme messages available at the end of the twentieth century. Today new preachers also preach about *wasatiyya*; they have borrowed the role of preaching, the medium of television, and the message itself in order to gain authority. So while the new preachers, many of whom "found God" later in life, are easily distinguished from the "bearded" 'ulama', they represent a continuation of the change that preachers and presenters instituted through their use of media, changes that were necessitated by the political reality in twentieth-century Egypt.[4] The new preachers are men and women of their time, and they have changed, and will change, religious discourse in their own way.[5] This change is the continual change of tradition in which the temporality of discursive influence overlaps with past and future elements. Sha'rawi relied on the past to transform or maintain elements of 'ulama' authority in his time (exoteric and esoteric knowledge), and some of what he carried forward (perceived piety, television, and personal charisma) underwent further alteration in the future.

NOTES

INTRODUCTION

1. Charles Kurzman, *Modernist Islam, 1840–1940 : A Sourcebook* (Oxford: Oxford University Press, 2002), 4–6. Kurzman sees modernism, based on Albert Hourani, *Arabic Thought in the Liberal Age, 1798–1939* (London: Oxford University Press, 1962), as ending in 1940 and then combining with other Islamic discourses in the later twentieth century to become a subset of liberal Islam, which he defines as a "calling upon the past in the name of modernity." For the purposes of this book, I will consider modernist Islam and liberal Islam as the same.

2. Roxanne Leslie Euben, *Enemy in the Mirror: Islamic Fundamentalism and the Limits of Modern Rationalism* (Princeton, NJ: Princeton University Press, 1999), 16–19.

3. Euben, *Enemy in the Mirror*, 16–19.

4. Muhammad Mitwalli Sha'rawi, *Al-Fadhila wa-l-Radila* (Cairo: Al-Akbar Al-Yawm, 2000), 53–54.

5. This claim was countered by Tim Winter, who said that Sha'rawi could not have espoused Wahhabi ideology because Wahhabi ideology directly opposed Sha'rawi's mystical leanings. See Tim Winter, "Obituary: Sheikh Mohamed Sha'rawi," *The Independent* (London), 23 June 1998.

6. Kate Zebiri, *Mahmud Shaltut and Islamic Modernism* (Oxford: Clarendon Press, 1993), 182. Zebiri quotes from Hava Lazarus-Yafeh, "Muhammad Mutawalli Al-Sha'rawi: A Portrait of a Contemporary Alim in Egypt," in *Islam, Nationalism, and Radicalism in Egypt and the Sudan*, ed. Gabriel Warburg and Uri M. Kupferschmidt (New York: Praeger Publishers, 1983), 281–97.

7. Marshall G. S. Hodgson, *The Venture of Islam: Conscience and History in a World Civilization*, vol. 1 (Chicago: University of Chicago Press, 1974), 250–51. Christopher Melchert critiques Hodgson's categories, claiming that Hodgson did not give enough

detail about what differentiated the later piety-minded (who became, for Hodgson, shari'a-minded) from other types of pious figures. See Christopher Melchert, "The Piety of the Hadith Folk," *International Journal of Middle East Studies* 34, no. 3 (2002): 425–39.

8. See Hamid Dabashi, *Authority in Islam: From the Rise of Muhammad to the Establishment of the Umayyads* (New Brunswick, New Jersey: Transaction Publishers, 1989). Dabashi gives in-depth treatment to this hadith in chapter 5.

9. See chapter 1 of Arthur F. Buehler, *Sufi Heirs of the Prophet: The Indian Naqshbandiyya and the Rise of the Mediating Sufi Shaykh* (Columbia: University of South Carolina Press, 1998).

10. See chapter 5 of Dabashi, *Authority in Islam*. Also see Liyakat N. Takim, *The Heirs of the Prophet: Charisma and Religious Authority in Shi'ite Islam* (Albany: State University of New York Press, 2006), especially chapter 1, where he gives extensive coverage to the Prophetic tradition: "The scholars are the heirs of the Prophet." See also Khaled Abou El Fadl, *Speaking in God's Name: Islamic Law, Authority and Women* (Oxford: Oneworld Publications, 2001), 12.

11. Chris Eccel, *Egypt Islam and Social Change: Al-Azhar in Conflict and Accommodation* (Berlin: Klaus Schwarz Verlag, 1984), chapter 1.

12. Ira Lapidus, "Islamic Revival and Modernity: The Contemporary Movements and the Historical Paradigms," *Journal of Economic and Social History of the Orient* 40, no. 4 (1997): 448.

13. See Gudrun Kramer and Sabine Schmidtke, "Introduction: Religious Authority and Religious Authorities in Muslim Societies: A Critical Overview," in *Speaking for Islam: Religious Authorities in Muslim Societies*, ed. Gudrun Kramer and Sabine Schmidtke (Leiden, Netherlands: Brill, 2006), 10; see also Takim, *The Heirs of the Prophet*, chapter 1.

14. Abou El Fadl, *Speaking in God's Name*, 18–19, chapter 2.

15. Johannes Pedersen, "The Criticism of the Islamic Preacher," *Die Welt des Islams* 2, no. 4 (1953): 215–31.

16. Pedersen, "Criticism of the Islamic Preacher," 217; Abu al-Faraj 'Abd al-Rahman ibn 'Ali Ibn al-Jawzi, *Ibn al-Jawzi's Kitab al-Qssass w'l-Mudhakkurin*, trans. Merlin Swartz (Beirut: Dar El-Machreq Éditeurs, 1971).

17. Patrick D. Gaffney, *The Prophet's Pulpit: Islamic Preaching in Contemporary Egypt* (Berkeley: University of California Press, 1994), chapter 1.

18. Linda Gale Jones, *The Power of Oratory in the Medieval Muslim World* (New York: Cambridge University Press, 2012), 18–20; Jonathan Berkey, *Popular Preaching and Religious Authority in the Medieval Islamic Near East* (Seattle: University of Washington Press, 2001); Pedersen, "Criticism of the Islamic Preacher," 215–31; Ibn al-Jawzi, *Ibn al-Jawzī's Kitāb al-Quṣāṣ w'l-Mudhakkirīn*, 215–31; Gaffney, *Prophet's Pulpit*, 30–34.

19. Indira Gesink, "'Chaos on the Earth': Subjective Truths versus Communal Unity in Islamic Law and the Rise of Militant Islam," *American Historical Review* 108, no. 3 (June 2003): 713; Muhammad Qasim Zaman, *Modern Islamic Thought in a*

Radical Age: Religious Authority and Internal Criticism (Cambridge: Cambridge University Press, 2012), 75–76.

20. Gesink, "'Chaos on the Earth,'" 711.

21. Ira Lapidus, "Islamic Revival and Modernity: The Contemporary Movements and the Historical Paradigms," *Journal of Economic and Social History of the Orient* 40, no. 1 (1997): 118

22. My thanks to Rizwan Zamir for suggesting this term.

23. Talal Asad, *Genealogies of Religion: Discipline and Reasons of Power in Christianity and Islam* (Baltimore, MD: Johns Hopkins University Press, 1993), 210.

24. These types of theories are most often referenced as poststructuralist, but in the latter part of this book, I will also attempt to bring together hermeneutics, media studies, and social semiotics.

25. Johan Fornäs, "The Crucial In Between: The Centrality of Mediation in Cultural Studies," *European Journal of Cultural Studies* 3, no. 1 (January 2000): 49–52.

26. See Ernest Gellner, *Muslim Society* (Cambridge: Cambridge University Press, 1983); Baoz Shoshan *Popular Culture in Medieval Cairo*, Cambridge Studies in Islamic Civilization (Cambridge: Cambridge University Press, 1993), argues that one need not disregard texts to study popular culture. See also Jonathan Berkey, *Popular Preaching* and *The Transmission of Knowledge in Medieval Cairo: A Social History of Islamic Education* (Princeton, NJ: Princeton University Press, 1992).

27. Dale F. Eickelman and Jon W. Anderson, "Redefining Muslim Publics," in *New Media in the Muslim World: The Emerging Public Sphere*, 2nd ed., ed. Dale F. Eickelman and Jon W. Anderson (Bloomington: Indiana University Press, 2003), 1–19; Jon W. Anderson, "Electronic Media and New Muslim Publics," in *Muslims and Modernity: Culture and Society since 1800*, ed. Robert Hefner (Cambridge: Cambridge University Press, 2011), 651.

28. Marshall McLuhan, *Understanding Media: The Extension of Man* (Cambridge: Massachusetts Institute of Technology, 1994), chapter 1.

CHAPTER 1

1. The subtitles of two of Sha'rawi's interview-based autobiographies reflect this narrative. One is "From Village to Protector (*qīma*)" and another is "From Daqadous to Government Ministry (*al-wizāra*)."

2. Nilüfer Göle, "Snapshots of Islamic Modernities," *Daedalus* 129, no. 1 (2000): 91.

3. S. N. Eisenstadt, "Multiple Modernities," *Daedalus* 129, no. 1 (2000): 1–3.

4. The degree to which the 'ulama' were tied to the state before Muhammad 'Ali's time is a point of scholarly debate. Scholars like Wael Hallaq have argued that there was a separation of the two that allowed each to function independently from the other. Others don't see as great a shift resulting from the modernization process but still recognize a change. See, for example, Ahmed Atif, *The Fatigue of the Shari'a* (New York: Palgrave Macmillan, 2012).

5. There have been many works written recently about modern changes and their effects on Egyptian religious institutions and the 'ulama', especially in reference to al-Azhar. Among them are Malika Zeghal, *Gardiens de l'Islam: Les Oulémas D'al Azhar dans L'egypte Contemporaine* (Paris: Presses de la Fondation nationale des sciences politiques, 1996). For English sources, see Malika Zeghal, "Religion and Politics in Egypt: The Ulema of Al-Azhar, Radical Islam, and the State (1952–94)," *International Journal of Middle East Studies* 31, no. 3 (1999): 371–99; Gregory Starrett, *Putting Islam to Work: Education, Politics, and Religious Transformation in Egypt* (Berkeley: University of California Press, 1998); Jakob Skovgaard-Petersen, *Defining Islam for the Egyptian State: Muftis and Fatwas of the Dar Al-Ifta*, Social, Economic, and Political Studies of the Middle East and Asia, vol. 59 (Leiden, Netherlands: Brill, 1997); Tamir Moustafa, "Conflict and Cooperation between the State and Religious Institutions in Contemporary Egypt," *International Journal of Middle East Studies* 32, no. 1 (2000): 3–22; Meir Hatina, "Historical Legacy and the Challenge of Modernity in the Middle East: The Case of Al-Azhar in Egypt," *The Muslim World* 93, no. 1 (2003): 51–68. For a more politically oriented view, see Carrie Rosefsky Wickham, *Mobilizing Islam: Religion, Activism, and Political Change in Egypt* (New York: Columbia University Press, 2002).

6. Moustafa, "Conflict and Cooperation," 3–22.

7. Moustafa, "Conflict and Cooperation," 4.

8. Hatina, "Historical Legacy," 51–68.

9. Moustafa, "Conflict and Cooperation," 8–11, has an in-depth discussion of the 1961 reforms and their implications, but Moustafa emphasizes the undermining of the authority of al-Azhar too widely. For a corrective to this view, see Zeghal, "Religion and Politics in Egypt," 371–99.

10. See Omid Safi, *The Politics of Knowledge in Premodern Islam: Negotiating Ideology and Religious Inquiry* (Chapel Hill: University of North Carolina Press, 2006), 96–100. See also George Makdisi, *The Rise of Colleges* (Edinburgh: Edinburgh University Press, 1981). In chapters 1 and 2, Makdisi considers the role and curriculum of different institutions of learning in various places. Outside official institutions, learning was even more diverse; see Jonathan Porter Berkey, *The Transmission of Knowledge in Medieval Cairo: A Social History of Islamic Education*, Princeton Studies on the Near East (Princeton, NJ: Princeton University Press, 1992), 193–201.

11. Makdisi, *The Rise of Colleges*, 70–90.

12. Makdisi, *The Rise of Colleges*, 10–27. Even the curricula in schools were varied; see page 80.

13. Starrett, *Putting Islam to Work*, 25–30. Zeghal, "Religion and Politics in Egypt," 371–99.

14. See Moustafa, "Conflict and Cooperation," 9–10.

15. Starrett, *Putting Islam to Work*, chapter 2. See also D. F. Eickelman, "Mass Higher Education and the Religious Imagination in Contemporary Arab Societies," *American Ethnologist* 19, no. 4 (1992): 257.

16. Franz Rosenthal, *Knowledge Triumphant: The Concept of Knowledge in Medieval Islam*, Brill Classics in Islam (Boston: Brill, 2007), chapter 1.

17. Rosenthal, *Knowledge Triumphant*, 32.

18. Rosenthal, *Knowledge Triumphant*, 248.

19. Rosenthal, *Knowledge Triumphant*, 166–68.

20. Starrett, *Putting Islam to Work*, especially chapter 2. See also Dale Eickelman and John Anderson, "Print, Islam, and the Prospects for Civic Pluralism: New Religious Writings and Their Audiences," *Journal of Islamic Studies* 8, no. 1 (1997): 43–62.

21. Omar Carlier, "Les Oulemas d'Al Azhar," *Vingtième Siècle. Revue d'histoire* 53 (January–March 1997): 169–171; Muhammad Qasim Zaman, *The Ulama in Contemporary Islam: Custodians of Change* (Princeton, NJ: Princeton University Press, 2002), chapter 6; Meir Hatina, *'Ulama', Politics, and the Public Sphere: An Egyptian Perspective*, Utah series in Turkish and Islamic Studies (Salt Lake City: University of Utah Press, 2010), 20–30.

22. Hatina, *'Ulama', Politics, and the Public Sphere*; Zaman, *The Ulama in Contemporary Islam*, chapter 1; Zeghal, "Religion and Politics in Egypt," 371–99.

23. Professor Yunan Labib Rizk, "Al-Azhar's 1934" *Al-Ahram Weekly*, no. 690 (May 13–19, 2004), accessed June 9, 2015, http://weekly.ahram.org.eg/2004/690/chrncls.htm.

24. George Annesley, *The Rise of Modern Egypt: A Century and a Half of Egyptian History, 1798–1957* (Edinburgh: Pentland Press, 1994), 194.

25. Meir Hatina, ed., *Guardians of Faith in Modern Times: 'Ulama' in the Middle East* (Leiden, Netherlands: Brill, 2009), 117–18.

26. Ron Shaham, "Western Scholars on the Role of the 'Ulama' in Adapting the Shari'a to Modernity: A Critical Review," in *Guardians of Faith in Modern Times: 'Ulama' in the Middle East*, ed. Meir Hatina (Leiden, Netherlands: Brill, 2009), 171–90; Raymond William Baker, *Islam without Fear: Egypt and the New Islamists* (Cambridge, MA: Harvard University Press, 2003); Zeghal, *Gardiens de l'Islam*, 373–99.

27. Zeghal, *Gardiens de l'Islam*, 373.

28. Zeghal, "Religion and Politics in Egypt," 380.

29. Zeghal, "Religion and Politics in Egypt," 380.

30. See Jakob Skovgaard-Petersen, "Yusuf Qaradawi and Al-Azhar," in *Global Mufti: The Phenomenon of Yusuf Al-Qaradawi*, ed. Bettina Graf and Jakob Skovgaard-Petersen (New York: Columbia University Press, 2009), 28–30.

31. Moustafa, "Conflict and Cooperation," 12.

32. Moustafa, "Conflict and Cooperation," 12.

33. See Nathan J. Brown, "Post Revolutionary Al-Azhar," *The Carnegie Papers* (Washington, DC: Carnegie Endowment for International Peace, September 2011), 5. Brown says that this complex has even had control over censuring content in publications that it considers "offensive to Islam."

34. Zeghal, "Religion and Politics in Egypt," 380–90.

35. Stating that an 'alim memorized the Qur'an at a young age has been important in biographies of the 'ulama' since medieval times. It is considered proof of the

capacity of the individual for religious learning because premodern Islamic primary education centered on Qur'anic memorization.

36. Muhammad Mitwalli Sha'rawi in interviews given to Mahmud Fawzi, *Al-Shaykh al-Sha'rawi: Min al-Qaryah ila al-Qimah* (Cairo: Dar al-Nashr Hatih, 1992), 40–41.

37. Engineer 'Abd al-Rahman, personal interview, Sha'rawi Center, Daqadous, Egypt, June 2008.

38. Muhammad Mitwalli Sha'rawi in interviews given to Mahmoud Fawzi, *Al-Shaykh al-Sha'rawi*, 43–44.

39. Ziad Fahmy, *Ordinary Egyptians: Creating the Modern Nation through Popular Culture* (Stanford, CA: Stanford University Press, 2011), 138–41.

40. Fahmy, *Ordinary Egyptians*, 148–49.

41. Muhammad Mitwalli Sha'rawi in interviews given to Mahmoud Fawzi, *Al-Shaykh al-Sha'rawi*, 43.

42. Ahmed Abdalla, *The Student Movement and National Politics in Egypt: 1923–1973* (Cairo: The American University of Cairo Press, 2008), 50–60.

43. Muhammad Mitwalli Sha'rawi in interviews given to Mahmoud Fawzi, *Al-Shaykh al-Sha'rawi*, 40.

44. Muhammad Mitwalli Sha'rawi in interviews given to Mahmoud Fawzi, *Al-Shaykh al-Sha'rawi*, 41–44.

45. Ahmed Abdalla, *The Student Movement*, 50–60.

46. Brynjar Lia, *The Society of the Muslim Brothers in Egypt: The Rise of an Islamist Mass Movement, 1928–1942* (Ithaca, NY: Ithaca Press, 2006), 224–26.

47. "The Opinion of Imam Sha'rawi on the Muslim Brotherhood," accessed January 5, 2015, http://www.youtube.com/watch?feature=endscreen&v=smI-Pp22Z90 &NR=1. My thanks to Adham Hashish for directing me to this video clip.

48. Interview, Cairo, Egypt, June and July 2008.

49. Muhammad Mitwalli Sha'rawi as told to Muhammad Safwat Amin al-Iskandariyah, *Hayati min Daqadus ila al-Wuzara: Al-Shaykh Muhammad Mitwalli Sha'rawi* (Cairo: Sharika Qaytbay lil-Tiba'ah wa-al-Nashr wa-al-Tawzi', 1992), 112–13.

50. Engineer 'Abd al-Rahman, personal interview, Daqadous, Egypt, June 21, 2008.

51. 'Abd al-Rahim al-Sha'rawi, personal interview, Cairo, Egypt, June 26.

52. 'Abd al-Rahim al-Sha'rawi, personal interview, June 26

53. 'Abd al-Rahim al-Sha'rawi, personal interview, Cairo, Egypt, June 26.

54. Muhammad Mitwalli Sha'rawi in interviews given to Mahmoud Fawzi, *Al-Shaykh al-Sha'rawi*, 10.

55. Professor William Quandt, conversation with author, University of Virginia, 2009.

56. Muhammad Mitwalli Sha'rawi in interviews given to Mahmoud Fawzi, *Al-Shaykh al-Sha'rawi*, 60–70. Here Sha'rawi was referring to the fact that many Algerians who took part in the revolution and had important roles in the new government had been students at al-Azhar and had even received some funding for the revolution from the Egyptian government.

57. Engineer 'Abd al-Rahman, personal interview, Daqadous, Egypt, June 21, 2008.

58. 'Abd al-Rahim al-Sha'rawi, Cairo, June 29, 2008.

59. Muhammad Mitwalli Sha'rawi as told to al-Iskandariyah, *Hayati min Daqadus ila al-Wuzara*, 18.

60. Lila Abu-Lughod, *Dramas of Nationhood: The Politics of Television in Egypt, The Lewis Henry Morgan Lectures* (Chicago: University of Chicago Press, 2005), 10–15.

61. Abu-Lughod, *Dramas of Nationhood*, 10.

62. http://www.ertu.org/tv_channel, accessed January 6, 2012. Even today the website of the Egyptian Radio and Television Union (ERTU) describes its television mission over four decades as that of fighting problems and dealing with "issues that face the community (*al-mujtama'*)," offering information about topics such as "community problems" and "national holidays."

63. Abu-Lughod, *Dramas of Nationhood*, 10–13.

64. Quote from an Egyptian director of television recounted in Abu-Lughod, *Dramas of Nationhood*, 111.

65. Andrew Hammond, *Popular Culture in the Arab World: Arts, Politics, and the Media* (Cairo: American University in Cairo Press, 2007), 25.

CHAPTER 2

1. Andrew Hammond, *Popular Culture in the Arab World: Art, Politics and the Media* (Cairo: American University in Cairo Press, 2007), 92; Muhammad Thabit, *Al- Sha'rawi wa al-Sulta* (Cairo: Dar al-Rawda li-l-Nashr wa al-Tawz', 2004), 20–30. Muhammad Jalal, *La . . . Ya Shaykh Sha'rawi* (Cairo: al-Tab'ia al-Thania, 1990). Both Hammond and Jalal portray this relationship as nefarious and Sha'rawi as a powerful influence over Sadat, but neither provide convincing proof of this view.

2. Hammond, *Popular Culture in the Arab World*, 93.

3. Specifically Qur'an 17:1–10.

4. Noor Attia and 'Abd al-Ra'uf, e-mail correspondence, March 2009.

5. Muhammad Mitwalli Sha'rawi, interviewed with Mahmoud Fawzi, *Al-Shaykh al-Sha'rawi: Min al-Qaryah ila al-Qimah* (Cairo: Dar al-Nashr Hatihh, 1992).

6. Muhammad Mitwalli Sha'rawi in interviews given to Mahmud Fawzi, *Al-Shaykh al-Sha'rawi: Min al-Qaryah ila al-Qimah* (Cairo: Dar al-Nashr Hatih, 1992). The story is repeated this way throughout the book.

7. Mahmoud Ayoub, *A Muslim View of Christianity: Essays on Dialogue*, ed. Irfan A. Omar (Maryknoll, NY: Orbis Books, 2009), 195.

8. Muhammad Mitwalli Sha'rawi, *Tafsir al-Sha'rawi: Khawatir Fadilat al-Shaykh Muhammad Mitwalli al-Sha'rawi Hawla al-Qur'an al-Karim*, vol. 3 (Cairo: Akhbar al-Yawm), 1010–40.

9. Muhammad Mitwalli Sha'rawi, *Min Fayd al-Rahman fi Tarbyat al-Insan: Min Qawl Muhammad Mitwalli Sha'rawi*, vol. 2 (Cairo: Wizara al-Rafa Idara al-Shu'un al-Diniyya, 1996), 183.

10. Sha'rawi, *Tafsir al-Sha'rawi*, vol. 5, 3188–89.

11. Sha'rawi, *Min Fayd al-Rahman fi Tarbyat al-Insan*, 30–31.

12. Reem Bassiouney, *Language and Identity in Modern Egypt* (Edinburgh: Edinburgh University Press, 2014), 45.

13. Saba Mahmood, "Religious Freedom, the Minority Question, and Geopolitics in the Middle East," *Comparative Studies in Society and History* 54, no. 2 (April 2012): 421.

14. Mahmood, "Religious Freedom," 436.

15. Mariz Tadros, *Copts at the Crossroads: The Challenges of Building Inclusive Democracy in Egypt* (Cairo: American University in Cairo Press, 2013), 7–10.

16. Vardit Rispler-Chaim, "Postmortem Examinations in Egypt," in *Islamic Legal Interpretation: Muftis and their Fatwas*, ed. Muhammad Khalid Masud, Brinkley Messick, and David S. Powers (Cambridge, MA: Harvard University Press, 1996), 278–86.

17. Abdulaziz Sachedina, *Islamic Biomedical Ethics: Principles and Application* (Oxford: Oxford University Press, 2009), 176–78.

18. Sachedina, *Islamic Biomedical Ethics*, 49–52.

19. Sherine Hamdy, "Re-thinking Islamic Jurisprudence in Egypt's Organ Transplant Debate," in *Muslim Medical Ethics: From Theory to Practice*, ed. Jonathan E. Brockopp and Thomas Eich (Columbia: University of South Carolina Press, 2008), 50. Sha'rawi was not the only 'alim who held this view of God's rights over the human body even after death; see Sachedina, *Islamic Biomedical Ethics*, 190–200.

20. Hamdy, "Re-thinking Islamic Jurisprudence," 81–3. These are Hamdy's translations of an article Sha'rawi wrote that appeared in the Egyptian government's religious newspaper, *Al-Liwa' al-Islami* on February 26, 1987.

21. Muhammad Mitwali Sha'rawi, *Al-Qada' wa-l-Qadr* (Cairo: Akhbar al-Yawm, 1993), 35.

22. Hamdy, "Re-thinking Islamic Jurisprudence," 50.

23. Muhammad Mitwalli Sha'rawi, *Tafsir al-Sha'rawi: Khawatir Fadilat al-Shaykh*, vol. 2 of Muhammad Mitawali Sha'rawi (Cairo: Akhbr al Yawm, 1999), 701.

24. Barbara Stowasser, "Old Shaykhs, Young Women, and the Internet: The Rewriting of Women's Political Rights in Islam," *The Muslim World* 91, no. 1–2 (2001): 100–102.

25. Stowasser, "Old Shaykhs, Young Women, and the Internet," 111–17.

26. Muhammad Mitwalli Sha'rawi, *Al-Fatawa: Kullu Ma Yahimu al-Muslimu fi Hayatihi wa Yawmihi wa Ghadihi* (Cairo: al-Makaba al-Tawfiqiyya, 1999), 508–10.

27. Sha'rawi, *Al-Fatawa*, 509–10.

28. Sha'rawi, *Al-Fatawa*, 509–10.

29. Sha'rawi, *Al-Fatawa*, 509.

30. Mohammed A. Tag-Eldin et al., "Prevalence of Female Genital Cutting among Egyptian Girls," *Bulletin of the World Health Organization* 86, no. 4 (April 2008), accessed January 4, 2015, http://www.who.int/bulletin/volumes/86/4/07 -042093/en/.

31. UNICEF, "Female Genital Mutilation and Cutting," UNICEF Data: Monitoring the Situation of Children and Women, accessed August 28, 2014, http://data.unicef.org/child-protection/fgmc.

32. See Abdulaziz Sachedina, "Woman, Half-the-Man? The Crisis of Male Epistemology in Islamic Jurisprudence," in *Perspectives on Islamic Law, Justice and Society*, ed. Ravindra S. Khare (Lanham, MD: Rowman and Littlefield, 1999), 145–160.

33. Sha'rawi, *Min Fayd al-Rahman fi Tarbiyyat al-Insan*, 203–206.

34. Lila Abu-Lughod, "Do Muslim Women Really Need Saving? Anthropological Reflections on Cultural Relativism and Its Others," *American Anthropologist* 104, no. 3 (2002): 783–94.

35. Saba Mahmood, "Feminist Theory, Embodiment, and the Docile Agent: Some Reflections on the Egyptian Islamic Revival," *Cultural Anthropology* 16, no. 2 (2001): 202–35.

36. Saba Mahmood, *Politics of Piety: The Islamic Revival and the Feminist Subject* (Princeton, NJ: Princeton University Press, 2005), 27.

37. Mahmood, *Politics of Piety*, 31.

38. Sha'rawi, *Al-Fatawa*, 473–75.

39. Sha'rawi, *Min Fayd al-Rahman fi Tarbiayat al-Insan*, 203–206.

40. See, for example, chapter 3 of Tarek Osman's, *Egypt on the Brink: From Nasser to the Muslim Brotherhood* (New Haven, CT: Yale University Press, 2010).

41. 'Abd al-Rahim al-Sha'rawi, personal interview, Cairo, Egypt, July 2008.

42. Geneive Abdo, *No God but God: Egypt and the Triumph of Islam* (New York: Oxford University Press, 2000), 10. Later Abdo names the radical as Omer 'Abd Al-Kafi, who does not deserve this misleading label. She also connects him to Shaykh Sha'rawi because both have influenced women's choices to put on the veil (146–48).

43. Eman Abdullah, "Actress Recalls How She Chose a Life of Piety," *Gulf News* (United Arab Emirates: December 17, 1999).

44. Hammond, *Popular Culture in the Arab World*, 92–93.

CHAPTER 3

1. Linda G. Jones, *The Power of Oratory in the Medieval Muslim World* (New York: Cambridge University Press, 2012), 160–163; Jonathan P. Berkey, *Popular Preaching and Religious Authority in the Medieval Islamic Near East* (Seattle: University of Washington Press, 2001), 22–36; Johannes Pedersen, "The Criticism of the Islamic Preacher," *Die Welt des Islams* 2, no. 4 (1953): 215–31.

2. Catherine Bell, *Ritual Theory, Ritual Practice* (New York: Oxford University Press, 1992), 210–11.

3. Khalil 'Athamina, "Al-Qasas: Its Emergence, Religious Origin and Its Socio-Political Impact on Early Muslim Society," *Studia Islamica*, no. 76 (1992): 64.

4. 'Athamina, "Al-Qasas," 64.

5. 'Athamina, "Al-Qasas," 64.

6. I was able to see Shaykh Sha'rawi's collection of books, specifically those that had been important to him later in his life, while visiting his library in his home village of Daqadous in the summer of 2008. A few authors were well represented there, including Ibn al-Jawzi. Ibn al-Jawzi wrote hundreds of books on many topics ranging from theology, to Qur'anic interpretation, to preaching.

7. Abu al-Faraj 'Abd al-Rahman Ibn al-Jawzi, *Ibn al-Jawzi's Kitab al-Quṣṣāṣ w'l-Mudhakkurin*, trans. Merlin Swartz (Beirut: Dar El-Machreq Éditeurs, 1971), 104–105.

8. Ibn al-Jawzi, *Ibn al-Jawzi's Kitab al-Quṣṣāṣ w'l-Mudhakkurin*, 110.

9. Ibn al-Jawzi, *Ibn al-Jawzi's Kitab al-Quṣṣāṣ w'l-Mudhakkurin*, Arabic, 93; English 179.

10. Pedersen, "The Criticism of the Islamic Preacher," *Die Welt des Islams* 2, no. 4 (1953): 215–31.

11. Carl F. Petry, *The Civilian Elite of Cairo in the Later Middle Ages* (Princeton, NJ: Princeton University Press, 1981), 261; Pedersen, "The Criticism of the Islamic Preacher," 270; Ibn al-Jawzi, *Ibn al-Jawzi's Kitab al-Quṣṣāṣ w'l-Mudhakkurin*, 97.

12. Pedersen, "The Criticism of the Islamic Preacher," 217.

13. Jones, *The Power of Oratory*, 18–20; Berkey, *Popular Preaching*, 22–36; Pedersen, "The Criticism of the Islamic Preacher," 215–31; Patrick D. Gaffney, *The Prophet's Pulpit: Islamic Preaching in Contemporary Egypt* (Berkeley: University of California Press, 1994), 30–34.

14. Jones, *The Power of Oratory*, 81.

15. Jones, *The Power of Oratory*, 18–20; Berkey, *Popular Preaching*, 22–36; Pedersen, "The Criticism of the Islamic Preacher," 215–31; Gaffney, *The Prophet's Pulpit*, 30–34.

16. Jones, *The Power of Oratory*, 83.

17. Jones, *The Power of Oratory*, 91.

18. Bell, *Ritual Theory*, 221–23.

19. Berkey, *Popular Preaching*, 64–69.

20. Pedersen, "The Criticism of the Islamic Preacher," 218.

21. See Pedersen, "The Criticism of the Islamic Preacher," 226–28. See also Boaz Shoshan, *Popular Culture in Medieval Cairo* (New York: Cambridge University Press, 1993), 12–15. See Petry, *The Civilian Elite of Cairo*, 220–74, for how fluid the two categories were and for how they manifested in different occupations.

22. Richard T. Antoun, *Muslim Preacher in the Modern World: A Jordanian Case Study in Comparative Perspective* (Princeton, NJ: Princeton University Press, 1989), 13. Here Antoun borrows from Redfield's classic study.

23. Gaffney, *The Prophet's Pulpit*, 30.

24. Gaffney, *The Prophet's Pulpit*, 52.

25. See chapter 3 of Jones, *The Power of Oratory*. Here she argues that Muslim preachers did not use local vernacular in their sermons.

26. Bell, *Ritual Theory*, 110–12.

27. Armando Salvatore, *Islam and the Political Discourse of Modernity* (Reading, UK: Ithaca Press, 1997), 250.

28. Bettina Graf, "The Concept of Wasitiyya in the Work of Yusuf Qaradawi," in *Global Mufti: The Phenomenon of Yusuf Qaradawi*, ed. Bettina Graf and Jakob Skovgaard-Petersen (New York: Columbia University Press, 2009), xi, 225–27, 262.

29. Graf, "The Concept of Wasitiyya," 225–27.

30. Volume 1, Book 2, Number 38: Bukhari Narrated Abu Huraira. See Ibn Hajar al-'Asqlani, *Fath al-Bari bi-Sharh Sahih al-Bukhari: Al-Juz' al-Awal* (Cairo: Maktaba Misr, 2001), 102.

31. Graf, "The Concept of Wasitiyya," 229.

32. 'Abd al-Ra'uf, personal interview, Zamalek, Cairo, Egypt, July 2009.

33. 'Abd al-Ra'uf, personal interview, Sha'rawi Center, Cairo, Egypt 2008.

34. George Lakoff and Mark Johnson, *Metaphors We Live By* (Chicago, IL: University of Chicago Press, 1980), 453–86.

35. Lakoff and Johnson, *Metaphors We Live By*, 481.

36. Lakoff and Johnson, *Metaphors We Live By*, 484.

37. Lakoff and Johnson, *Metaphors We Live By*, 484.

38. *Ḥama' masnūn* is black fetid clay that has a certain odor. Edward William Lane and Stanley Lane-Poole, vol. 1 of *Arabic-English Lexicon* (Cambridge: Islamic Texts Society, 1984), 638.

39. This word can be synonymous with *ḥama' masnūn*, or it can mean a clay that can be, or has been, fired to become hard. Lane and Lane-Poole, *Arabic-English Lexicon*, 1711.

40. Muhammad Mitwalli Sha'rawi, *Min Fayd al-Rahman fi Tarbiyyat al-Insan: Min Qawl Muhammad Mitwalli Sha'rawi*, vol. 2 (Cairo: Wizara al-Rafa Idara al-Shu'un al-Diniyya, 1996), 3–4.

41. Sha'rawi, *Min Fayd al-Rahman fi Tarbiyyat al-Insan*, 7.

42. Sha'rawi, *Min Fayd al-Rahman fi Tarbiyyat al-Insan*, 7.

43. Sha'rawi, *Min Fayd al-Rahman fi Tarbiyyat al-Insan*, 4–6.

44. Stanley Hauerwas, "Self as Story: Religion and Morality from the Agent's Perspective," *Journal of Religious Ethics* 1 (Fall 1973): 73–85, especially 74.

45. Muhammad Mitwalli Sha'rawi, Muhammad Mitwalli Sha'rawi, *Tafsir al-Sha'rawi: Khawatir Fadilat al-Shaykh Muhammad Mitwalli al-Sha'rawi Hawla al-Qur'an al-Karim*, vol. 2 (Cairo: Akhbar al-Yawm), 236–39.

46. Sha'rawi, *Min Fayd al-Rahman fi Tarbiyyat al-Insan*, 29–30.

47. Granddaughter of Muhammad and sister of Husayn, Zaynab is a saint greatly venerated by Egyptians. She is the matron saint of Egypt and her shrine in Cairo is a very popular gathering place, especially for women. It is across the street from the Sha'rāwī Center in Cairo. See Nadia Abu-Zahra, *The Pure and Powerful: Studies in Contemporary Muslim Society* (Reading, UK: Ithaca Press, 1997), 116.

48. Sha'rawi, *Min Fayd al-Rahman fi Tarbiyyat al-Insan*, 30–34.

49. Muhammad Mitwalli, Sha'rawi, *Mu'jizat al-Qur'an* (Cairo: Akhbar al-Yawm, 1981), 50–51.

50. Sha'rawi, *Tafsir al-Sha'rawi*, 834–35.

51. Sha'rawi, *Tafsir al-Sha'rawi*, 835.

52. Sha'rawi, *Tafsir al-Sha'rawi*, 836.

53. Sha'rawi, *Tafsir al-Sha'rawi*, 837.

54. See Yvonne Yazback Haddad, "Operation Desert Storm and the War of the Fatwa," in *Islamic Legal Interpretation: Muftis and Their Fatwas*, eds. Muhammad Khalid Masud, Brinkley Messick, and David S. Powers (Cambridge, MA: Harvard University Press, 1996), 297–310.

55. Sha'rawi, *Mu'jizat al-Qur'an*, 65–69. Muhammad Asad, in his translation of these verses of sura Fussilat, says that this explanation of the overlapping time of the two stages is typical among exegetes.

56. Sha'rawi, *Mu'jizat al-Qur'an*, 88–89.

57. Sha'rawi, *Mu'jizat al-Qur'an*, 90.

CHAPTER 4

1. Umm Fatima (follower of Sha'rawi), interview in Cairo, June 2008.

2. See Jakob Skovgaard-Petersen, *Defining Islam for the Egyptian State: Muftis and Fatwas of the Dār Al-Iftā* (Leiden, Netherlands: Brill, 1997), 6–10. He relies here on chapter 3 of Brinkley Messick's *The Calligraphic State: Textual Domination and History in a Muslim Society* (Berkeley: University of California, 1993).

3. Indira Falk Gesink, "'Chaos on the Earth': Subjective Truths versus Communal Unity in Islamic Law and the Rise of Militant Islam," *The American Historical Review* 108, no. 3 (June 2003), 710–33.

4. Wael B. Hallaq, "Ijtihad," in *The Oxford Encyclopedia of the Modern Islamic World*, ed. John L. Esposito (New York: Oxford University Press, 1995), 178–81; D. D. B. MacDonald, "Idjtihad," in *Encyclopaedia of Islam*, 2nd ed., ed. P. Bearman, T. Bianquis, C. E. Bosworth, E. van Donzel, and W. P. Heinrichs (Brill Online, 2015), http://referenceworks.brillonline.com.www2.lib.ku.edu/entries/encyclopaedia-of -islam-2/id-j-tiha-d-COM_0351; Wael B. Hallaq, "Were the Gates of Ijtihad Closed?" *International Journal of Middle East Studies* 16, no. 1 (March 1984): 3–41; Sherman A. Jackson, *Islamic Law and the State: The Constitutional Jurisprudence of Shihab al-Din al-Qarafi* (Leiden, Netherlands: Brill, 1996), 70–80; Bernard Weiss, "Interpretation in Islamic Law: The Theory of Ijtihad," *The American Journal of Comparative Law* 26, no. 2 (Spring 1978): 199–212.

5. As'ad Abu Khalil, "Revival and Renewal," in *The Oxford Encyclopedia of the Modern Islamic World*, ed. John L. Esposito (New York: Oxford University Press, 1995), 431; Ella Landau-Tasseron, "The 'Cyclical Reform': A Study of the *Mujaddid* Tradition," *Studia Islamica*, no. 70 (1989): 87–90.

6. For explanation of the requirements of a *mujtahīd* (one who performs *ijtihād*), see Hallaq, "Ijtihād," 179–80. On page 180, Hallaq also discusses how different *mujtahids* were classified in the beginning of the eleventh century. As for the complexity of the task of the *mujtahīd*, see Weiss, *Spirit of Islamic Law* (Athens: University of Georgia Press, 1998), 209–10.

7. Skovgaard-Petersen, *Defining Islam for the Egyptian State*.

8. MacDonald, "Idjithad." *Ijtihād* was connected specifically to independent judgments in regard to the law. For a discussion of the history of ijtihād within the context of Sunni Islamic law, see Hallaq, "Were the Gates of Ijtihād Closed?" 3–41. See also Jackson, *Islamic Law and the State*, introduction, 76–79; Weiss, "Interpretation in Islamic Law," 199–212.

9. Landau-Tasseron, "'Cyclical Reform,'" 87–90.

10. Gesink, "Chaos on the Earth," 712; Hallaq, "Were the Gates of Ijtihād Closed?" 3–41; Jackson, *Islamic Law and the State*; Weiss, "Interpretation in Islamic Law," 199–212; Wael B. Hallaq, *Shari'a: Theory, Practice, and Transformations* (Cambridge: Cambridge University Press, 2009), 357–71.

11. Gesink, "Chaos on the Earth," 711.

12. Abu Dawud 37:4278, accessed, June 12, 2015, http://www.usc.edu/org/cmje/religious-texts/hadith/abudawud/037-sat.php#037.4278.

13. Khalil, "Revival and Renewal," 431.

14. Khalil, "Revival and Renewal," 435.

15. Nehemia Levtzion and John Obert Voll, eds., *Eighteenth-Century Renewal and Reform in Islam*, 1st ed. (Syracuse, NY: Syracuse University Press, 1987), 35.

16. John Obert Voll, "Renewal and Reform in Islamic History," in *Voices of Resurgent Islam*, edited by John Esposito (New York: Oxford University Press, 1983), 34–36.

17. See Levtzion and Voll, *Eighteenth-Century Renewal and Reform in Islam*, 3–5. See also John O. Voll, "Revivalism and Social Transformations in Islamic History," *The Muslim World* 76, no. 3–4 (1986): 170–72.

18. Voll, "Renewal and Reform in Islamic History," 35.

19. Albert Hourani, *Arabic Thought in the Liberal Age, 1798–1939* (Cambridge: Cambridge University Press, 1983), chapter 6.

20. Hourani, *Arabic Thought in the Liberal Age*, 228.

21. Gesink, "Chaos on the Earth," 712

22. See Hallaq, "Ijtihād," 181; Bernard Haykel, *Revival and Reform in Islam: The Legacy of Muhammad al-Shawkani* (Cambridge: Cambridge University Press, 2003), 78; John Obert Voll's discussion of the Salayfiyya in his *Islam, Continuity and Change in the Modern World* (Boulder, CO: Westview Press, 1982), 251–53; John L. Esposito, *Islam and Politics*, 3rd ed. (Syracuse, NY: Syracuse University Press, 1991), 298–300.

23. Gesink, "Chaos on the Earth," 712.

24. Hourani, *Arabic Thought in the Liberal Age*, chapter 3.

25. Hallaq, "Ijtihād," 181; Haykel, *Revival and Reform in Islam*, 78.

26. Arthur Golschmidt, *Biographical Dictionary of Modern Egypt* (Boulder, CO: Lynne Rienner, 2000), 123.

27. Muhammad 'Abduh, *Risalat al-Tawhid* (Cairo: al-Matba'ah al-'Amirah, 1906), 32.

28. Muhammad Mitwalli Sha'rawi, *Al-Qada' wa-l-Qadr* (Cairo: Akhbar al-Yawm, 1993), 58.

29. Frank Griffel, *Al-Ghazali's Philosophical Theology* (Oxford: Oxford University Press, 2009), chapters 5 and 6.

30. 'Abduh, *Risālat al-Tawhid*, 158.

31. 'Abduh, *Risālat al-Tawhid*, 202.

32. Muhammad Mitwalli Sha'rawi, *Min Fayd al-Rahman fi Tarbiyyat al-Insan: min Qawl Muhammad Mitwalli Sha'rawi*, vol. 2 (Cairo: Wizara al-Rafa Idara al-Shu'un al-Diniyya 1996), 40.

33. Muhammad Mitwalli Sha'rawi, *Mu'jizat al-Qur'an* (Cairo: Akhbar al-Yawm, 1981), 87.

34. 'Abd al-Ra'uf, lecture and question-and-answer session, Al-Husayn Square, Cairo, Egypt, June 2008.

35. Muhammad Mitwalli Sha'rawi, *Muhammad Mitwalli al-Sha'rawi Hawla al-Qur'an al-Karim*, vol. 1 (Cairo: Akhbar al-Yawm, 1980), 55–56.

36. Sha'rawi, *Al-Qada' wa-l-Qadr*, 68.

37. Catherine Bell, *Ritual Theory, Ritual Practice* (New York: Oxford University Press, 1992), chapter 4.

38. Sha'rawi, *Al-Qada' wa-l-Qadr*, 68.

39. Sha'rawi, *Al-Qada' wa-l-Qadr*, 25–26.

40. Sha'rawi, *Al-Qada' wa-l-Qadr*, 58.

41. Sha'rawi, *Al-Qada' wa-l-Qadr*, 62–63.

42. Sha'rawi, *Al-Qada' wa-l-Qadr*, 65.

43. Sha'rawi, *Al-Qada' wa-l-Qadr*, 71–72.

44. Sha'rawi, *Al-Qada' wa-l-Qadr*, 72.

45. Sha'rawi, *Al-Qada' wa-l-Qadr*, 76–77.

46. This idea is reminiscent of the classic Ash'arite position that God's justice is not just because it fits a particular definition of justice, what God does is the definition of justice. See Sherman A. Jackson, *Islam and the Problem of Black Suffering* (Oxford: Oxford University Press, 2009), chapter 3.

47. Sha'rawi, *Min Fayd al-Rahman fi Tarbiyyat al-Insan*, 179.

48. Translated literally, the phrase *harakat al- hayāti* means "life movements." But Edward William Lane claims that *haraka* can mean movement, or it can signify that someone moves something, someone was in a state of motion, or put oneself in a state of motion. He also states that *hayā* can refer to life in general, or it can signify "the faculty of sensation and the faculty of intellect or everlasting life, which one attains by that *hayā* which is intelligence and knowledge." Taking these possibilities into account, I translate *harakat al- hayāti* in the sense that Sha'rawi used it, and Lane explained it, to mean independent volition because whether in moving things or oneself, an individual displays volition. Volition can also be enacted through the use of independent faculties of knowledge and sensation for the purposes of this life and the afterlife. See Edward William Lane and Stanley Lane-Poole, *Arabic-English Lexicon* (Cambridge: Islamic Texts Society, 1984), 682 and 553.

49. Sha'rawi, *Min Fayd al-Rahman fi Tarbiyyat al-Insan*, 198.

50. 'Abd al-Ra'uf, interview with author, Zamalek, Cairo, July 2008; 'Abd al-Ra'uf, lecture and question-and-answer session, Husayni Square, Cairo, Egypt, July 2008.

51. "From the hadith about Hajj: God is proud in front of his angels because the crowds of people show how much his people love him. They come to Hajj asking for his mercy and forgiveness. So God says to his angels: 'I hereby inform you that I have forgiven them.' This is stated in all books of hadith (abwāb al-Ḥajj) and many other hadith books." Shaykh 'Abd al-Ra'uf, e-mail correspondence with author, March 2009.

52. 'Abd al-Ra'uf, interview, Cairo, July 2008.

53. The scale for Sha'rawi was "that which straightens the movement of life in the universe."

54. Al-āḥra ("the other)" here means other in terms of those inside and outside Islam. I do not think it makes sense to read the whole passage as "to the other (Muslim)" because it is obvious from the next part of the sentence that this other is the neighbor. In keeping with the hadith, when Sha'rawi refers to Muslims loving other Muslims, he uses the word brother ('akh); when referring to the love between people universally, he uses the word neighbor (jār).

55. Sha'rawi, Min Fayd al-Rahman fi Tarbiyyat al-Insan, 205–206.

56. "'Not one of you [will] believe completely until he loves for his brother what he loves for himself'" becomes "We find the whole universe connected in love . . . connecting whoever loves for his neighbor what he loves for himself."

57. Sha'rawi, Min Fayd al-Rahman fi Tarbiyyat al-Insan, 179.

CHAPTER 5

1. Muhammad Mitwalli Sha'rawi, Al-Ghayb (Cairo: Akbar Al-Yawm, 1999), 8.

2. Gregory Starrett, Putting Islam to Work: Education, Politics, and Religious Transformation in Egypt (Berkeley: University of California Press, 1998), 30.

3. Muhammad Mitwalli Sha'rawi, Al-Shaykh al-Sha'rawi: Min al-Qarya ila al-Qimah (Cairo: Dar al-Nashr Hatih, 1992), 49.

4. Muhammad Mitwalli Sha'rawi, Al-Shaykh al-Sha'rawi, 49. Sha'rawi's opinion of the Muslim Brotherhood can be seen in this popular YouTube clip: "Al-Shaarawi on the Muslim Brotherhood" accessed October 1, 2010, www.youtube.com/watch?v=UraOAacsr38.

5. Muhammad Mitwalli Sha'rawi, Min Fayd al-Rahman fi Tarbiyyat al-Insan: Min qawl Muhammad Mitwalli Sha'rawi, al-juz' al-thani (Cairo: Wizara al-Rafa Idara al-Shu'un al-Diniyya, 1996), 34–35.

6. Sha'rawi, Min Fayd al-Rahman fi Tarbiyyat al-Insan, 34–35.

7. Interview with Mahmoud Fawzi, Muhammad Mitwalli Sha'rawi, Al-Shaykh al-Sha'rawi: Min al-Qarya ila al-Qima, 99–100.

8. Muhammad Jalal, La . . . Ya Shaykh Sha'rawi (Cairo: al-Tab'iyya al-Taniya, 1990).

9. Interview with Mahmoud Fawzi, Muhammad Mitwalli Sha'rawi, Al-Shaykh al-Sha'rawi: Min al-Qarya ila al-Qima, 82.

10. Carrie Rosefsky Wickham, *The Muslim Brotherhood: Evolution of an Islamist Movement* (Princeton, NJ: Princeton University Press 2013), 48. Wickham quotes one of the leaders of the Muslim Brotherhood explaining in 1984 why they were running candidates in elections: "Our goal is not what you would call a political victory but rather what concerns us is achieving a victory for God and the application of his Law . . ."

11. Wickham, *The Muslim Brotherhood*, 47.

12. Wickham, *The Muslim Brotherhood*, 48.

13. Wickham, *The Muslim Brotherhood*, 34.

14. Wickham, *The Muslim Brotherhood*, 34.

15. Qutb, Qutb, Sayyid, *Ma'alim fi al-Tariq* (Cairo: Dar al-Shuruq, 1970), chapter 4.

16. Roxanne L. Euben and Muhammad Qasim Zaman, ed., "Neglected Duty" in *Princeton Readings in Islamist Thought: Texts and Contexts from al-Banna to Bin Laden* (Princeton, NJ: Princeton University Press 2009), 327–44.

17. Euben and Zaman, ed., "Neglected Duty," 327–44.

18. J. J. G. Jansen, "The Creed of Sadat's Assassins, 'The Contents of the Forgotten Duty' Analysed," *Die Welt des Islams* 25, no. 1/4 (1985): 15.

19. Giles Kepel, *Jihad: The Trials of Political Islam* (London: I.B. Taurus, 2006), 86.

20. Kepel, *Jihad*, 86.

21. Euben and Zaman, ed., "Neglected Duty," 341.

22. Jansen, "The Creed of Sadat's Assassins," 1–30. On page 11, in Jansen's discussion of Farag's ideas about corrupt cabinet ministers, he says: "Would an Egyptian reader of these lines be able not to think of Shaikh Al-Sha'rāwī, Cabinet Minister of Awqāf . . . ?"

23. Jansen, "The Creed of Sadat's Assassins," 17.

24. Interview with Mahmoud Fawzi, Muhammad Mitwalli Sha'raw, *Al-Shaykh al-Sha'rawi: Min al-Qarya ila al-Qima*, 49.

25. I recorded this clip in Cairo on June 28, 2013, from Al-Hayat television.

26. Sha'rawi, *Min Fayd al-Rahman fi Tarbyat al-Insan*, 30–40; Muhammad Mitwalli Sha'rawi, *Al-Shaykh al-Sha'rawi*, 35–45.

27. "Fight against them until there is no more oppression and all worship is devoted to God alone. But if they desist than all hostility shall cease. Save against those who willfully do wrong. Fight during the sacred months if you are attacked: for a violation of sanctity is [subject to the law of] just retribution. Thus, if anyone commits aggression against you, attack him just as he has attacked you—but remain conscious of God, and know that God is with those who are conscious of him."

28. Muhammad Mitwalli Sha'rawi, *Tafsīr al-Sha'rāwī: Khawatir Fadilat al-Shaykh Muhammad Mitwalli Sha'rawi, Hawla al-Qur'an al-Karim*, vol. 2 (Cairo: Akhbar al Yawm, 1999), 1045.

29. Sha'rawi, *Min Fayd al-Rahman fi Tarbyat al-Insan*, 21.

30. Sha'rawi, *Min Fayd al-Rahman fi Tarbyat al-Insan*, 25.

31. In Euben and Zaman, ed., "Neglected Duty," Farag interprets this verse to apply to his historic moment and the impending fall of Western Christendom instead of interpreting it how the exegetes had understood it for centuries as pertaining specifically to Muḥammad's time. See Jansen, "The Creed of Sadat's Assassins," 6–7.

32. Sha'rawi, *Al-Ghayb*, 59–60.

33. Sha'rawi, *Al-Ghayb*, 10–11.

34. Sha'rawi, *Al-Ghayb*, 6.

35. Sha'rawi, *Al-Ghayb*, 6.

36. Sha'rawi, *Al-Ghayb*, chapter 3.

37. Sha'rawi, *Al-Ghayb*, 60–61.

38. Sha'rawi, *Min Fayd al-Rahman fi Tarbiyyat al-Insan*, 7–8.

39. Sha'rawi, *Al-Ghayb*, 8–9.

CHAPTER 6

1. William Chittick, "Mysticism in Islam," lecture delivered at the David M. Kennedy Center for International Studies, Brigham Young University, May 2003, 5–8.

2. Chittick, "Mysticism in Islam," 8.

3. Omid Safi, "Bargaining with Baraka: Persian Sufism, Mysticism, and Premodern Politics," *The Muslim World* 90, nos. 3–4 (2000): 278.

4. Ibrahim El-Houdaiby, "The Identity of al-Azhar and Its Doctrine," accessed January 2015, http://www.jadaliyya.com/pages/index/6638/the-identity-of-al-azhar-and-its-doctrine.

5. El-Houdaiby, "The Identity of al-Azhar and Its Doctrine."

6. Samuli Schielke, "Hegemonic Encounters: Criticism of Saints-Day Festivals and the Formation of Modern Islam in Late 19th- and Early 20th-Century Egypt," *Die Welt des Islams, New Series* 47, no. 3–4 (2007): 327.

7. Schielke, "Hegemonic Encounters," 329.

8. Schielke, "Hegemonic Encounters," 330.

9. Muhammad 'Abduh, *Risalat al-Tawhid* (Cairo: al-Matba'ah al-'Amirah, 1906), 34.

10. Richard Gauvain, "Salafism in Modern Egypt: Panacea or Pest?," *Political Theology* 11, no. 6 (2010): 808, accessed January 4, 2015, doi:10.1558/poth.v11i6.802.

11. Meir Hatina, "Religious Culture Contested: The Sufi Ritual of Dawsa in Nineteenth-Century Cairo," *Die Welt des Islams* 47, no. 1 (2007): 33–62.

12. Hatina, "Religious Culture Contested," 50.

13. Hatina, "Religious Culture Contested," 44–46.

14. Hatina, "Religious Culture Contested," 53.

15. Hatina, "Religious Culture Contested," 34.

16. Itzchak Weismann, "The Politics of Popular Religion: Sufis, Salafis, and Muslim Brothers in 20th-Century Hamah," *International Journal of Middle East Studies* 37 (2005): 39–58.

17. Gauvain, "Salafism in Modern Egypt," 808.

18. Gauvain, "Salafism in Modern Egypt," 822.

19. Gauvain, "Salafism in Modern Egypt," 822.

20. Mia Shams al-Din, "Opposing Currents: Internal Rifts May Risk the Credibility of Egypt's Religious Institutions," *Egypt Independent*, February 25 (2013), accessed December 21, 2014, http://www.egyptindependent.com/news.

21. Gauvain, "Salafism in Modern Egypt," 815.

22. Gauvain, "Salafism in Modern Egypt," 819.

23. Gauvain, "Salafism in Modern Egypt," 819.

24. Valerie J. Hoffman, *Sufism, Mystics, and Saints in Modern Egypt*, Studies in Comparative Religion (Columbia: University of South Carolina Press, 1995), chapter 9.

25. Hoffman, *Sufism, Mystics, and Saints*, chapter 1. Hoffman says that she received this answer frequently from shaykhs when she asked them, "What is Sufism?"

26. For more on this modern divide, see Elizabeth Sirriyeh, *Sufis and Anti-Sufis: The Defense, Rethinking and Rejection of Sufism in the Modern World* (Surrey, England: Curzon, 1999), 25–40.

27. Hoffman, *Sufism, Mystics, and Saints*, 117–18.

28. Hoffman, *Sufism, Mystics, and Saints*, 118.

29. Julian Johansen, *Sufism and Islamic Reform in Egypt: The Battle for Islamic Tradition*. Oxford Oriental Monographs (Oxford: Clarendon Press,1996), 61.

30. I heard this definition from many people I met who were visiting the tombs of saints throughout Cairo.

31. Still both mosques and tombs are usually crowded with people waiting in line to talk to the saints buried there. Every time I visited I saw people weeping at these sites while they talked to the tombs. Sayyida Nafisa's tomb is usually packed on Thursday evening by women who come to pray besides her tomb.

32. Stephanie Lacroix, "Between Revolution and Apoliticism: Nasir al-Din al-Albani and His Impact on the Shaping of Contemporary Salafism," in *Global Salafism: Islam's New Religious Movement*, ed. Roel Meijer (New York: Oxford University Press, 2013), 58–81.

33. Lacroix, "Between Revolution and Apoliticism," 58–85.

34. "al-Albaani about ash-Sharaawi, Kishk and the al-Azhar university," accessed November 2014, http://ahlulbidahwalhawa.com/2013/05/28/al-albaani.

35. "al-Albaani about ash-Sharaawi," http://ahlulbidahwalhawa.com/2013/05/28/al-albaani.

36. Muhammad Mitwalli Sha'rawi, *Al-Ghayb* (Cairo: Akhbar al-Yawm, 1990), 114.

37. "*Wahdat al-Shuhud*," in *The Oxford Dictionary of Islam Online*, ed. John L. Esposito, accessed April 14, 2009, http://www.oxfordislamicstudies.com/article/opr/t125/e2465. See also Marshall Hodgson, *The Venture of Islam: Conscience and History in a World Civilization*, vol. 2 (Chicago, IL: University of Chicago Press, 1974), 462–67.

38. "*Wahdat al-Shuhud*," http://www.oxfordislamicstudies.com/article/opr/t125/e2465; Hodgson, *The Venture of Islam*, vol. 2, 462–67.

39. "*Wahdat al-Shuhud*," http://www.oxfordislamicstudies.com/article/opr/t125/e2465.

40. Hafiz A. Ghaffar Khan, "Shah Wali Allah (Qutb al-Din Ahmad al-Rahim, 1703–1762)," in *Islamic Philosophy*, subject ed. Oliver Leaman, from *The Routledge Encyclopedia of Philosophy*, ed. Edward Craig, 1998, Routledge Online, accessed December 22, 2014, http://www.muslimphilosophy.com/ip/rep.htm.

41. Khan, "Shah Wali Allah," Routledge Online.

42. Sha'rawi, *Al-Ghayb*, 6.

43. Sha'rawi, *Al-Ghayb*, 6.

44. Sha'rawi, *Al-Ghayb*, 16–17.

45. William Chittick, "Ibn Arabi," in *The Stanford Encyclopedia of Philosophy*, ed. Edward N. Zalta, accessed June 2014, http://plato.stanford.edu/archives/spr2014/entries/ibn-arabi/.

46. William Chittick, "Presence with God," *Journal of the Muhyiddin Ibn Arabi Society* 20 (1996), accessed April 14, 2009, http://www.ibnarabisociety.org/articles/presence.html.

47. Chittick, "Presence with God."

48. Chittick, "Presence with God."

49. Sha'rawi, *Al-Ghayb*, 76.

50. Sha'rawi, *Al-Ghayb*, 70.

51. Sha'rawi, *Al-Ghayb*, 70.

52. Muhammad Mitwalli Sha'rawi, *Mu'jizat al-Qur'an*, vol. 2 (Cairo: Akhbar al-Yawm, 1981), 198–99.

53. Sha'rawi, *Mu'jizat al-Qur'an*, vol. 2, 59.

54. Reza Shah Kazemi, "The Notion and Significance of Ma'rifa in Sufism," *Journal of Islamic Studies* 12, no. 2 (2002): 156.

55. Kazemi, "The Notion and Significance," 159.

56. Kazemi, "The Notion and Significance," 163–64.

57. Sha'rawi, *Al-Ghayb*, 115.

58. Vincent Cornell, *Realm of the Saint: Power and Authority in Moroccan Sufism* (Austin: University of Texas Press, 1998), 35–38.

59. Thomas Emil Homerin, "Ibn Arabi in the People's Assembly: Religion, Press, and Politics in Sadat's Egypt," *Middle East Journal* 40, no. 3 (Summer 1986): 463.

60. Homerin, "Ibn Arabi in the People's Assembly," 466.

61. Homerin, "Ibn Arabi in the People's Assembly," 470.

62. "And [know that true servants of God are those who never bear witness to what is false, and [who], whenever they pass by [people engaged in] frivolity, pass on with dignity; and who, whenever they are reminded of their Sustainer's messages, do not throw themselves upon them [as if] deaf and blind; and who pray "O our Sustainer! Grant that our spouses and our offspring be a joy to our eyes, and cause us to be foremost among those who are conscious of you! [Such as] these will be rewarded for all their patient endurance [in life] with a high station [in paradise], and will be met therein with a greeting of welcome and peace."

63. Safi, "Bargaining with Baraka," 267.

64. Daphna Ephrat, *Spiritual Wayfarers, Leaders in Piety: Sufis and the Dissemination of Islam in Medieval Palestine*, 1st ed., Harvard Middle Eastern Monographs (Cambridge: Harvard University Press, 2008), 98–100.

65. See John Renard, *Friends of God: Islamic Images of Piety, Commitment, and Servanthood* (Berkeley: University of California Press, 2008), 140–42; Cornell, *Realm of the Saint*, 35–38.

66. Safi "Bargaining with Baraka," 267.

67. Matthew Keufler, *The Making and Unmaking of a Saint: Hagiography and Memory in the Cult of Gerald of Aurillac* (Philadelphia: University of Pennsylvania Press, 2014), 3–5.

68. Thomas J. Heffernan, *Sacred Biography: Saints and Their Biographers in the Middle Ages* (New York: Oxford University Press, 1988), 5–6.

69. Jawid Mojaddedi, *The Biographical Tradition in Sufism: The Tabaqat Genre from al-Sulami to Jami* (Surrey, England: Curzon, 2001), 51–53.

70. Keufler, *The Making and Unmaking of a Saint*, 7.

71. Charles F. Keyes, "Charisma: From Social Life to Sacred Biography," in *Charisma and Sacred Biography*, ed. Michael A Williams, *Journal of the American Academy of Religion* 48, no. 3 and 4 (1982): 2–4.

72. Carl Ernst, *Ruzbihan Baqli: Mysticism and the Rhetoric of Sainthood in Persian Sufism* (Surrey, England: Curzon 1996). On pages 121–25, Ernst contrasts Baqli's autobiographical accounts of his life to the hagiographies written by his followers.

73. See Wendy Doniger O'Flaherty, *Other People's Myths* (New York: Macmillan, 1988), chapter 7.

74. Keyes, "Charisma: From Social Life to Sacred Biography," 13.

75. Bruce B. Lawrence, "The Chishtiya of Sultanate India: A Case Study of Biographical Complexities in South Asian Islam," in *Charisma and Sacred Biography*, ed. Michael A. Williams, *Journal of the American Academy of Religion* 48, no. 3 and 4 (1982): 49.

76. Lawrence, "The Chishtiya of Sultanate India," 49.

77. Mojaddedi, *Biographical Tradition in Sufism*, 1–3.

78. Mojaddedi, *Biographical Tradition in Sufism*, 3.

79. Roy Mottahedeh, "The Patricians of Nishapur: A Study in Medieval Islamic Social History by R. W. Bulliet," *Journal of the American Oriental Society* 95, no. 3 (July–September 1975): 491–95.

80. Bernd Radtke, and John O'Kane, *The Concept of Sainthood in Early Islamic Mysticism* (Surrey, England: Curzon, 1996), 86. The quote is taken from a translation from Al-Hikam al-Tirmidhi: *The Life of the Friends of God*. Al-Tirmidhi lived in the ninth century C.E.

81. Radtke and O'Kane, *The Concept of Sainthood*, 124.

82. Radtke and O'Kane, *The Concept of Sainthood*, 15–31.

83. Ernst, *Ruzbihan Baqli*, 112–113. Ruzbihan Baqli died in 1209 C.E.

84. Ernst, *Ruzbihan Baqli*, 112–113.

85. Ernst, *Ruzbihan Baqli*, 116.

86. Lawrence, "The Chishtiya of Sultanate India," 51. This is part of a reprinted list from the work of Simon Digby.

87. Daphna Ephrat, *Spiritual Wayfarers, Leaders in Piety: Sufis and the Dissemination of Islam in Medieval Palestine* (Cambridge, MA: Harvard University Press, 2008), 10.

88. Lawrence, "The Chishtiya of Sultanate India," 60–62.

89. Ephrat, *Spiritual Wayfarers*, 10–14.

90. Mojaddedi, *Biographical Tradition in Sufism*.

91. Ernst, *Ruzbihan Baqli*, 14.

92. Lawrence, "The Chishtiya of Sultanate India," 52–53.

93. Lawrence, "The Chishtiya of Sultanate India," 52–53.

94. "Omar Abdelkafy: The Greatness of Sheikh Sharawy," accessed June 29, 2014, https://www.youtube.com/watch?v=J12oz-Kas6U.

95. Mawlids are festivals held at the graves of saints usually on the date of their births. For information on mawlids in Egypt today, see Hoffman, *Sufism, Mystics, and Saints*, especially 107–17; Julian Johansen, *Sufism and Islamic Reform in Egypt: The Battle for Islamic Tradition* (Oxford: Clarendon Press, 1996). For information on medieval performances, see Jonathan Berkey, *Popular Preaching and Religious Authority in the Medieval Islamic near East* (Seattle: University of Washington Press, 2001); Boaz Shoshan, *Popular Culture in Medieval Cairo* (New York: Cambridge University Press, 1993). For the yearly festival in Daqadous, see Samuli Schielke, "Pious Fun at Saints Festivals in Modern Egypt," *ISIM Newsletter* 7 (2001). 23.

96. Schielke, *Snacks and Saints: Mawlid Festivals and the Politics of Festivity: Piety and Modernity in Contemporary Egypt* (Leiden, Netherlands: ISIM dissertation, 2005), 89.

97. Schielke, *Snacks and Saints*, 90.

98. 'Abd al-Rahim al-Sha'rawi, conversations with author, Sha'rawi Center, Cairo, Egypt, July 2008.

99. Schielke, *Snacks and Saints*, 100.

100. 'Abd al-Rahim al-Sha'rawi, conversations with author, Sha'rawi Center, Cairo, Egypt, July 2008.

101. Engineer 'Abd al-Rahman, interview, Sha'rawi Center, Daqadous, Egypt, July 2008.

102. All of the following stories were gathered from interviews I conducted with Engineer 'Abd al-Rahman at the Sha'rawi Center in Daqadous in June 2008 and 'Abd al-Rahim al-Sha'rawi at the Sha'rawi Center in Cairo in June 2008. The last story was told at a lecture given by 'Abd al-Ra'uf al-Hanafi, in Cairo, Egypt, in July 2008.

103. 'Abd Al-Ra'uf, lecture, Cairo, Egypt, July 2008.

104. Al-Ghazali, *The Rememberence of Death and the Afterlife*, Book XL of The Revival of the Religious Sciences (*Ihya 'Ulum al-Din*) (Cambridge, England: Islamic Texts Society 1989), 156. This hadith is recorded in the book of Bukhari, volume 9,

book 87, number 187, accessed June 15, 2105, http://www.iupui.edu/~msaiupui/087.sbt
.html.

105. Kristin Zahra Sands, *Sufi Commentaries on the Quran in Classical Islam*, Routledge Studies in the Quran (London: Routledge, 2006), 3.

106. Safi, "Bargaining with Baraka," 267.

107. Frederick De Jong, *Turuq and Turuq-Linked Institutions in Nineteenth Century Egypt: A Historical Study in Organizational Dimensions of Islamic Mysticism* (Leiden, Netherlands: Brill, 1978), 39.

108. Sarah al-Masry, "Sufi Islam in Egypt," *Daily News Egypt*, September 21, 2012, accessed June 15, 2015, http://www.dailynewsegypt.com/2012/10/21/sufi-islam
-in-egypt/.

CHAPTER 7

1. Norman Fairclough, *Analysing Discourse: Textual Analysis for Social Research* (New York: Routledge, 2003), 230.

2. For studies in language ideology, see Jan Blommaert, "Language Ideology," in *Encyclopedia of Language & Linguistics*, ed. Keith Brown (Oxford: Elsevier, 2006), 510–22; Jan Blommaert, *Discourse: A Critical Introduction* (Cambridge: Cambridge University Press, 2005); Kathryn A. Woolard, "Language Ideology: Issues and Approaches," *Pragmatics* 2, no. 3 (1992): 235–49; Dell Hymes, *Foundations of Sociolinguistics: An Ethnographic Approach* (Philadelphia: University of Pennsylvania Press, 1974); Michael Silverstein, "The Uses and Utility of Ideology: Some Reflections," *Pragmatics* 2, no. 3 (1992): 311–23.

3. Shannon Sullivan, *Living Across and Through Skins: Transactional Bodies, Pragmatism, and Feminism* (Bloomington: Indiana University Press, 2002), 9.

4. Kathryn A. Woolard, quoted in Susanne Stadbauer, "Language Ideologies in the Arabic Diglossia of Egypt," *Colorado Research in Linguistics* 22 (Boulder: University of Colorado, June 2010): 2.

5. Kathryn Clark and Michael Holquist, *Bakhtin* (Cambridge, MA: Harvard University Press, 1984), 210.

6. Dell Hymes, quoted in Blommaert, *Discourse: A Critical Introduction*, 70.

7. Blommaert "Language Ideology," 512.

8. Silverstein, "The Uses and Utility of Ideology," 316–17.

9. Hymes, *Foundations of Sociolinguistics*, 49.

10. Hymes *Foundations of Sociolinguistics*, 48–52.

11. Mikhail Bakhtin, *Speech Genres and Other Late Essays*, ed. Carly Emerson and Michael Holquist, trans. Carly Emerson and Michael Holquist (Austin: University of Texas, 1986), 170.

12. Silverstein, "The Uses and Utility of Ideology," p. 319.

13. Niloofar Haeri, *Sacred Language, Ordinary People: Dilemmas of Culture and Politics in Egypt* (New York: Palgrave Macmillan, 2003), 26–45.

14. Susanne Stadbauer, "Language Ideologies in the Arabic Diglossia of Egypt," *Colorado Research in Linguistics*, 22 (Boulder: University of Colorado, June 2010): 3.

15. Stadbauer "Language Ideologies," 5.

16. Haeri, *Sacred Language, Ordinary People*, 20–23.

17. Blommaert "Language Ideology," 512.

18. Marius Canard, "Da'wa," *Encyclopaedia of Islam*, 2nd ed. (Brill Online, 2013).

19. Christian Troll, "Two Conceptions of Da'wa in Islam," *Archives des sciences sociales des religions* 87, no. 1 (1994): 116.

20. From many verses in the Qur'an, for example, 3:110, 3:104, 7: 157, 9:107. For an explanation of this tradition in Islamic history, see Michael Cook, *Commanding the Right and Forbidding the Wrong in Islamic Thought* (Cambridge: Cambridge University Press, 2010).

21. Troll, "Two Conceptions of Da'wa in Islam," 116–20.

22. For a genealogy of the term and how it is understood today, see Saba Mahmood, *Politics of Piety: The Islamic Revival and the Feminist Subject* (Princeton, NJ: Princeton University Press, 2005), 57–59.

23. Cook, *Commanding the Right and Forbidding the Wrong*, 505–49.

24. Mahmood, *Politics of Piety*, 63.

25. Mahmood, *Politics of Piety*, 63.

26. Cook, *Commanding the Right and Forbidding the Wrong*, 19.

27. Silverstein, "The Uses and Utility of Ideology," 320.

28. Muhammad Mitwalli Sha'rawi, *Min Fayd al-Rahman fi Tarbyat al-Insān: Min Qawl Muhammad Mitwalli Sha'rawi*, vol. 2 (Cairo: Wizara al-Rafa Idara al-Shu'un al-Diniyya, 1996), 16

29. Sha'rawi was not the first one to qualify *bi-llatī hiya ahsan* as the most kindly manner because *ahsan* is connected to goodness, although in this instance he qualified the meaning of goodness.

30. Sha'rawi, *Min Fayd al-Rahman fi Tarbiyyat al-Insan*, 16–18.

31. Wolfram Bublitz, and Axel Hubler, "Introduction to Metapragmatics in Use," in *Metapragmatics in Use*, ed. Wolfram Bublitz and Axel Hubler (Philadelphia, PA: John Benjamin Publishing Company, 2007), 7.

32. Muhammad Mitwalli Sha'rawi, *Al-Qada' wa-l-Qadar* (Cairo: Akhbar al-Yawm, 1993), 73.

33. Sha'rawi, *Min Fayd al-Rahman fi Tarbiyyat al-Insan*, 19.

34. "Doing Dawah—Sheikh Shaarawy," accessed January 3, 2015, https://www.youtube.com/watch?v=AahFTkYlKNk

35. "He was not on the right or left but in the middle (*wasat*). He solved many problems by choosing the simplest solution, as did the Prophet; he always chose the most moderate way because he wanted to be welcoming and to make people love religion [he did not want them] to fear. He always mentioned paradise before hell and he would always say how good deeds lead people to heaven before he would say how bad

deeds lead to hell. Many preachers are using this method now in *da'wa* (summoning through preaching)." 'Abd al-Rahim al-Sha'rawi, Sha'rawi Center, Cairo, Egypt, 2008.

36. Mikhail Bakhtin, *The Dialogic Imagination: Four Essays*, ed. and tran. Michael Holquist (Austin: University of Texas Press, 1992), 294.

37. Edward William Lane and Stanley Lane-Poole, "Minhaj," in *Arabic-English Lexicon*, vol. 2, ed. Edward William Lane (Cambridge: Islamic Texts Society, 1984), 2856.

38. Dale F. Eickelman and James P. Piscatori, *Muslim Politics*, Princeton Studies in Muslim Politics (Princeton, NJ: Princeton University Press, 1996), especially chapter 1.

39. Sayyid Qutb, *Ma'alim fi al-Tariq* (Cairo: Dar al-Shuruq, 1970), 49.

40. Roxanne Leslie Euben, *Enemy in the Mirror: Islamic Fundamentalism and the Limits of Modern Rationalism* (Princeton, NJ: Princeton University Press, 1999), 52.

41. Armando Salvatore, *Islam and the Political Discourse of Modernity*, 1st ed., International Politics of the Middle East Series (Berkshire, New York: Ithaca, 1997), 190.

42. William E. Shepard, "Islam as a 'System' in the Later Writings of Sayyid Qutb," *Middle Eastern Studies* 25, no. 1 (1989): 36–37.

43. Euben, *Enemy in the Mirror*, p. 37.

44. See Salvatore, *Islam and the Political Discourse of Modernity*, 204–205; Shepard, "Islam as a 'System' in the Later Writings of Sayyid Qutb," 31–50.

45. Sha'rawi, *Min Fayd al-Rahman fi Tarbiyyat al-Insan*, 11.

46. Sha'rawi, *Tafsir al-Sha'rawi: Khawatiru fadilati al-Muhammad Mitwalli al-Sha'rawi Hawla al-Qur'an al-Karim*, vol. 1 (Cairo: Akhbar al-Yawm, 1980), 25.

47. Sha'rawi's reversal at the end of the quote still reifies Islam, presenting it as an active entity that can rule a passive subject.

48. Mikhail Bakhtin, *Speech Genres and Other Late Essays*, trans. Vern W. McGee (Austin: University of Texas Press, 1986), 69.

49. John Fiske, *Television Culture* (New York: Routledge, 1987), 90.

50. Bakhtin, *Speech Genres and Other Late Essays*, 69.

51. Charles Hirschkind, *The Ethical Soundscape: Cassette Sermons and Islamic Counterpublics* (New York: Columbia University Press, 2006), chapter 2.

52. Hirschkind, *Ethical Soundscape*, 106–108.

53. The Qur'an (2: 258) does not specify with whom Abraham disputed.

54. "Shaykh Sha'rawi to Husni Mubarak," accessed January 2015, http://www.youtube.com/watch?v=NGEEIn_Cpi4&feature=PlayList&p=56DAB157FC3C8344&playnext=1&index=31.

55. Armando Salvatore, "Staging Virtue: The Disembodiment of Self-Correctness and the Making of Islam as Public Norm," in *Islam, Motor or Challenge of Modernity*, ed. Georg Stauth, Yearbook of the Sociology of Islam (Hamburg: Lit Verlag, 1998), 96.

CHAPTER 8

1. Catherine Bell, *Ritual Theory, Ritual Practice* (New York: Oxford University Press, 1998), 140–42.

2. H. R. Jauss, "The Identity of the Poetic Text in the Changing Horizon of Understanding," in *Reception Study: From Literary Theory to Cultural Studies*, ed. James L. Machor and Philip Goldstein (New York: Routledge, 2001), 68.

3. Patricia T. Clough, "The Affective Turn: Political Economy, Biomedia and Bodies," in *The Affect Theory Reader*, ed. Melissa Gregg and Gregory J. Seigworth (Durham, NC: Duke University Press, 2010), 212.

4. Clough, "The Affective Turn," 212.

5. Gregory J. Seigworth and Melissa Gregg, "An Inventory of Shimmers," in *The Affect Theory Reader*, ed. Melissa Gregg and Gregory J. Seigworth (Durham, NC: Duke University Press, 2010), 2.

6. Linda Jones, *The Power of Oratory in the Medieval Muslim World* (Cambridge: Cambridge University Press, 2012), chapter 1.

7. Dale Eickelman and Jon Anderson, "Redefining Muslim Publics," in *New Media in the Muslim World: The Emerging Public Sphere*, ed. Dale Eickelman and Jon Anderson (Bloomington: Indiana University Press, 2003), 1–19.

8. Patrick Eisenlohr, "The Anthropology of Media and the Question of Ethnic and Religious Pluralism," *Social Anthropology* 19, no. 1 (2011): 40–55; Eickelman and Anderson, "Redefining Muslim Publics," 10; Peter Van der Veer, *Imperial Encounters: Religion and Modernity in India and Britain* (Princeton, NJ: Princeton University Press, 2001).

9. See Qasim Zaman, "Epilogue: Competing Conceptions of Religious Education," in *Schooling Islam: The Culture and Politics of Modern Muslim Education*, ed. Robert Heffner and Qasim Zaman (Princeton, NJ: Princeton University Press, 2007), 242–69.

10. Dale F. Eickelman and James P. Piscatori. *Muslim Politics*. Princeton Studies in Muslim Politics. Princeton, NJ: Princeton University Press, 1996. Also see Dorthea Schulz, "Promises of (Im)mediate Salvation: Islam, Broadcast Media, and the Remaking of Religious Experience in Mali," American Ethnologist 33, no. 2 (2006): 110–29; Bryan Turner, "Religious Authority and the New Media," *Theory, Culture & Society* 24, no. 2 (2007): 117–34.

11. Brinkley Messick, "Media Muftis: Radio Fatwas in Yemen," in *Islamic Legal Interpretation: Muftis and Their Fatwas*, ed. Muhammad Khalid Masud, Brinkley Messick, and David S. Powers (Cambridge, MA: Harvard University Press), 310–23.

12. John Fiske, "Television, Polysemy and Popularity," *Critical Studies in Mass Communication* 3, no. 4 (1996): 392.

13. Fiske, "Television, Polysemy and Popularity," 392.

14. Ideas about religious authority being non-coercive have their beginnings in the writings of Max Weber. See "The Three Types of Legitimate Rule." *Berkeley Publications in Society and Institutions* 4, no. 1 (1958): 1–11. In the Islamic context see: Hamid Dabashi, *Authority in Islam: From the Rise of Muhammad to the Establishment of the Umayyads* (New Brunswick, NJ: Transaction Publishers, 1989), chapter 5; Liyakat N. Takim, *The Heirs of the Prophet: Charisma and Religious Authority in Shi'ite Islam* (Albany: State University of New York Press, 2006); Khaled Abou El

Fadl, *Speaking in God's Name: Islamic Law, Authority and Women* (Oxford: One-world Publications, 2001), 12.

15. Charles Hirschkind, *The Ethical Soundscape: Cassette Sermons and Islamic Counterpublics*, Cultures of History (New York: Columbia University Press, 2006), chapter 4.

16. Carrie Rosefsky Wickham, *The Muslim Brotherhood: Evolution of an Islamist Movement* (Princeton, NJ: Princeton University Press, 2013), 32–34.

17. Lila Abu-Lughod, *Dramas of Nationhood: The Politics of Television in Egypt*, The Lewis Henry Morgan Lectures (Chicago: University of Chicago Press, 2005).

18. Salwa Ismail, "Islamism, Re-Islamization and the Fashioning of Muslim Selves: Refiguring the Public Sphere," *Muslim World Journal of Human Rights* 4, no. 1 (2007): 1–21; Armando Salvatore, "Staging Virtue: The Disembodiment of Self-Correctness and the Making of Islam as Public Norm." In *Islam, Motor or Challenge of Modernity*, edited by Georg Stauth, *Yearbook of the Sociology of Islam* (Hamburg: Lit Verlag, 1998): 90–92.

19. Pierre Bourdieu, *On Television*, translated by Pricilla Parkhurst Ferguson (New York: The New Press, 1998), 17

20. Bourdieu, *On Television*, 18

21. Bourdieu, *On Television*, 21

22. Bourdieu, *On Television*, 47.

23. Bourdieu, *On Television*, 44–47.

24. Bourdieu, *On Television*, 22

25. David Morgan, *The Sacred Gaze: Religious Visual Culture in Theory and Practice*, 1st ed. (University of California Press, 2005), 33. "Privileging of participant experience through analysis and interpretation of images and ways of seeing that configure the agents, practices, conceptualities, and institutions that put images to work."

26. Catherine Bell, *Ritual Theory, Ritual Practice* (New York: Oxford University Press, 1998), 140–142.

27. Lawrence Grossberg interviewed by Gregory J. Seigworth and Melissa Gregg, "Affect's Future: Rediscovering the Virtual in the Actual," in *The Affect Theory Reader*, edited by Melissa Gregg and Gregory J. Seigworth (Durham: Duke University Press, 2010), 328.

28. Information gathered during my visits to Cairo.

29. Catherine Bell, *Ritual Theory, Ritual Practice*, 140–142.

30. Eve Kosofsky Sedgwick, *Touching, Feeling: Affect, Pedagogy, Performativity* (Durham, NC: Duke University Press, 2003), 7. Here she quotes Paul de Man.

31. Sedgwick, *Touching, Feeling*, 8.

32. Sedgwick, *Touching, Feeling*, 7.

33. Judith Butler, *Excitable Speech: The Politics of the Performative* (New York: Routledge, 1997), 157–59.

34. Shannon Sullivan, *Living Across and Through Skins: Transactional Bodies, Pragmatism, and Feminism* (Bloomington: Indiana University Press, 2002), 102–103.

35. Seigworth and Gregg, "An Inventory of Shimmers," 1.

36. Seigworth and Gregg, "An Inventory of Shimmers," 1.

37. Seigworth and Gregg, "An Inventory of Shimmers," 1.

38. Sullivan, *Living Across and Through Skins*, 4.

39. Sullivan, *Living Across and Through Skins*, 51.

40. Sullivan, *Living Across and Through Skins*, 3.

41. Sullivan, *Living Across and Through Skins*, 9.

42. Eric Shouse, "Feeling, Emotion, Affect," *Journal of Media and Culture* 8, no. 6, accessed December 15, 2014, http://www.journal.media-culture.org.au/0512/03 -shouse.php.

43. Shouse, "Feeling, Emotion, Affect."

44. Silvan Tomkins, "Affect Theory," in *Approaches to Emotion*, ed. Klaus R. Scherer and Paul Ekman (New York: Psychology Press, 2009), 183.

45. Tomkins, "Affect Theory," 183.

46. Yasmin Moll, "Islamic Televangelism: Religion, Media and Visuality in Contemporary Egypt," *Arab Media & Society*, no. 10 (Spring 2010): 23.

47. Moll, "Islamic Televangelism," 23.

48. Shouse, "Feeling, Emotion, Affect."

49. Shouse, "Feeling, Emotion, Affect."

50. Shouse, "Feeling, Emotion, Affect."

51. Grossberg, interview by Seigworth and Gregg, "Affect's Future," 330.

52. Grossberg, interview by Seigworth and Gregg, "Affect's Future," 328.

53. Grossberg, interview by Seigworth and Gregg, "Affect's Future," 328.

54. Butler, *Excitable Speech*, 157–59.

55. Shouse, "Feeling, Emotion, Affect."

56. Tomkins, *Exploring Affect: The Selected Writings of Silvan S. Tompkins*, ed. Virginia E. Demos (New York: Press Syndicate of the University of Cambridge, 1995), 8.

57. Annemarie Schimmel, *Calligraphy and Islamic Culture* (New York: New York University Press, 1990), 107–10.

58. David Morgan, *The Sacred Gaze: Religious Visual Culture in Theory and Practice* (Berkeley: University of California, 2005), 62.

59. Yusuf Al-Qaradawi, *The Lawful and the Prohibited in Islam* (Malaysia: Islamic Book Trust, 2001), 110–15.

60. Oleg Grabar, *The Mediation of Ornament* (Princeton, NJ: Bollingen, 1995), 104.

61. Schimmel "Caligraphy and Islamic Culture," 110.

62. Seyyed Hossein Nasr, "The Spiritual Message of Islamic Calligraphy," in *Religion, Art, and Visual Culture: A Cross-Cultural Reader*, ed. S. Brent Plate (New York: Palgrave, 2002), 113.

63. Beth Buggenheim, "Islam and the Media of Devotion in and out of Senegal," *Visual Anthropology Review* 26, no. 2 (2010): 93.

64. Brian Larkin, "Islamic Renewal, Radio and the Surface of Things," in *Aesthetic Formations: Media, Religion, and the Senses*, ed. Birgit Meyer (New York: Palgrave Macmillan, 2009), 121–23.

65. Larkin, "Islamic Renewal, Radio and the Surface," 121–23.

CONCLUSION

1. Ira Lapidus, "Islamic Revival and Modernity: The Contemporary Movements and the Historical Paradigms," *Journal of Economic and Social History of the Orient* 40, no. 4 (1997): 448.

2. Mikhail Bakhtin, *The Dialogic Imagination: Four Essays* (Austin: University of Texas Press, 1992), 294.

3. I recorded this clip in Cairo on June 28, 2013, from Al-Hayat television.

4. Robert F. Worth, "Preaching Moderate Islam and Becoming a TV Star," *New York Times,* January 2, 2009. Worth looks at one Saudi preacher, Younr Ahmad al-Shugairi, who calls his immensely popular show *khawātir* (thoughts), which is also what Sha'rawi called his televised Qur'anic interpretations.

5. 'Ali Jaafar, "Muslim Preachers Take to TV," *Variety,* posted April 4, 2008, http://www.variety.com/article/VR1117983548?refcatid=2826. See also Jessica Winegar, "Preachers and the State," *ISIM Review* 22 (Autumn 2008): 28–29. For a story about women issuing religious edicts (*fatāwā*) on television, see Sharon Otterman, "Fatwas and Feminism: Women, Religious Authority and Islamic TV," *TBS Journal* 16 (2006), http://www.tbsjournal.com/Otterman.html.

BIBLIOGRAPHY

ARABIC-LANGUAGE SOURCES

Books on Preaching and Related Topics

'Abduh, Muhammad. *Risalat al-Tawhid*. Cairo: al-Matba'ah al-'Amirah, 1906.

Abu Faris, Muhammad 'Abd al-Qadir. *Mushkilat awajuh al-'amal al-Islami*. Amman: Dar al-Furqan, 2006.

al-'Asqlani, Ibn Hajar. *Fath al-Bari bi-Sharh Sahih al-Bukhari*. Cairo: Maktaba Misr, 2001.

Al-Khawali, Muhammad 'Abd al-'Aziz. *Islah al-Wa'z al-Dini*. Cairo: Fati'a al Jadid, 1969.

Mahmud, 'Ali 'Abd al-Halim. *Iqh al-Da'wah ila Allah*. Cairo: Dar al-Wafa', 1990.

Qutb, Sayyid. *Ma'alim fi al-Tariq*. Cairo: Dar al-Shuruq, 1970.

Rifa'i, 'Ali. *Al-Tarbiyya al-Asasiya fi al Khutba al- Minbariya*. Cairo: Maktaba wa-Matbaqa Muhammad 'Ali Sabij, 1963.

———. *Wahi al-Nahda al-Wataniya*. Cairo: Maktaba wa matbaqa Muhammad 'Ali Sabij, 1964.

Shalabi, Ra'uf. *Saykuluzhiyat al-Ra'y wa-al-Da'wa*. Cairo: Matba'at al-Fajr al-Jadid, 1985.

Biographies and Books about Sha'rawi

Al-Jamili, Doktur al-Sayid. *Al-Shaykh al-Sha'rawi: Hayatahu wa Fiqrahu*. Cairo: al-Muhtar al-Islami, 1980.

Fawzi, Muhmud. *Al-Shaykh al-Sha'rawi wa Yas'alunaka 'an al-Dunya wa al-Akhira*. Cairo: al-Watan lil-Nashr, 1993.

Hasan, Muhammad Mahjub Muhammad. *Al-Shaykh al-Sha'rawi min al-Qaryah ila al-Alimiyya*. Cairo: Maktaba al-Turath al-Islami, 1990.

Isma'il, Muhammad. *Mawaqif . . . wa Qadaya fil Hayat al-Shaykh Sha'rawi*. Cairo: Maktaba al-Iyawat, 1989.

Jalal, Muhammad. *La . . . Ya Shaykh Sha'rawi*. Cairo: al-Tab'ia al-Thania, 1990.

Thabit, Muhammad. *Al-Sha'rawi wa al-Sulta*. Cairo: Dar al-Rawda lil-Nashr wa al-awz', 2004.

Thabit, Muhammad and Khalid Ghadbah Lillah. *Hawla Bayan al-Shaykh al-Sha'rawi: Didda kul min Tawfiq al-Hakim wa-Yusuf Idris wa-Zaki Najib Mahmud*. Cairo: Dar al Thabit, 1983.

Zayd, Muhammad. *Madhakkirat Imam al-Du'a*. Cairo: Dar al-Shuruk, 1998.

Interviews and Lectures

al-Hanafi, 'Abd al-Ra'uf. Personal interviews. Cairo, Egypt, June 29, July 5, July 19, 2008.

———. Lecture. Husayni Square, Cairo, Egypt, July 3 and July 17, 2009.

———. Lecture. Shaykh Sha'rawi Center, Cairo, Egypt, July 4.

———. Lecture and question-and-answer session. Husayni Square, Cairo, Egypt, July 7, 2008.

al-Rahman, Engineer 'Abd. Personal interview. Daqadous, Egypt, June 21, 2008.

al-Sha'rawi, 'Abd al-Rahim. Personal interviews. Cairo, Egypt, June 26 and June 29, 2008.

Works by Muhammad Mitwalli Sha'rawi

Sha'rawi, Muhammad Mitwalli. *Al-Fadhila wa-l-Radila*. Cairo: Al-Akbar Al-awm, 2000.

———. *Al-Fatawa*. Cairo: al-Maktaba al-Tawfiqiyya, 1989.

———. *Al-Ghayb*. Cairo: Akhbar al-Yawm, 1990.

———. *Al-Mar'ah al-Muslimah*. Cairo: Dar al-Sahwah, 1982.

———. *Al-Qada' wa-l-Qadr*. Cairo: Akhbar al-Yawm, 1993.

———. *Al-Shaykh al-Sha'rawi: Min al-Qaryah ila al-Qimah*. Cairo: Dar al-Nashr Hatih, 1992.

———. *Al-Tarbia al-Islamiyya*. Cairo: Maktaba al Turath al-Islamiyya, 1984.

———. *Al-Tariq ila al-Qur'an*. Cairo: Dar al-Wataniyya lil-Nashr, 1999.

———. *Fatawa kul Mayahum al-Muslim fi Hayatihi Yawmihi wa Ghaddihi*. Cairo: al-Maktaba al-Tawfiqiyya, 1997.

———. *Hayati min Daqadus ila al-Wuzara: Al-Shaykh Muhammad Mitwalli Sha'rawi*. Cairo: Sharika Qaytbay lil-Tiba'ah wa-al-Nashr wa-al-Tawzi', 1992.

———. *Min Fayd al-Rahman fi Tarbiyyat al-Insan: Min Qawl Muhammad Mitwalli Sha'rawi, al-juz' al-thani*. Cairo: Wizara al-Rafa Idara al-Shu'un al-Diniyya, 1996.

———. *The Miracles of the Qur'an*. London: Dar al-Taqwa Publishers, 1999.

———. *Mu'jizat al-Qur'an*. Cairo: Akhbar al-Yawm, 1981.

———. *Tafsir al-Sha'rawi: Khawatir Fadilat al-Shaykh Muhammad Mitwalli al-Sha'rawi Hawla al-Qur'an al-Karim*. Cairo: Akhbar al-Yawm, 1999.

ENGLISH LANGUAGE BIBLIOGRAPHY

Abdo, Geneive. *No God but God: Egypt and the Triumph of Islam.* New York: Oxford University Press, 2000.

Abdulkader, Tayob. *Islam and Societal Norms: Approaches to Modern Muslim Intellectual History.* Leiden, Netherlands: Brill, 2007.

Abdullah, Eman. "Actress Recalls How She Chose a Life of Piety." *Gulf News* (United Arab Emirates), December 17, 1999.

Abou El Fadl, Khaled. *Rebellion and Violence in Islamic Law.* Cambridge: Cambridge University Press, 2001.

———. *Speaking in God's Name: Islamic Law, Authority and Women.* Oxford: Oneworld Publications, 2001.

Abu-Lughod, Lila. "Do Muslim Women Really Need Saving? Anthropological Reflections on Cultural Relativism and Its Others." *American Anthropologist* 104, no. 3 (September 2002): 783–90.

———. *Dramas of Nationhood: The Politics of Television in Egypt.* The Lewis Henry Morgan Lectures. Chicago: University of Chicago Press, 2005.

———. "Movie Stars and Islamic Moralism in Egypt." *Social Text,* no. 42 (Spring 1995): 53–67.

Abu-Mannah, Butrus. *Studies on Islam and the Ottoman Empire in the 19th Century, 1826–1876.* Istanbul, Turkey: Isis Press, 2001.

Abu-Zahra, Nadia. *The Pure and Powerful: Studies in Contemporary Muslim Society.* 1st ed. Reading, Berkshire, UK: Ithaca Press, 1997.

Afsaruddin, Asma. "Exegeses of 'Moderation'": Negotiating the Boundaries of Pluralism and Exclusion." *The Good Society* 16, no. 2 (2007): 1–9.

Al-Azmeh, Aziz. "Islamic Legal Theory and the Appropriation of Reality." In *Islamic Law: Historical and Social Contexts,* edited by Aziz al-Azmeh, 250–65. London: Routledge, 1988.

Al-Din, Mia Shams. "Opposing Currents: Internal Rifts May Risk the Credibility of Egypt's Religious Institutions." *Egypt Independent,* February 25, 2013. http://www.egyptindependent.com/news (accessed December 21, 2014).

Al-Ghazali, Abu Hamid. *The Rememberence of Death and the Afterlife: Kitab Dhikr Al-Mawt Wa-Ma Ba'dahu.* Translated by T. J. Winter. Book XL of The Revival of the Religious Sciences (Ihya ulum al-din). Cambridge: Islamic Texts Society.

Al-Jawzi, Ibn, and Merlin L. Swartz. *Kitab al-Qusas wa-l-Mudhakkirin.* Edited and translated by Merlin L. Swartz. Beruit: Dar al-Mashriq, 1971.

Al-Khateeb, Motaz. "Yusuf al-Qaradawi as an Authoritative Reference (Marj'iyya)." In *Global Mufti: The Phenomenon of Yusuf al-Qaradawi,* edited by Bettina Gräf and Jakob Skovgaard-Petersen, xi, 262. New York: Columbia University Press, 2009.

Anderson, Benedict. *Imagined Communities: Reflections on the Origin and Spread of Nationalism.* New ed. New York: Verso, 2006.

Anderson, Jon W. "Electronic Media and New Muslim Publics." In *Muslims and Modernity: Culture and Society since 1800*, edited by Robert Hefner, 648–60. Cambridge: Cambridge University Press, 2010.

Annesley, George. *The Rise of Modern Egypt: A Century and a Half of Egyptian History, 1798–1957*. Edinburgh: Pentland Press, 1994.

Antoun, Richard T. *Muslim Preacher in the Modern World: A Jordanian Case Study in Comparative Perspective*. Princeton, NJ: Princeton University Press, 1989.

Appadurai, Arjun. *Modernity at Large: Cultural Dimensions of Globalization*. Minneapolis: University of Minnesota Press, 1996.

Armbrust, Walter. *Mass Culture and Modernism in Egypt*. Cambridge: Cambridge University Press, 1996.

Asad, Muhammad. *The Message of the Qur'an*. Gibraltar: Dar al-Andalus Limited, 1980.

Asad, Talal. *Formations of the Secular: Christianity, Islam, Modernity*. Cultural Memory in the Present. Stanford, CA: Stanford University Press, 2003.

———. *Genealogies of Religion: Discipline and Reasons of Power in Christianity and Islam*. Baltimore, MD: Johns Hopkins University Press, 1993.

———. "Reading a Modern Classic: W. C. Smith's "The Meaning and End of Religion." *History of Religions* 40, no. 3 (2001): 205–22.

Athamina, Khalil. "Al-Qasas: Its Emergence, Religious Origin and Its Socio-Political Impact on Early Muslim Society." *Studia Islamica*, no. 76 (1992): 53–74.

Ayoub, Mahmoud. *A Muslim View of Christianity: Essays on Dialogue*. Edited by Irfan A. Omar. Maryknoll, NY: Orbis Books, 2009.

Badawi, Muhammad Zaki. *The Reformers of Egypt: A Critique of Al-Afghani, 'Abduh, and Ridha*. Muslim Institute Papers 2. Slough, England: Open Press, 1976.

Baker, Raymond. *Islam without Fear: Egypt and the New Islamists*. Cambridge, MA: Harvard University Press, 2003.

Bakhtin, Mikhail. *The Dialogic Imagination: Four Essays*. Edited and translated by Michael Holquist. Austin: University of Texas Press, 1992.

———. *Speech Genres and Other Late Essays*. Translated by Vern W. McGee. Austin: University of Texas Press, 1986.

Bassiouney, Reem. *Language and Identity in Modern Egypt*. Edinburgh: Edinburgh University Press, 2014.

Bell, Catherine. *Ritual Theory, Ritual Practice*. New York: Oxford University Press, 1992.

Berkey, Jonathan P. "Madrasas Medieval and Modern: Politics, Education, and the Problem of Muslim Identity." In *Schooling Islam: The Culture and Politics of Modern Muslim Education*, edited by Robert W. Hefner and Muhammad Qasim Zaman, 40–59. Princeton, NJ: Princeton University Press, 2007.

———. *Popular Preaching and Religious Authority in the Medieval Islamic Near East*. Publications on the Near East. Seattle: University of Washington Press, 2001.

———. *The Transmission of Knowledge in Medieval Cairo: A Social History of Islamic Education.* Princeton Studies on the Near East. Princeton, NJ: Princeton University Press, 1992.

Black, Antony. *The History of Islamic Political Thought: From the Prophet to the Present.* New York: Routledge, 2001.

Blau, Peter M. "Critical Remarks on Weber's Theory of Authority." *The American Political Science Review* 57, no. 2 (June 1, 1963): 305–16.

Blommaert, Jan. *Discourse: A Critical Introduction.* Cambridge: Cambridge University Press, 2005.

———. "Language Ideology." In *Encyclopedia of Language & Linguistics,* 2nd ed., vol. 6, Keith Brown, Editor-in Chief, Oxford: Elsevier, 2006.

Bourdieu, Pierre. *Outline of a Theory of Practice.* Translated by Richard Nice. Cambridge: Cambridge University Press, 1977.

———. *On Television.* New York: The New Press, 1998.

Brown, Nathan. "Post Revolutionary Al-Azhar." *Carnegie Papers, Carnegie Endowment for International Peace,* Washington, DC, October 3, 2011.

Bublitz, Wolfram, and Axel Hubler. "Introduction to Metapragmatics in Use." In *Metapragmatics in Use,* edited by Wolfram Bublitz and Axel Hubler, 1–29. Philadelphia, PA: John Benjamin Publishing Company, 2007.

Buehler, Arthur F. *Sufi Heirs of the Prophet: The Indian Naqshbandiyya and the Rise of the Mediating Sufi Shaykh.* Columbia: University of South Carolina Press, 1998.

Buggenheim, Beth. "Islam and the Media of Devotion in and out of Senegal." *Visual Anthropology Review* 26, no. 2 (2010): 81–95.

Butler, Judith. *Excitable Speech: The Politics of the Performative.* New York: Routledge, 1997.

Canard, M. "Da'wa." In *Encyclopaedia of Islam.* 2nd ed. Brill Online, accessed June 17, 2015, http://referenceworks.brillonline.com/entries/encyclopaedia-of-islam-/dawa-SIM_1738.

Carey, James W. *Communication as Culture: Essays on Media and Society.* Boston: Unwin Hyman, 1989.

Charles, D. Smith. "Imagined Identities, Imagined Nationalisms: Print Culture and Egyptian Nationalism in Light of Recent Scholarship. A Review Essay of Israel Gershoni and James P. Jankowski's, *Redefining the Egyptian Nation, 1930–1945.*" *International Journal of Middle East Studies* 29, no. 4 (1997): 607–22.

Chittick, William. "Ibn Arabi." In *The Stanford Encyclopedia of Philosophy* (Spring 2014 ed., edited by Edward N. Zalta, accessed July 2014, http://plato.stanford.edu/archives/spr2014/entries/ibn-arabi/.

———. "Mysticism in Islam." Lecture delivered at the David M. Kennedy Center for International Studies, Brigham Young University, May 2003.

Chodkiewicz, Michel. "The Diffusion of Ibn Arabi's Doctrine." *Journal of the Muhyiddin Ibn Arabi Society,* 9 (1991). Accessed June 16, 2015, www.ibnarabisociety.org/articles/diffusion.html.

Clark, Kathryn, and Michael Holquist. *Bakhtin*. Cambridge, MA: Harvard University Press, 1984.

Clough, Patricia T. "The Affective Turn: Political Economy, Biomedia and Bodies." In *The Affect Theory Reader*, edited by Melissa Gregg and Gregory J. Seigworth, 206–25. Durham, NC: Duke University Press, 2010.

Commins, David. *Islamic Reform: Politics and Social Change in Late Ottoman Syria*. Studies in Middle Eastern History. New York: Oxford University Press, 1990.

———. "Social Criticism and Reformist Ulama of Damascus." *Studia Islamica*, no. 78 (1993): 169–80.

Cook, Michael. *Commanding the Right and Forbidding the Wrong in Islamic Thought*. Cambridge: Cambridge University Press, 2010.

Cornell, Vincent J. *Realm of the Saint: Power and Authority in Moroccan Sufism*. 1st ed. Austin: University of Texas Press, 1998.

Crone, Patricia, and Martin Hinds. *God's Caliph: Religious Authority in the First Centuries of Islam*. University of Cambridge Oriental Publications. Cambridge: Cambridge University Press, 1986.

Dabashi, Hamid. *Authority in Islam: From the Rise of Muhammad to the Establishment of the Ummayads*. New Brunswick, NJ: Transaction Publishers, 1989.

De Jong, Frederick. "Opposition to Sufism in Twentieth Century Egypt (1900–1970): A Preliminary Survey." In *Islamic Mysticism Contested: Thirteen Centuries of Controversies and Polemics*," edited by Frederick De Jong and Bernd Radtke, 310–24. Leiden, Netherlands: Brill, 1999.

———. *Turuq and Turuq-Linked Institutions in Nineteenth Century Egypt: A Historical Study in Organizational Dimensions of Islamic Mysticism*. Leiden, Netherlands: Brill, 1978.

Doniger, Wendy. *Other Peoples' Myths: The Cave of Echoes*. New York: Macmillan, 1988.

Eccel, Chris. *Egypt Islam and Social Change: al-Azhar in Conflict and Accommodation*. Berlin: Klaus Schwarz Verlag, 1984.

Eickelman, Dale. "Communication and Control in the Middle East: Publication and Its Discontents." In *New Media in the Muslim World: The Emerging Public Sphere*, edited by Dale F. Eickelman and Jon W. Anderson, 33–45. Indiana Series in Middle East Studies. Bloomington: Indiana University Press, 2003.

———. "Mass Higher Education and the Religious Imagination in Contemporary Arab Societies." *American Ethnologist* 19, no. 4 (1992): 643–55.

Eickelman, Dale, and John Anderson. "Print, Islam, and the Prospects for Civic Pluralism: New Religious Writings and Their Audiences." *Journal of Islamic Studies* 8, no. 1 (January 1, 1997): 43–62.

———. "Redefining Muslim Publics." In *New Media in the Muslim World: The Emerging Public Sphere*, edited by Dale F. Eickelman and Jon W. Anderson, 1–19. Indiana Series in Middle East Studies. Bloomington: Indiana University Press (2003).

Eickelman, Dale, and James P. Piscatori. *Muslim Politics*. Princeton Studies in Muslim Politics. Princeton, NJ: Princeton University Press, 1996.

Eisenlohr, Patrick. "The Anthropology of Media and the Question of Ethnic and Religious Pluralism." *Social Anthropology* 19, no. 1 (2011): 40–55.

Eisenstadt, S. N. "Multiple Modernities." *Daedalus* 129, no. 1 (2000): 1–29.

El-Houdaiby, Ibrahim. "The Identity of al-Azhar and Its Doctrine." http://www .jadaliyya.com/pages/index/6638/the-identity-of-al-azhar-and-its-doctrine (accessed January 2015).

Ephrat, Daphna. *Spiritual Wayfarers, Leaders in Piety: Sufis and the Dissemination of Islam in Medieval Palestine*. Harvard Middle Eastern Monographs. 1st ed. Cambridge, MA: Center for Middle Eastern Studies of Harvard University, 2008. Distributed by Harvard University Press.

Ernst, Carl. *Ruzbihan Baqli: Mysticism and the Rhetoric of Sainthood in Persian Sufism*. Surrey, England: Curzon, 1996.

Esposito, John L. *Islam and Politics*. 3rd ed. Syracuse, NY: Syracuse University Press, 1991.

Euben, Roxanne Leslie. *Enemy in the Mirror: Islamic Fundamentalism and the Limits of Modern Rationalism*. Princeton, NJ: Princeton University Press, 1999.

Euben, Roxanne Leslie, and Muhammad Qasim Zaman, ed. "Neglected Duty." Translated by Johannes J. G. Jansen. In *Princeton Readings in Islamist Thought: Texts and Contexts from al-Banna to Bin Laden*, 327–44. Princeton, NJ: Princeton University Press, 2009.

Fadl, Khaled Abou El. *Rebellion and Violence in Islamic Law*. Cambridge: Cambridge University Press, 2001.

———. *Speaking in God's Name: Islamic Law, Authority and Women*. 1st ed. Oxford: Oneworld Publications, 2001.

Fahmy, Ziad. *Ordinary Egyptians: Creating the Modern Nation through Popular Culture*. Stanford, CA: Stanford University Press, 2011.

Fairclough, Norman. *Analysing Discourse: Textual Analysis for Social Research*. New York: Routledge, 2003.

———. *Media Discourse*. New York: Bloomsbury USA, 1995.

Fiske, John. *Television Culture*. London: Routledge, 1987.

———. "Television, Polysemy and Popularity." *Critical Studies in Mass Communication* 3, no. 4 (1986): 391–408.

Fornäs, Johan. "The Crucial In Between: The Centrality of Mediation in Cultural Studies." *European Journal of Cultural Studies* 3, no. 1 (January 2000): 49–52.

Frank, Richard M. "Moral Obligation in Classical Muslim Theology." *Journal of Religious Ethics* 11, no. 2 (1983): 204–23.

Gaffney, Patrick D. *The Prophet's Pulpit: Islamic Preaching in Contemporary Egypt*. Comparative Studies on Muslim Societies. Berkeley: University of California Press, 1994.

Gauvain, Richard. "Salafism in Modern Egypt: Panacea or Pest?" *Political Theology* 11, no. 6 (2010): 802–25. doi:10.1558/poth.v11i6.802 (accessed January 4, 2015).

Gellner, Ernest. *Muslim Society*. Cambridge: Cambridge University Press, 1983.

Gellner, Ernest, and John Breuilly. *Nations and Nationalism*. Ithaca, NY: Cornell University Press, 2008.

Gershoni, I., and James P. Jankowski. *Redefining the Egyptian Nation, 1930–1945*. Cambridge Middle East Studies. Cambridge: Cambridge University Press, 1995.

Gesink, Indira Falk. "'Chaos on the Earth': Subjective Truths versus Communal Unity in Islamic Law and the Rise of Militant Islam." *The American Historical Review* 108, no. 3 (June 2003): 710–33.

Giddens, Anthony. *Central Problems in Social Theory: Action, Structure, and Contradiction in Social Analysis*. London: Macmillan, 1979.

Ginsburg, Faye D., Lila Abu-Lughod, and Brian Larkin. *Media Worlds: Anthropology on New Terrain*. Berkeley: University of California Press, 2002.

Göle, Nilüfer. "Snapshots of Islamic Modernities." *Daedalus* 129, no. 1 (2000): 91–117.

Golschmidt, Arthur. *Biographical Dictionary of Modern Egypt*. Boulder, CO: Lynne Rienner, 2000.

Grabar, Oleg. *The Mediation of Ornament*. Princeton, NJ: Bollingen, 1995.

Graf, Bettina. "The Concept of Wasitiyya in the Work of Yusuf Al-Qaradawi." In *Global Mufti: The Phenomenon of Yusuf Qaradawi*, edited by Bettina Gräf and Jakob Skovgaard-Petersen, 213–38. New York: Columbia University Press, 2009.

Griffel, Frank. *Al-Ghazali's Philosophical Theology*. Oxford: Oxford University Press, 2009.

Grossberg, Lawrence. "Affect's Future: Rediscovering the Virtual in the Actual." In *The Affect Theory Reader*, edited by Melissa Gregg and Gregory J. Seigworth, 309–38. Durham, NC: Duke University Press (2010).

Haeri, Niloofar. *Sacred Language, Ordinary People: Dilemmas of Culture and Politics in Egypt*. New York: Palgrave Macmillan, 2003.

Hall, Stuart. "Encoding/Decoding." In *Culture, Media, Language: Working Papers in Cultural Studies, 1972–79*, edited by Stuart Hall, Dorthea Hobson, Andrew Lowe and Paul Willis, 128–38. New York: Routledge, 1991.

Hallaq, Wael B. *Shari'a: Theory, Practice, and Transformations*. Cambridge: Cambridge University Press, 2009.

———. "Were the Gates of Ijtihad Closed?" *International Journal of Middle East Studies* 16, no. 1 (March 1984): 3–41.

Hamdy, Sherine. "Re-thinking Islamic Jurisprudence in Egypt's Organ Transplant Debate." In *Muslim Medical Ethics: From Theory to Practice*, edited by Jonathan E. Brockopp and Thomas Eich, 78–97. Columbia: University of South Carolina Press, 2008.

Hammond, Andrew. *Popular Culture in the Arab World: Arts, Politics, and the Media*. Cairo: American University in Cairo Press, 2007.

Hatina, Meir. *Guardians of Faith in Modern Times: 'Ulama' in the Middle East*. Leiden, Netherlands: Brill, 2009.

———. "Historical Legacy and the Challenge of Modernity in the Middle East: The Case of Al-Azhar in Egypt." *The Muslim World* 93, no. 1 (2003): 51–68.

———. *Identity Politics in the Middle East: Liberal Thought and Islamic Challenge in Egypt*. Library of Modern Middle East Studies. London: Tauris Academic Studies, 2007.

———. "Religious Culture Contested: The Sufi Ritual of Dawsa in Nineteenth-Century Cairo." *Die Welt des Islams, New Series* 47, no. 1 (2007): 33–62.

———. *'Ulama', Politics, and the Public Sphere: An Egyptian Perspective*. Salt Lake City: University of Utah Press, 2010.

Haykel, Bernard. *Revival and Reform in Islam: The Legacy of Muhammad al-Shawkani*. Cambridge: Cambridge University Press, 2003.

Heffernan, Thomas J. *Sacred Biography: Saints and Their Biographers in the Middle Ages*. New York: Oxford University Press, 1988.

Heyd, Uriel. "The Ottoman Ulema and Westernization in the Time of Selim III and Mahmud II." In *Studies in Islamic History and Civilization*, edited by Uriel Heyd, 29–59. Jerusalem: Hebrew University, 1961.

Hinds, Martin and El-Said Badawi, *A Dictionary of Egyptian Arabic: Arabic-English*. Beirut: Librairie du Liban, 1986.

———. *Studies in Islamic History and Civilization*. Jerusalem: Hebrew University, 1961.

Hirschkind, Charles. "Cassette Ethics: Public Piety and Popular Media in Egypt." In *Religion, Media, and the Public Sphere*, edited by Birgit Meyer and Annelies Moors, 29–51. Bloomington: Indiana University Press, 2006.

———. *The Ethical Soundscape: Cassette Sermons and Islamic Counterpublics*. Cultures of History. New York: Columbia University Press, 2006.

Hobsbawm, E. J. *Nations and Nationalism since 1780: Programme, Myth, Reality*. 2nd ed. Cambridge: Cambridge University Press, 1992.

Hodgson, Marshall G. S. *The Venture of Islam: Conscience and History in a World Civilization*. 3 vols. Chicago: University of Chicago Press, 1974.

Hoffman, Valerie J. *Sufism, Mystics, and Saints in Modern Egypt*. Studies in Comparative Religion. Columbia: University of South Carolina Press, 1995.

Hoffman-Ladd, Valerie J. "Polemics on the Modesty and Segregation of Women in Contemporary Egypt." *International Journal of Middle East Studies* 19, no. 1 (1987): 23–50.

Homerin, Emil Thomas, "Ibn Arabi in the People's Assembly: Religion, Press, and Politics in Sadat's Egypt," *Middle East Journal* 40, no. 3 (Summer 1986): 462–77.

Hoover, Stewart M. "The Cultural Construction of Religion in the Media Age." In *Practicing Religion in the Age of the Media: Explorations in Media, Religion, and Culture*, edited by Stewart M. Hoover and Lynn Schofield Clark, 1–7. New York: Columbia University Press, 2002.

Hoover, Stewart M., and Shalini S. Venturelli. "The Category of the Religious: The Blindspot of Contemporary Media Theory?" *Critical Studies in Mass Communication* 13, no. 3 (September 1, 1996): 251–65.

Hourani, Albert. *Arabic Thought in the Liberal Age, 1798–1939*. Cambridge: Cambridge University Press, 1983.

Hourani, George F. "Ghazali on the Ethics of Action." *Journal of the American Oriental Society* 96, no. 1 (1976): 69–88.

———. *Reason and Tradition in Islamic Ethics.* Cambridge: Cambridge University Press, 1985.

Hymes, Dell. *Foundations of Sociolinguistics: An Ethnographic Approach.* Philadelphia: University of Pennsylvania Press, 1974.

Ismail, Salwa. "Islamism, Re-Islamization and the Fashioning of Muslim Selves: Refiguring the Public Sphere." *Muslim World Journal of Human Rights* 4, no. 1 (September 2007): 2567–2890

Jackson, Sherman A. *Islam and the Problem of Black Suffering.* Oxford: Oxford University Press, 2009.

———. *Islamic Law and the State: The Constitutional Jurisprudence of Shihāb al-Dīn al-Qarāfī.* Leiden, Netherlands: Brill, 1996.

Jauss, H. R. "The Identity of the Poetic Text in the Changing Horizon of Understanding." In *Reception Study: From Literary Theory to Cultural Studies,* edited by James L. Machor and Philip Goldstein, xvii, 393. New York: Routledge, 2001.

Jensen, J. J. G. "The Creed of Sadat's Assassins: The Contents of 'The Forgotten Duty' Analysed." *Die Welt des Islams* 25, no. 1/4 (1985): 1–30.

Johansen, Julian. *Sufism and Islamic Reform in Egypt: The Battle for Islamic Tradition.* Oxford Oriental Monographs. Oxford: Clarendon Press, 1996.

Jones, Linda G. *The Power of Oratory in the Medieval Muslim World.* New York: Cambridge University Press, 2012.

Kazemi, Reza Shah. "The Notion and Significance of Ma'arifa in Sufism." *Journal of Islamic Studies* 12, no. 2 (2002): 155–81.

Keddie, Nikki R. *Scholars, Saints, and Sufis: Muslim Religious Institutions in the Middle East since 1500.* Berkeley: University of California Press, 1972.

Kepel, Giles. *Jihad: The Trials of Political Islam.* London: I.B. Taurus, 2006.

Keufler, Matthew. *The Making and Unmaking of a Saint: Hagiography and Memory in the Cult of Gerald of Aurillac.* Philadelphia: University of Pennsylvania Press, 2014.

Keyes, Charles F. "Charisma: From Social Life to Sacred Biography." In *Charisma and Sacred Biography,* edited by Michael A Williams. *Journal of the American Academy of Religion* 48, no. 3 and 4 (1982): 2–4.

Khalil, As'ad Abu. "Revival and Renewal." In *The Oxford Encyclopedia of the Modern Islamic World,* edited by John L. Esposito, volume 3, 118–20. New York: Oxford University Press, 1995.

Kress, Gunther R. *Literacy in the New Media Age.* Literacies. London: Routledge, 2003.

Kurzman, Charles. *Liberal Islam: A Source Book.* New York: Oxford University Press, 1998.

———. *Modernist Islam, 1840–1940: A Sourcebook.* Oxford: Oxford University Press, 2002.

Lacroix, Stephanie. "Between Revolution and Apoliticism: Nasir al-Din al-Albani and His Impact on the Shaping of Contemporary Salafism." In *Global Salafism:*

Islam's New Religious Movement, edited by Roel Meijer, 58–81. New York: Oxford University Press, 2013.

Laffan, Michael Francis. *Islamic Nationhood and Colonial Indonesia: The Umma Below the Winds.* Soas/Routledge Curzon Studies on the Middle East. London: Routledge Curzon, 2003.

Lakoff, George, and Mark Johnson. *Metaphors We Live By.* Chicago: University of Chicago Press, 1980.

Landau-Tasseron, Ella. "The 'Cyclical Reform': A Study of the Mujaddid Tradition." *Studia Islamica,* no. 70 (1989): 79–117.

Lane, Edward William, and Stanley Lane-Poole. *Arabic-English Lexicon.* 2 vols. Cambridge: Islamic Texts Society, 1984.

Lapidus, Ira M. "Islamic Revival and Modernity: The Contemporary Movements and the Historical Paradigms." *Journal of the Economic and Social History of the Orient* 40, no. 4 (1997): 444–60.

Larkin, Brian. "Islamic Renewal, Radio and the Surface of Things." In *Aesthetic Formations: Media, Religion, and the Senses,* edited by Birgit Meyer, 117–37. New York: Palgrave Macmillan, 2009.

Lawrence, Bruce B. "The Chisthiya of Sultanate India: A Case Study of Biographical Complexities in South Asian Islam." In *Charisma and Sacred Biography,* edited by Michael A Williams, *Journal of the American Academy of Religion* 48, no. 3 and 4 (1982): 47–67.

Lazarus-Yafeh, Hava. "Muhammad Mutawalli Al-Sha'rawi: A Portrait of a Contemporary Alim in Egypt." In *Islam, Nationalism, and Radicalism in Egypt and the Sudan,* edited by Gabriel Warburg and Uri M. Kupferschmidt, 285–300. New York: Praeger Publishers, 1983.

Levtzion, Nehemia, and John Obert Voll. *Eighteenth-Century Renewal and Reform in Islam.* 1st ed. Syracuse, NY: Syracuse University Press, 1987.

MacDonald, D. B. "Idjtihad." In *Encyclopaedia of Islam,* 2nd ed, edited by P. Bearman, T. Bianquis, C. E. Bosworth, E. van Donzel, W. P. Heinrichs. Brill Online, 2015. http://referenceworks.brillonline.com.www2.lib.ku.edu/entries/encyclopaedia-of-islam-2/id-j-tiha-d-COM_0351.

MacGregor, Geddes. *Dictionary of Religion and Philosophy.* New York: Paragon House, 1989.

Mahmood, Saba. "Feminist Theory, Embodiment, and the Docile Agent: Some Reflections on the Egyptian Islamic Revival." *Cultural Anthropology* 16, no. 2 (2001): 202–36.

———. *Politics of Piety: The Islamic Revival and the Feminist Subject.* Princeton, NJ: Princeton University Press, 2005.

———. "Religious Freedom, the Minority Question, and Geopolitics in the Middle East." *Comparative Studies in Society and History* 54, no. 2 (April 2012): 418–46.

Makdisi, George. *The Rise of Colleges: Institutions of Learning in Islam and the West.* Edinburgh: Edinburgh University Press, 1981.

Mandaville, Peter. *Transnational Muslim Politics: Reimagining the Umma.* New York: Routledge, 2003.

al-Masry, Sarah. "Sufi Islam in Egypt." *Daily News Egypt*, September 21, 2012, accessed June 15, 2015, http://www.dailynewsegypt.com/2012/10/21/sufi-islam-in -egypt/.

Melchert, Christopher. "The Piety of the Hadith Folk." *International Journal of Middle East Studies* 34, no. 3 (2002): 425–39.

Messick, Brinkley, "Media Muftis: Radio Fatwas in Yemen." In *Islamic Legal Interpretation: Muftis and Their Fatwas*, edited by Muhammad Khalid Masud, Brinkley Messick, and David S. Powers, 310–23. Cambridge, MA: Harvard University Press, 1996.

Meyer, Birgit, and Annelies Moors. "Introduction." In *Religion, Media, and the Public Sphere*, edited by B. Meyer and A. Moors, 1–22. Bloomington: Indiana University Press, 2006.

Mojaddedi, Jawid. *The Biographical Tradition in Sufism: The Tabaqat Genre from al-Sulami to Jami.* Surrey, England: Curzon, 2001.

Moll, Yasmin. "Islamic Televangelism: Religion, Media and Visuality in Contemporary Egypt." *Arab Media and Society*, no. 10 (Spring 2010): 1–27.

Morgan, David. *The Sacred Gaze: Religious Visual Culture in Theory and Practice.* Berkeley: University of California Press, 2005.

Mottahedeh, Roy. "*The Patricians of Nishapur: A Study in Medieval Islamic Social History* by R. W. Bulliet." *Journal of the American Oriental Society* 95, no. 3 (July–September, 1975): 491–95.

Moustafa, Tamir. "Conflict and Cooperation between the State and Religious Institutions in Contemporary Egypt." *International Journal of Middle East Studies* 32, no. 1 (2000): 3–22.

Murata, Sachiko, and William C. Chittick. *The Vision of Islam.* Visions of Reality. New York: Paragon House, 1994.

Nafi, Basheer M. "Taṣawwuf and Reform in Pre-Modern Islamic Culture: In Search of Ibrahim Al-Kurani." *Die Welt des Islams* 42, no. 3 (2002): 307–55.

Nasr, Seyyed Hossein. "The Spiritual Message of Islamic Calligraphy." In *Religion, Art, and Visual Culture: A Cross-Cultural Reader,* edited by S. Brent Plate, 112–18. New York: Palgrave, 2002.

O'Flaherty, Wendy Doniger. *Other People's Myths.* New York: Macmillan, 1988.

Omar, Carlier. "Zeghal Malika, Gardiens de l'Islam: Les ulamas d'al Azbar dans l'Egypte contemporaine." *Vingtième Siècle. Revue d'histoire* (1997): 169–71.

Osman, Tarek. *Egypt on the Brink: From Nasser to the Muslim Brotherhood.* New Haven, CT: Yale University Press, 2010.

Pedersen, Johannes. "The Criticism of the Islamic Preacher." *Die Welt des Islams* 2, no. 4 (1953): 215–31.

Petry, Carl F. *The Civilian Elite of Cairo in the Later Middle Ages.* Princeton, NJ: Princeton University Press, 1981.

Qaradawi, Yusuf. *The Lawful and the Prohibited in Islam.* Malaysia: Islamic Book Trust, 2001.

Radtke, Bernd, and John O'Kane, *The Concept of Sainthood in Early Islamic Mysticism*. Surrey, England: Curzon, 1996.

Rajagopal, Arvind. *Politics after Television: Religious Nationalism and the Reshaping of the Indian Public*. Cambridge: Cambridge University Press, 2001.

Renard, John. *Friends of God: Islamic Images of Piety, Commitment, and Servanthood*. Berkeley: University of California Press, 2008.

Ricoeur, Paul. *History and Truth*. Northwestern University Studies in Phenomenology & Existential Philosophy. Evanston, IL: Northwestern University Press, 1965.

———. "Toward a Hermeneutic of the Idea of Revelation." *The Harvard Theological Review* 70, no. 1/2 (1977): 1–37.

Rispler-Chaim, Vardit. "Postmortem Examinations in Egypt." In *Islamic Legal Interpretation: Muftis and Their Fatwas*, edited by Muhammad Khalid Masud, Brinkley Messick, and David S. Powers, 278–86. Cambridge, MA: Harvard University Press, 1996.

Rizk, Yunan Labib. "Al-Azhar's 1934." *Al-Ahram Weekly*, May 13–19, 2004.

Rosenthal. *Knowledge Triumphant: The Concept of Knowledge in Medieval Islam*. Leiden, Netherlands: Brill, 2006.

Sachedina, Abdulaziz Abdulhussein. *Islamic Biomedical Ethics: Principles and Application*. New York: Oxford University Press, 2009.

———. "Woman, Half-the-Man? The Crisis of Male Epistemology in Islamic Jurisprudence." In *Perspectives on Islamic Law, Justice and Society*, edited by Ravindra S. Khare, 145–57. Lanham, MD: Rowman and Littlefield, 1999.

Saeed, Abdullah. *Islamic Thought: An Introduction*. New York: Routledge, 2006.

Safi, Omid. "Bargaining with Baraka: Persian Sufism, Mysticism, and Pre-Modern Politics." *The Muslim World* 90, no. 3–4 (2000): 259–88.

———. *The Politics of Knowledge in Premodern Islam: Negotiating Ideology and Religious Inquiry*. Chapel Hill: University of North Carolina Press, 2006.

Salvatore, Armando. *Islam and the Political Discourse of Modernity*. International Politics of the Middle East Series. 1st ed. Reading, UK: Ithaca, 1997.

———. "Muslim Traditions and Modern Techniques of Power." In *Yearbook of the Sociology of Islam*, edited by Armando Salvatore, 9–45. Mèunster: Lit Verlag, 2001.

———. *The Public Sphere: Liberal Modernity, Catholicism, Islam*. New York: Palgrave Macmillan, 2007.

———. "Social Differentiation, Moral Authority and Public Islam in Egypt: The Path of Mustafa Mahmud." *Anthropology Today* 16, no. 2 (2000): 12–25.

———. "Staging Virtue: The Disembodiment of Self-Correctness and the Making of Islam as Public Norm." In *Islam, Motor or Challenge of Modernity*, edited by Georg Stauth, 87–121. *Yearbook of the Sociology of Islam*. Hamburg: Lit Verlag, 1998.

———. "Tradition and Modernity within Islamic Civilization and the West." In *Islam and Modernity: Key Issues and Debates*, edited by Muhammad Khalid

Masud, Armando Salvatore, and Martin van Bruinessen, 4–32. Edinburgh: Edinburgh University Press, 2009.

Salvatore, Armando, and Dale F. Eickelman. "Introduction." In *Public Islam and the Common Good*, edited by Armando Salvatore and Dale F. Eickelman, 1–32. Leiden, Netherlands: Brill, 2004.

Sands, Kristin Zahra. *Sufi Commentaries on the Quran in Classical Islam*. Routledge Studies in the Quran. London: Routledge, 2006.

Schacht, Joseph. *An Introduction to Islamic Law*. Oxford: Oxford University Press, 1982.

Schielke, Samuli. "Hegemonic Encounters: Criticism of Saints-Day Festivals and the Formation of Modern Islam in Late 19th- and Early 20th-Century Egypt." *Die Welt des Islams, New Series* 47, no. 3–4 (2007): 319–55.

———. "Pious Fun at Saints Festivals in Modern Egypt." *ISIM Newsletter* 7 (2001): 23.

———. *Snacks and Saints. Mawlid Festivals and the Politics of Festivity: Piety and Modernity in Contemporary Egypt*. Leiden, Netherlands: ISIM Dissertation, 2005.

Schimmel, Annemarie. *Calligraphy and Islamic Culture*. New York: New York University Press, 1990.

———. *Mystical Dimensions of Islam*. Chapel Hill: University of North Carolina Press, 1975.

Schulz, Dorthea. "Promises of (Im)mediate Salvation: Islam, Broadcast Media, and the Remaking of Religious Experience in Mali." *American Ethnologist* 33, no. 2 (2006): 210–29.

Sedgwick, Eve Kosofsky. *Touching, Feeling: Affect, Pedagogy, Performativity*. Durham, NC: Duke University Press, 2003.

Seigworth, Gregory J., and Melissa Gregg. "An Inventory of Shimmers." In *The Affect Theory Reader*, edited by Melissa Gregg and Gregory J. Seigworth, 1–25. Durham, NC: Duke University Press, 2010.

Shaham, Ron. "Western Scholars on the Role of the 'Ulama' in Adapting the Shari'a to Modernity: A Critical Review." In *Guardians of Faith in Modern Times: 'Ulama' in the Middle East*, edited by Meir Hatina, 171–95. Leiden, Netherlands: Brill, 2009.

Shakir, Abu Muhammad 'Abd al-Ra'uf. *The Islamic Ruling Concerning at-Tasweer*. Philadelphia, PA: Zakee Muwwakkil, 1998.

Shepard, William E. "Islam as a 'System' in the Later Writings of Sayyid Qutb." *Middle Eastern Studies* 25, no. 1 (1989): 31–50.

Sherman Jackson. "Jihad and the Modern World." *Journal of Islamic Law and Culture* 7, no. 1 (2002): 1–25.

Shoshan, Boaz. *Popular Culture in Medieval Cairo*. Cambridge Studies in Islamic Civilization. New York: Cambridge University Press, 1993.

Shouse, Eric. "Feeling, Emotion, Affect." *Journal of Media and Culture* 8, no. 6 (December 2005). http://www.journal.media-culture.org.au/0512/03-shouse.php.

Silverstein, Michael. "The Uses and Utility of Ideology: Some Reflections." *Pragmatics* 2, no. 3 (1992): 311–23.

Sirriyeh, Elizabeth. *Sufis and Anti-Sufis: The Defense, Rethinking and Rejection of Sufism in the Modern World.* Surrey, England: Cuzon, 1999.

Skovgaard-Petersen, Jakob. *Defining Islam for the Egyptian State: Muftis and Fatwas of the Dar al-Ifta.* Social, Economic, and Political Studies of the Middle East and Asia. Leiden, Netherlands: Brill, 1997.

———. "Yusuf Qaradawi and Al-Azhar." In *Global Mufti: The Phenomenon of Yusuf Qaradawi,* edited by Bettina Graf and Jakob Skovgaard-Petersen, 27–54. New York: Columbia University Press, 2009.

Smith, Anthony D. *Chosen Peoples.* Oxford: Oxford University Press, 2003.

Soloveitchik, Joseph. *Halakhic Man.* Philadelphia, PA: Jewish Publication Society of America, 1983.

Sreberny, Annabelle, and 'Ali Mohammadi. *Small Media, Big Revolution: Communication, Culture, and the Iranian Revolution.* Minneapolis: University of Minnesota Press, 1994.

Stacher, Joshua A. "Post-Islamist Rumblings in Egypt: The Emergence of the Wasat Party." *Middle East Journal* 56, no. 3 (2002): 415–32.

Stadbauer, Susanne. "Language Ideologies in the Arabic Diglossia of Egypt." Colorado Research in Linguistics. Vol. 22. Boulder: University of Colorado, 2010, 1–19.

Starrett, Gregory. *Putting Islam to Work: Education, Politics, and Religious Transformation in Egypt.* Comparative Studies on Muslim Societies. Berkeley: University of California Press, 1998.

Stolow, Jeremy. "Communicating Authority, Consuming Tradition: Jewish Orthodox Outreach Literature and Its Reading Public." In *Religion, Media, and the Public Sphere,* edited by Birgit Meyer and Annelies Moors, 73–91. Bloomington: Indiana University Press, 2006.

Stowasser, Barbara. "Old Shaykhs, Young Women, and the Internet: The Rewriting of Women's Political Rights in Islam." *The Muslim World* 91, no. 1–2 (2001): 99–120.

Sullivan, Shannon. *Living Across and Through Skins: Transactional Bodies, Pragmatism, and Feminism.* Bloomington: Indiana University Press, 2002.

Tadros, Mariz. *Copts at the Crossroads: The Challenges of Building Inclusive Democracy in Egypt.* Cairo: American University in Cairo Press, 2013.

Takim, Liyakat N. *The Heirs of the Prophet: Charisma and Religious Authority in Shi'ite Islam.* Albany: State University of New York Press, 2007.

Tomkins, Silvan. "Affect Theory." In *Approaches to Emotion,* edited by Klaus R. Scherer and Paul Ekman, 163–95. New York: Psychology Press, 2009.

Torfing, Jacob. *New Theories of Discourse: Laclau, Mouffe, and Zizek.* Oxford: Blackwell Publishers, 1999.

Troll, Christian. "Two Conceptions of Da'wa in India: Jama'at Islami and Tablighi Jama'at. *Archives des Sciences Sociales des Religions,* 87, no. 1 (1994): 115–33.

Turner, Bryan. "Religious Authority and the New Media." *Theory, Culture & Society* 24 no. 2 (2007): 117–34.

Veer, Peter Van der. *Imperial Encounters: Religion and Modernity in India and Britain*. Princeton, NJ: Princeton University Press, 2001.

Voll, John O. *Islam, Continuity and Change in the Modern World*. Boulder, CO: Westview Press, 1982.

———. "Renewal and Reform in Islamic History," in *Voices of Resurgent Islam*, edited by John Esposito, 32–47. New York: Oxford University Press, 1983.

———. "Revivalism and Social Transformations in Islamic History." *The Muslim World* 76, no. 3–4 (1986): 168–80.

Vries, Hent de, and Samuel Weber. *Religion and Media*. Cultural Memory in the Present. Stanford, CA: Stanford University Press, 2001.

Wallace, Mark I. "From Phenomenology to Scripture? Paul Ricoeur's Hermeneutical Philosophy of Religion." *Modern Theology* 16, no. 3 (2000): 301–13.

Weber, Max. "The Three Types of Legitimate Rule." *Berkeley Publications in Society and Institutions* 4, no. 1 (1958): 1–11.

Weber, Max, Guenther Roth, and Claus Wittich. *Economy and Society: An Outline of Interpretive Sociology*. 2 vols. Berkeley: University of California Press, 1978.

Weismann, Itzchak. "The Politics of Popular Religion: Sufis, Salafis, and Muslim Brothers in 20th-Century Hamah." *International Journal of Middle East Studies* 37 (2005): 39–58.

Weiss, Bernard. "Interpretation in Islamic Law: The Theory of Ijtihad." *The American Journal of Comparative Law* 26, no. 2 (Spring 1978): 199–212.

———. *The Spirit of Islamic Law*. Athens: University of Georgia Press, 1998.

Whittingham, Martin. *Al-Ghazali and the Qur'an: One Book, Many Meanings*. Culture and Civilization in the Middle East. New York: Routledge, 2007.

Wickham, Carrie Rosefsky. *Mobilizing Islam: Religion, Activism, and Political Change in Egypt*. New York: Columbia University Press, 2002.

———. *The Muslim Brotherhood: Evolution of an Islamist Movement*. Princeton, NJ: Princeton University Press, 2013.

———. "The Path to Moderation: Strategy and Learning in the Formation of Egypt's Wasat Party." *Comparative Politics* 36, no. 2 (2004): 205–28.

Winegar, J. "Purposeful Art between Television Preachers and the State." *ISIM Review* 22 (2008): 28.

Woolard, Kathryn A. "Language Ideology: Issues and Approaches." *Pragmatics* 2, no. 3 (1992): 235–49.

Yazbak, Mahmoud. "Nabulsi Ulama in the Late Ottoman Period, 1864–1914." *International Journal of Middle East Studies* 29, no. 1 (1997): 71–91.

Zaman, Muhammad Qasim. *The Ulama in Contemporary Islam: Custodians of Change*. Princeton, NJ: Princeton University Press, 2007.

Zaman, Qasim. "Consensus and Religious Authority in Modern Islam: The Discourses of the 'Ulama'." In *Speaking for Islam: Religious Authorities in Muslim Societies*, edited by Gudrun Kramer and Sabine Schmidtke, 153–81. Social, Economic and Political Studies of the Middle East and Asia. Leiden, Netherlands: Brill, 2006.

———. "Epilogue: Competing Conceptions of Religious Education." In *Schooling Islam: The Culture and Politics of Modern Muslim Education*, edited by Robert Heffner and Qasim Zaman, 242–96. Princeton, NJ: Princeton University Press, 2007.

———. "The 'Ulama' and Contestations on Religious Authority." In *Islam and Modernity: Key Issues and Debates*, edited by Muhammad Khalid Masud, Armando Salvatore, and Martin van Bruinessen, 206–37. Edinburgh: Edinburgh University Press, 2009.

Zebiri, Kate. *Mahmud Shaltut and Islamic Modernism*. Oxford: Oxford University Press, 1993.

Zeghal, Malika. *Gardiens de l'Islam: Les OuléMas d'al Azhar dans l'Egypte contemporaine*. Paris: Presses de la Fondation Nationale des Sciences Politiques, 1996.

———. "Religion and Politics in Egypt: The Ulema of Al-Azhar, Radical Islam, and the State (1952–94)." *International Journal of Middle East Studies* 31, no. 3 (1999): 371–99.

INDEX